A CONCISE HISTORY OF POLAND

Poland is a country which sporadically hits the headlines of the Anglo-Saxon world. It has suffered the dubious distinction of being wiped off the political map in 1795, to be resurrected after the First World War, only to suffer apparent annihilation during the Second and reduction to satellite status of the Soviet Union, to emerge in the van of resistance to Soviet domination during the 1980s. Yet the history of Poland remains comparatively little known. This book offers a primarily political outline of its turbulent and complex past, from medieval times to the present day, and is the only brief history of the country available in English.

The pre-1795 Polish state had become a byword for political weakness before its erasure from the map; yet from the fifteenth to the seventeenth century it was one of the dominant forces of central and eastern Europe. It was also the scene of a remarkable experiment in consensual, constitutional politics, in an area embracing much of not only what is present-day Poland, but also Lithuania, Ukraine and Belarus. Under foreign rule in the nineteenth century, different patterns of political, economic and social development accentuated regional differences, and the emergence of several mutually antagonistic ethnic and linguistic nationalisms undermined the traditions of the pre-partition Polish-Lithuanian Commonwealth. The book traces Poland's painful rebirth after the First World War, the achievements and failings of the inter-war Polish state, and the traumatic ordeal of the Second World War. Finally, it describes how Polish society was altered by – and how it responded to – forty-five years of communism. The book ends with a review of Poland's emergence from that experience and its search for a new direction.

JERZY LUKOWSKI is Senior Lecturer in Modern History, University of Birmingham. His publications include *Liberty's folly: the Polish-Lithuanian Commonwealth in the eighteenth century* (1991) and *The partitions of Poland 1772, 1793, 1795* (1999)

HUBERT ZAWADZKI teaches history at Abingdon School. His publications include *A man of honour: Adam Czartoryski as a statesman of Russia and Poland 1795–1831* (1993).

CAMBRIDGE CONCISE HISTORIES

This is a series of illustrated 'concise histories' of selected individual countries, intended both as university and college textbooks and as general historical introductions for general readers, travellers and members of the business community.

First titles in the series:

Other titles are in preparation

A Concise History of Poland

JERZY LUKOWSKI

and

HUBERT ZAWADZKI

CAMBRIDGE
UNIVERSITY PRESS

PUBLISHED BY THE PRESS SYNDICATE OF THE UNIVERSITY OF CAMBRIDGE
The Pitt Building, Trumpington Street, Cambridge, United Kingdom

CAMBRIDGE UNIVERSITY PRESS
The Edinburgh Building, Cambridge CB2 2RU UK
40 West 20th Street, New York NY 10011–4211, USA
477 Williamstown Road, Port Melbourne, VIC 3207, Australia
Ruiz de Alarcón 13, 28014 Madrid, Spain
Dock House, The Waterfront, Cape Town 8001, South Africa

http://www.cambridge.org

First published 2001
Reprinted 2002

Printed in the United Kingdom at the University Press, Cambridge

Typeface 10/13pt Sabon   System 3B2   [CE]

A catalogue record for this book is available from the British Library

Library of Congress Cataloguing in Publication data
Lukowski, Jerzy.
A concise history of Poland / Jerzy Lukowski and Hubert Zawadzki.
p.   cm. – (Cambridge concise histories)
Includes bibliographical references and index.
ISBN 0 521 55109 9 (hardback) – ISBN 0 521 55917 0 (paperback)
1. Poland – History.   I. Zawadzki, Hubert.
II. Title.   III. Series.

DK 4140.L85 2001   943.8–dc21   00–067438

ISBN 0 521 55109 9 hardback
ISBN 0 521 55917 0 paperback

For

Lesley and Francesca

CONTENTS

ILLUSTRATIONS

PLATES

MAPS

PREFACE

Writing Concise Histories is an activity more rewarding than satisfactory. The begetters know how much has been omitted; readers, no matter how much or how little they know, have to put up with those omissions. This present offering in the Cambridge Concise Histories series is no exception. It is, however, the first to have been written by two authors, one an eighteenth-century specialist, the other more at home in the nineteenth century. Neither of us felt quite up to the undertaking of an all-embracing treatment of Poland's entire past; if some of the difficulties which such an undertaking might have created become apparent to our readers, then we will have achieved something.

For there have been at least two 'Polands'. One disappeared from the political map of Europe in 1795. For over one hundred and twenty years afterwards, it either did not exist, or did so in the form of spluttering, half-formed entities, which had a kind of relationship with what had gone before, but a relationship so uncertain, be it at a wider political level or be it at that of the individual 'Pole', that it is almost impossible to define it in any satisfying detail. The state that emerged in the aftermath of the First World War was very different indeed from the one which met its end in the late eighteenth century; these differences are even more striking in the state which appeared after the Second World War, following an excision from the political map more brutal than anything the country had endured before.

The links between the two 'Polands', the one pre-1795, the other post-1918, remain indissoluble. Poles have always had to rebuild their past, not least because of the systematic attempts to deprive them of it. The most tangible sign of that of course is Warsaw itself: the so-called Old and New Towns are bijou replicas not just of structures destroyed by the Germans during the Second World War but of buildings going back to the old, pre-1795 state and to the Middle Ages. And similar extensive reconstruction has taken place in Gdańsk, Wrocław and Poznań – to mention only the most notable examples. Here historians enter very treacherous waters. To say that there are two Polands is not so much a necessary simplification as a gross distortion. Indeed, virtually anything that can be said about 'Poland' by one observer can be plausibly demonstrated to be false by another. Its territories in their length and breadth have been the abode not only of the Slavonic people who call themselves 'Poles' but also of (among others) Germans, Jews, Armenians, Lithuanians, Ukrainians, Byelorussians, Tatars – and these, in turn, have often intermarried, absorbed each other's cultures and faiths, become one another. As late as the 1850s, one in five marriages in the city of Poznań (or, as it was known to its then Prussian rulers, Posen) was between Poles and Germans. Across wide stretches of territory, for much of their history, the degree of intermarriage between Poles and Lithuanians/Ukrainians/Byelorussians was at least as high. It remains reflected today in the frequent incidence in the Polish population of surnames of diverse linguistic-ethnic origins (a comparable diversity can, of course, be found among Poland's neighbours). In the great and bloody ethnic untanglings that have blighted the twentieth century, these people were often forced to choose their 'ethnic identity', whatever this concept (scientifically bizarre but conventionally indispensable) is understood to mean.

For much of its history, Poland was very much a border region of more or less peacefully co-existing peoples and cultures. From the late Middle Ages onwards, its elites evolved a remarkable consensual political culture, without which the Polish state would probably have fallen apart under the strains of accommodating its differences. These divergences and the less than satisfactory mechanisms of consensus brought the Polish state close to disintegration during the seventeenth century and, we can see with hindsight, contributed massively to its destruction by the end of the eighteenth. While there is much to criticize in that failed political and constitutional experiment, it is worth pointing out that the governance of multi-ethnic political entities in our own times has left at least as much to be desired. The ruling elites' consensual commitments translated into a strong attachment to 'liberty', which, in turn, helped those who considered themselves to be Poles to survive the nineteenth century, yet also helped to bring about the catastrophically unsuccessful insurrections of 1830–1 and 1863–4.

By the late nineteenth century, amid universally burgeoning nationalisms, the old notion of the Pole as a nobleman who could readily accommodate more than one 'ethnic' identity showed itself to be unsustainable romantic nostalgia. Some within the diverse ethnic groups living on territories which once formed part of the Polish state would indignantly deny that they ever shared a common homeland. Poland's current homogeneity is very much an enforced product of the Second World War and its immediate aftermath. It is also something not seen in Poland since at least the middle of the fourteenth century. The pasts of Poland and its neighbours are too intertwined for easy, compartmentalized analysis. The nation-state is not yet dead, but, if it were, a reading of Poland's history might be much facilitated. It may not matter very much to a Briton or American (not that these labels are without their own pitfalls) that a Pole will refer to the city of L'viv (in Ukraine) as Lwów; it would probably not matter to a Ukrainian. But it might matter to a Ukrainian if the label Lwów is applied to L'viv in a book such as this, aimed at a wider, non-Polish or non-Ukrainian readership. In such a context, 'Lwów' might say something which 'L'viv' does not (and vice versa): a descriptor with a baggage of Polish overtones and belongings; whereas to a Pole, in the same context, 'L'viv' might well appear a denial of the Polish character of a great trading city which was once part of Poland. Seemingly innocuous 'Lemberg' – how Lwów/L'viv was labelled by Austrian bureaucrats – is a hopeless anachronism. Comparable alarms and suspicions can still be generated over other descriptors: Gdańsk/Danzig; Toruń/Thorn; Wilno/Vilnius; Grodno/Gardinas/ Hrodna; even Oświęcim/Auschwitz. If this is a particularly acute problem for historians of Poland (even if born in Britain) seeking to project their past for the benefit of others, it is a problem found throughout much of eastern Europe and bedevils the writing of any history of the region. In this context, the early part of this book is careful to use the term Rus' (not Russia) for the regions to Poland's east – if we cannot avoid the charge of furthering Polish terminological imperialism, we would certainly wish to avoid that of abetting its Muscovite variant.

We appreciate that our approach to such sensitivities will satisfy few who have any emotional involvement or even substantial knowledge of eastern Europe's past. There are too many of these pasts to be quietly reconciled. We have therefore eschewed consistency in the naming of parts: we are conscious that this will only lead to historical absurdities; we have sometimes avoided the issue altogether. We have used terminology which seems right for the period. Thus, in chapter 2, Vilnius appears as Vilnius; as Wilno in chapters 3, 4 and 5; as both Wilno and Vilnius in chapter 6; 'Thorn' and 'Danzig' in the early modern period are labels meant to reflect the Germanic character of their elites, integral components of the late Jagiellonian state and Polish-Lithuanian Commonwealth. English is insufficiently acquainted with east European toponymy to permit the consistent use of anglicized, and therefore neutral (?), descriptors such as Warsaw or Kiev. Even where such descriptors exist, current usage tends to the adoption of Polish forms (Kraków, rather than Cracow; even British football commentators have been known to struggle with Łódź, rather than Lodz). We are only too happy to encourage this development. We have listed some alternative versions in the index. Readers should feel at liberty to argue among themselves as to what form we should really have used. At a hopefully less contentious level, we have chosen to retain some established anglicizations of Polish proper names (thus, John Casimir, as opposed to Jan Kazimierz); and drop other anglicizations in favour of the Polish (Bolesław, Władysław or Stanisław, rather than Boleslas, Ladislas, or Stanislaus/Stanley). Once again, we have been guided by our own instincts rather than any spurious consistency, though we accept that what feels right to us will not seem so to others.

This is primarily a political history. It is here that we feel the need for a coherent narrative to be most pressing. This has meant some regrettable sacrifices: economic and social developments receive comparatively limited attention, particularly in the first three chapters. The Jews, so important in Poland's past life, receive far too little acknowledgement. To do them justice, and the many others who have received altogether too short shrift in these pages, would mean abandoning all hope of conciseness. For those who want their histories sprawling and expansive, we cannot do other than point them in the direction of Norman Davies' *God's playground: a history of Poland* (2 volumes, Oxford, Clarendon, 1981).

Numerous persons have helped and encouraged us, not least by pointing out our shortcomings. Our thanks for their advice and apologies for not always having followed it to Danuta Manikowska, Robert Frost, Robert Swanson, Chris Wickham, Jūratė Kiaupiėnė, Michael Laird and Richard Hofton. Graeme Murdock has provided pleasurably clear illumination of the darker crevasses of late medieval and early modern Hungarian and Balkan politics. Will Zawadzki and Anna Zawadzki have helped with the search for illustrations in the second half of the book. Will has also provided invaluable advice on the design of the maps, while Meg Zawadzki has removed some stylistic infelicities from the text. Our mistakes remain ours alone. We both owe a particular debt of gratitude to William Davies at Cambridge University Press: he has been a model of forbearance, patience, understanding and all-round helpfulness.

A NOTE ON POLISH PRONUNCIATION

The pronunciation of Slavonic languages, not least Polish, can be something of a problem for the uninitiated. The following can only be a very simplistic guide; it is not meant for philological or phonetic perfectionists.

ą:	similar to the French 'on' if crossed with the 'o' in 'dome'
ę:	similar to the French 'on', if crossed with the 'e' in 'get'
ó:	u, as in 'shook'
y:	i, as in 'bit'
ci:	short 'chee', as in 'chit'
si:	short 'she', as in 'ship'
Ć, ć:	'ch', as in 'chop'
cz:	as the above, but harsher
c:	'ts' as in 'pots', except in the combinations 'ci' and 'cz'
Ł, ł:	'w' as in 'wet'
ń:	slighty softened 'n' – as in Spanish 'ñ'
Ś, ś:	'sh' as in 'shut'
sz:	as the above, but harsher
rz, Ż, ż:	as the above, but with a 'z' sound (zh as in 'Zhukov')
w:	'v' as in vile
zi:	pronounced as first two letters of French 'gîte'
Ź, ź:	pronounced as first letter of French 'gîte'

I

POLAND, TO 1795

I

Piast Poland, ?–1385

The Romans never conquered Poland: a source of pride to its first native chronicler, Bishop Vincent of Kraków, writing around 1200, but a nuisance to the modern historian. Since Rome neither subjugated, nor abandoned Poland, there is no widely recognizable Year One from which to launch a historical survey. The year AD 966 has to serve, for in that year the ruler of what has come to be known as 'Poland' accepted (and imposed) Latin Christianity. We know as little about this event as we do about anything else that happened during the next hundred years or so. The written record begins to assume substantial proportions only in the fourteenth century. Some eighty years before Bishop Vincent, an unknown clergyman, possibly of French origin (hence his appellation Gall-Anonim, 'the anonymous Gaul') produced the earliest chronicle emanating directly from the Polish lands. Archaeological and toponymic evidence, the accounts of foreign observers and travellers, inform the historian little better than the folk memory on which Gall relied to locate the founder of the ruling house in a successful peasant adventurer called 'Piast',[1] who had overthrown a tyrannical predecessor, Popiel (supposedly gnawed to death by some very hungry mice), at some point in the ninth century AD.

The later twentieth century has added its own myths. In the forty or so years after the Second World War, Polish historiography was

---

[1] The label 'Piast' was attributed to the ruling dynasty only in the late seventeenth century by Silesian antiquarians. Medieval sources used formulae such as 'the dukes and princes of Poland' ('duces et principes Poloniae').

wont to depict a 'Piast Poland' whose boundaries were curiously congruent with those of the post-1945 state. This reflected more than an attempt by a deeply unpopular communist regime to legitimize itself by appeal to an original past. It was also symptomatic of a genuine need for stability after a thousand years of a history when borders were rarely fixed, but could contract and expand, twist and disappear within the span of a lifetime, taking in or discarding groups of people some of whom even today cannot wholly decide on their own identity: 'Poles'? 'Germans'? 'Ukrainians'? 'Jews'? 'Belorussians'? 'Lithuanians'?

'Polak' (*polonus, polanus, polenus* were the commonly used medieval Latin forms) derives from *pole*, plain – the land of the *Polanie*, living in the basin of the middle Warta river, in the western part of modern-day Poland. Some kind of distinct political unit emerged in this area between the sixth and ninth centuries AD, with well-established commercial and administrative centres in Gniezno and Poznań. The primacy of these western lands came to be acknowledged in the thirteenth century with their designation as 'Old' or 'Great' Poland (Wielkopolska, Polonia Maior) – as opposed to 'Little' Poland (Małopolska, Polonia Minor) to the south and south-east. What linked the Polanie to their neighbours and to so many peoples of the great Eurasian plain was language – *słowo* – the word: those who spoke intelligibly to one another were Słowianie, *Sclavinii*, Slavs – as opposed to the 'Dumb Ones' (*Niemcy*) who spoke no tongue intelligible to 'Poles' or 'Czechs' or 'Russians'. The 'Dumb Ones' were mainly from the Germanic world – Saxons, Franks, Bavarians, Lotharingians. In the unceasing border wars of the eighth and ninth centuries, the 'Dumb Ones' took so many Slavic tribesmen captive that their chroniclers were able to more than hold their own in the insult trade: *sclavus* replaced *servus* as the Latin word for 'slave'.

Linguistic community did not mean political solidarity. The Slav tribes of the lands between the Elbe and the Oder were as likely to be in conflict with their Polish/Silesian/Czech neighbours of the east as with incomers from the west. It was only in the course of the twelfth century that these marcherlands were effectively brought under the authority of German rulers. Only in 1157 did Slav Brunabor become German Brandenburg. In 965, the *knez*, the prince of the Polanie, Mieszko I, thwarted a troublesome alliance between the Christian Czechs and his pagan, Slav neighbours to the west by his marriage to Dobrava, daughter of Duke Boleslav I of Bohemia. Conversion in the following year allowed Mieszko to tap into the manpower, military technology and politics of the German Empire in a way that would have been inconceivable if he had remained a heathen. Most of the early clergy who came to Poland were German; Mieszko and his successors were as willing to conclude marriage alliances with the great families of the Empire as with the ruling dynasties of Scandinavia, Hungary and the Rus' lands. They were quite prepared to furnish the emperors with tribute and warriors in return for recognition of their lordship over the borderlands that they disputed with the German marcher lords. Mieszko's marriage to Dobrava was something of an aberration – the Piasts and the Bohemian Přemyslids had too many conflicting interests for family ties to take root.

According to the Arab-Jewish merchant, Ibrahim ibn Yakub, Mieszko had 3,000 heavily armed cavalry and infantry at his call. Even if this is a very flattering assessment (the emperor Otto I, ruling over lands perhaps five times as populous, had an army of 5,000 mounted knights), Mieszko's retinue of warriors was an impressive instrument, which enabled him to annex Silesia from his former Bohemian in-laws. His son, Bolesław I Chrobry, 'the Valiant' (992–1026), deprived them of the burgeoning commercial centre of Kraków and its southern hinterland, extending the Piast realm to the Carpathian mountains. The two rulers brought under their sway the Pomeranian lands between the Vistula and Oder deltas. It was probably Mieszko who founded the port town of Gdańsk around 980 to consolidate his grip on lands at the mouth of the Vistula. Bolesław's western forays, into lands still peopled by fellow Slavs, took him to the Elbe. In 1018, Emperor Henry II reluctantly acknowledged his rule over Militz and Lusatia, west of the Oder. In 1018, too, Bolesław intervened in Kiev, to secure his brother-in-law, Sviatopolk, on its throne. He was even briefly able to impose his rule over Bohemia, Moravia and much of modern-day Slovakia.

Almost annual expeditions for human and material plunder were essential to the 'economy' of the early medieval state. But Piast

Poland, with a population of probably below a million in lands densely tangled by forests, swamps and heaths, could not sustain such efforts indefinitely. The aggressive reigns of Mieszko II (1025–34), Bolesław II (1058–81) and Bolesław III (1102–38) were interwoven with periods of revolt, foreign invasion, and recovery. Even Chrobry faced serious rebellions in 1022 and 1025. He had to pull out of Bohemia and his successors had to abandon Moravia and Slovakia. His protégé, Sviatopolk, was driven out of Kiev by his brother, Yaroslav 'the Wise', as soon as Polish forces withdrew. Mieszko II had to abandon Militz and Lusatia; he lost his kingdom and his life to domestic revolt. Between 1034 and 1039, Poland may have been without a ruler at all (some chroniclers tried to fill the gap with a Bolesław the Forgotten, but he is just as likely to have been a Bolesław the Non-Existent), as it threatened to disintegrate under the pressures of pagan reaction and Bohemian invasion. Mieszko II's son, Casimir (Kazimierz) 'the Restorer' (1039–58), needed at least fifteen years to stitch his lands back together with Imperial and Kievan help. It was during his reign that Kraków began to establish itself as Poland's capital: the old political and metropolitan centre of Gniezno was so devastated by the disorders as to be temporarily uninhabitable.

Few, if any, of the Slav tribes east of the Elbe accepted Christianity gracefully. The Polanie and their associated tribes were no exception. Christianity was the price that had to be paid to escape the fate of their more obdurate fellow Slavs to the west, such as the Wends, who kept faith with the pagan ways and suffered one murderous Christian onslaught after another, until they lost their gods, their independence and their identity. Today, between the Elbe and the Oder, some 50,000 Sorbs survive with their language, an ethnic and linguistic reminder that the peoples who lived in these lands were once not German but Slav.

To the bulk of the populace, Christianity brought burdens which only exacerbated those imposed by the ruler's war bands and garrisons. Bolesław I took his role as Christian ruler sufficiently seriously to be regarded by the young emperor Otto III as his partner in the conversion of Slavonic Europe. In the person of Vojtěch (Adalbert) of Prague, Bolesław furnished Poland with its first, albeit adopted, martyr – in 997 Vojtěch was slain by the

1   One of the earliest surviving Polish churches: the collegiate church of the Blessed Virgin and St Alexis, *c.* 1150–61, at Tum, near Łęczyca, in western Poland.

heathens of Prussia whom the king hoped he would convert. He was canonized two years later. Like Vojtěch, most of the early clergy came from abroad. They were supported with tributes and tithes exacted by a brutal ruling apparatus. A significant native clergy did not begin to emerge until at least three or four generations after Mieszko I's conversion. The deeper Christianization of Poland began only with the coming of the monasteries and friars in the twelfth and thirteenth centuries. Until then, the Church remained an alien, unpopular institution, foisted on the people by a ruling elite in pursuit of its own political and expansionist ambitions. But it differentiated Poland from its eastern Slav neighbours in one crucial respect. The new bishops, with their dioceses and synods, with their political and economic privileges, with their ties to Rome, came eventually to open a door to the differentiation and variegation of political authority, limiting the ruler's monopoly on power. Further east, the traditions of Orthodoxy and Byzantine caesaropapism were to direct the lands of Rus' along a very different path of political development.

The new institution of kingship which accompanied Christianity found little wider echo. The Polish word for king, *król* – a corruption of 'Karol' (Charles, Charlemagne) – reflects its alien character. Bolesław I, Mieszko II and Bolesław II were Poland's only crowned monarchs before 1296. All faced revolts almost immediately after their coronations (1025, 1026 and 1076). Opposition came not just from the lower orders. Mieszko II was murdered by a disgruntled court official. Bolesław II emulated Chrobry in his forays into Kiev, Bohemia and Hungary; he backed the pope against the emperor in the Investiture Conflict; he was a generous benefactor of the Church – but it was an ecclesiastic, Bishop Stanisław of Kraków, who appears to have headed a reaction among the king's own notables against his demanding foreign policy. In 1078, Bolesław had him hacked to pieces, apparently for treason, and inadvertently produced Poland's first native martyr (Stanisław was to be canonized in 1253). Bolesław was deposed, exiled and replaced by his younger brother, Wodzisław Herman (1079–1102). Real power was exercized by the *palatinus*, Sieciech, head of the war bands and of the network of garrison-towns, the *grody*.

Wodzisław's elevation highlights a key weakness of the Piast state (though hardly one peculiar to it) – the absence of a secure means of succession. Shortly before his death in 992, Mieszko I placed Poland under direct papal jurisdiction, apparently in the hope that ecclesiastical influence might preserve the rights of his sons by his second marriage to the German princess Oda. Bolesław I settled the matter in his own way: he either exiled his rivals or had them blinded. Bishop Vincent's chronicle suggests a society in which any form of hereditary claim had to be reinforced with a more general acceptance of the individual ruler: Mieszko's lineal descendants may not have been wholly assured of their position until the consolidation of Christianity, in the late twelfth century. The presence of a younger brother provided a figurehead for a revolt against Bolesław II; the availability of Wodzisław's sons, Zbigniew and Bolesław, facilitated revolts against their father and his over-mighty palatine, Sieciech, in 1097 and 1100. When the emperor Henry V invaded in 1109, it was in support of Zbigniew (who also had the backing of the Church hierarchy) against his ruthless younger half-brother. Despite a formal reconciliation,

Bolesław III had Zbigniew blinded and killed in 1111. Bolesław's nickname, 'Wrymouth', may well refer to the ease with which he broke his oaths rather than to any physical deformity. He, too, tried to solve the problem of the succession, this time in more civilized fashion, in his testament of 1138, by a borrowing from Kievan practice: overall political authority would be vested in the *princeps*, the eldest of his five sons. The fertile southern provinces of Kraków and Sandomierz would form the territorial basis of the *princeps'* power, but he would also retain the right to make appointments to all the leading lay and ecclesiastical offices of the Piast patrimony. The younger brothers would be his viceroys in different provinces; the position of *princeps* would always be held by the eldest survivor. This expedient proved no more successful than in the Kievan state. Poland began to break up. In 1202, there were five Piast duchies; by 1250, nine; and by 1288, seventeen, at least ten of them in Silesia. Fratricidal strife inevitably followed. Even in the first, post-Wrymouth generation, the efforts of Mieszko III (ruling periodically between 1138 and 1202 – his nickname was 'the Old') to impose authoritarian rule provoked chronic revolts. In 1177, his siblings, nephews and his own son joined forces to assign the position of *princeps* to the youngest of Bolesław Wrymouth's sons, Casimir 'the Just'. He could still exercise real authority outside his own Kraków-Sandomierz lands, through his patronage of the Church and his power to appoint bishops. As canonical elections increasingly took hold, his successors were less well placed. Kraków retained a prestigious and symbolic role – no one could credibly lay claim to the title of *princeps* without control over it. Casimir the Just and his successors in the principate were, in effect, elected rulers. The idea that the *princeps* should always be the eldest Piast was tacitly abandoned. The position was filled by unanimous or majority agreement among the different Piast dukes. But, ever more, the consent of the Kraków-Sandomierz notables was sought; by the second half of the thirteenth century, the approval of the wealthy, largely German-speaking Kraków urban elite came to be essential.

Fragmentation may, paradoxically, have facilitated economic and cultural development. Rulers and their leading subjects had little choice but to expand their resources by intensive means, just

Map 1   Early Piast Poland, *c.* 1000.

Vilnius

LITHUANIAN TRIBES

TRIBES

Nieman

RUS'

Warsaw
MASOVIA

Bug

Vistula

SCALE

| 0 | 50 | 100 | 150 | 200 | 250 km |

| 0 | | 50 | | 100 | | 150 miles |

Kiev ●

Sandomierz

San

(MAŁOPOLSKA)

RUS'

● Košice

HUNGARY

like the lords of Germany's thinly populated eastern marches. From the early twelfth century, the lords of these territories began to attract new colonists with the promise of collective and individual exemptions from dues and services and the prospect of lighter burdens in the future. The settlement of the east Elbian lands developed into a major enterprise, as entrepreneurs and speculators, *locatores*, looked to enrich themselves by the provision of human capital – migrants from Franconia, Saxony and the Low Countries – to landowners desperate for the manpower without which even the most extensive estates were useless. The ruling elite of the Polish territories were as anxious as their German counterparts to attract settlers, or, as they were styled, 'guests', *hospites* – a recognition of the need to regard them as 'free' men. The *hospites* brought with them new, more compact field systems and technical innovations in the form of mills and heavier ploughs. In 1175, Duke Bolesław 'the Tall' (1163–1201) of Silesia allowed German Cistercians to settle colonists at Lubiąż on the Oder, exempting them from 'Polish law' – they were to remain free from the normal dues, services and burdens which a Polish prince might choose to impose on his subjects. A much more systematic and intensive programme of colonization under 'German law', *ius teutonicum*, was developed in Silesia by Bolesław's son, Henry 'the Bearded' (1201–38). 'German law' meant not the laws in Germany, but the more or less standard package of terms under which colonists from the German lands were settled east of the Elbe and Oder rivers. West of the Elbe, the bulk of the peasantry remained closely tied to their lords – unless they broke loose and made the difficult decision to settle in the east on more generous terms, albeit under harsher physical conditions. When, in 1229, Henry the Bearded began to run out of Germans, he took to locating Polish migrants under 'German law'. Other lords, dukes and ecclesiastics followed suit. There was some compensation – German law actually restricted the terms on which settlers might leave, by comparison with more open-ended Polish practice. By the middle of the fourteenth century, if not earlier, the bulk of the Polish peasantry, including a largely assimilated German element, could regard themselves as in some sense 'free'. But assimilation worked both ways. By the end of the thirteenth century, in central and northern Silesia, the more fertile areas most attractive to new settlers were becoming German, rather than Polish. By 1300, the once Polish village of Wlen, near Wrocław, had become the German Lähn; and Wrocław itself, to increasing numbers of its inhabitants, was becoming Breslau. Parallel influences were at work in Polish towns. Most were very small. The largest, Kraków and Wrocław, are unlikely to have numbered more than 5,000 inhabitants each in 1200. This was not enough to generate the wealth that Poland's rulers wanted. Seeking to attract merchants and craftsmen, they looked to the German lands, where, in the course of the eleventh century, more and more towns had succeeded in wresting a degree of genuine autonomy from their overlords: they appointed their own judges, administrators and magistrates. The towns' new status found legal expression in charters of rights and privileges. Magdeburg, the closest significant urban centre to Polish lands, had secured effective self-rule in 1188. Its pattern of an elected or co-opted bench of aldermen, sitting as magistrates, assisting a mayoral figure, the Vogt (in Poland, *wójt*), was to become almost universal in the Polish lands. In 1211, Henry the Bearded conferred Magdeburg law on the little Silesian town of Złotoryja; in 1258, Bolesław 'the Bashful' did the same for Kraków. Judicial appeals and other delicate questions were usually referred to Magdeburg itself for advice and adjudication. Before the thirteenth century was over, around one hundred Polish towns had Magdeburg-style municipal institutions.

The governing classes in these towns were increasingly Germans and German-speaking. Indigenous Polish peasants were forbidden (ineffectively) to live in Kraków, since princes and landlords feared the drain of manpower from their own estates. In Silesia, by the end of the Middle Ages, Polish was the language of the peasantry, although even in the countryside it began to go into stubborn retreat. In larger towns, Germans, or Poles assimilated as Germans, made up a majority. Those most likely to resent germanization were, to begin with, the native Polish clergy, who, as they found their feet, increasingly opposed the intrusion of Germans into their ranks. At the synod of Łęczyca in 1285, Archbishop Jakub Świnka of Gniezno warned that Poland might become a 'new Saxony' if German contempt for Polish language, customs, clergy and ordinary people went unchecked.

The local rulers of Silesia and western Pomerania were particularly exposed to German wealth and culture, whose charms outshone those of an impoverished and backward Poland. It was only towards the later thirteenth century, encouraged by clerics like Archbishop Świnka, that Polish developed enough sophistication to be suitable for the delivery of sermons. As a literary medium, it could scarcely compare with German before the early 1500s. Henry the Bearded of Silesia had enjoyed listening to the fireside tales of Polish peasant storytellers; his great-grandson, Henry IV Probus 'the Honourable' (1257–90) spoke German by preference and was proud to compose and perform poetry and song in the language, a veritable *Minnesänger*. Further east, German communities in the towns tended to be isolated islands. In the countryside, even in much of Silesia, German peasants were more likely be assimilated by native elements. The same went for German knights and adventurers attracted to the courts of Polish rulers.

The twelfth and thirteenth centuries also witnessed the transformation of the old Piast rulers' erstwhile warrior-bands into 'knights', *milites*, in the western European mould. Those soldiers who obtained enough land and peasants for themselves from their ruler to maintain a warhorse, weapons and armour, or who were sufficiently well placed to take part in the process of *locatio*, came to form a western-European style of military aristocracy. The less well-endowed, the *włodycy*, fell into the ranks of peasants. In principle, the knights held land in return for service (although the kinds of feudal homage ceremonies widespread in France and England were little practised). But as the Piast states fragmented, their rulers found they had to concede immunities and jurisdictional rights to their mounted fighting-men, just as they had had to to the Church. Those with enough chutzpah and resources simply appropriated these rights, so that by the turn of the thirteenth and fourteenth centuries, anyone who could plausibly claim to hold land by *ius militare*, that is, any *rycerz*, would exercise jurisdictional rights over it (the terminology hints at the strength of German influences in the thirteenth century – *rycerz* derives from *Ritter*, German for knight). The dukes reserved, at best, the right to hear appeals. As the dukes gave away, or were obliged to give away, their powers of jurisdiction, they found they had to resort to co-operation and collaboration with their leading subjects. When, in 1228, Władysław 'Spindleshanks' (1202–28) issued the Privilege of Cienia to the bishop of Kraków and the local *barones*, according them the right to be consulted at assemblies, *wiece*, which made laws and heard judicial cases, he was formalizing a situation that had been in the making at least since Wrymouth's reign, in the early twelfth century.

The Catholic Church contributed significantly to the survival of a sense of unity in the Polish lands. Gniezno, given metropolitan status in 999, was able to preserve its ecclesiastical authority over the five other sees of the old Piast state and ultimately to back the programmes of political unification which emerged. After all, the Church itself was one of the chief victims of political disorders. The hierarchy made strong efforts in the thirteenth century to deepen the parish and schools network and to tighten their links to the populace. As the largest landowner after the dukes, the Church had an urgent material interest in halting the processes of political fragmentation – which, in the final analysis, counterbalanced the positive social and economic developments of the twelfth and thirteenth centuries.

The rag-bag of Piast duchies could not hope to aspire to the forceful political role of Mieszko I and his immediate successors. To protect his north-eastern borders against the incursions of still-pagan Prussian and Yatwingian tribes, Conrad, duke of Masovia (Mazowsze) (1202–47), settled the crusading order of the Teutonic Knights on the left bank of the Vistula in 1227. The Poles stood no chance against the devastating Mongol onslaught which wreaked havoc across eastern and central Europe and which swept across Poland in 1241. Perhaps the ablest of the Silesian dukes, Henry 'the Pious', was slain at the battle of Legnica on 9 April. Only news of the death of their Great Khan Ögödei caused the Mongols to withdraw from their Polish and Hungarian conquests in December. They remained in the Crimea and in the steppe-lands of the Black Sea and the eastern Balkans, a new and long-lasting menace to south-eastern Poland. Virtually all semblance of orderly rule collapsed in their wake. Dukes became robber-barons, strong enough to aggravate their subjects' misery, too weak to impose order, let alone unity. Dwarf statelets emerged whose rulers could barely hold their own against their leading subjects. Who ruled in Kraków was no longer decided by the dukes, but by the barons, clergy and even townsmen of the area. Silesia was disintegrating. The duchy of Masovia threatened to go the same way. The local princes through whom the Piasts had always ruled in western Pomerania had broken loose during the twelfth century. Only the core lands of Wielkopolska and the principate lands of Kraków and Sandomierz remained more or less intact.

The road to even partial reunification was a tortuous one. In 1289, the nobles, knights and the bishop of Kraków chose as *princeps* Duke Bolesław II of Płock, in Masovia. Bolesław transferred his rights over the principate to his cousin, Władysław 'the Short' (Łokietek, literally 'Elbow-High'), ruler of the little duchies of Łęczyca, Kujawy and Sieradz. Łokietek, a princely thug, found that his penchant for brigandage won much support among knights and squires on their uppers. He was quite unacceptable in Kraków, whose townsmen handed over the capital to Henry IV Probus, the Honourable, duke of Wrocław/Breslau. It was Henry who took the first serious steps towards what would be so symbolically important for any reunification of the Polish lands. He began to negotiate with the papacy and with his patron, the emperor-elect Rudolf, for agreement to his coronation. Just before his childless death in June 1290 he bequeathed the duchy of Kraków to Duke Przemysł II of Wielkopolska. Przemysł was already suzerain of the port of Gdańsk and of eastern Pomerania. On paper, he had a stronger territorial power-base than any of his predecessors for over a century. The idea of a crowned head was much more attractive to a more latinized Poland than it had been in the early Piast state. Archbishop Świnka was all in favour: the recent canonization of Bishop Stanisław of Kraków, whose dismembered body had undergone a miraculous regrowth, provided an irresistible metaphor for Świnka's aspirations. Przemysł's only serious Polish rival was Łokietek, clinging on in the duchy of Sandomierz. Both men were, however, overshadowed by an ambitious and powerful foreign ruler, Vaclav II of Bohemia.

Vaclav was one of the Middle Ages' most successful territorial stamp-collectors. His father, Přemysl Otakar II (1253–78) – Přemysl to his Slav subjects, Otakar to his Germans – had built up a glittering court at Prague. Bohemia's mineral, commercial and agricultural wealth enabled him to support an ambitious programme of expansion, until his bid for leadership of the German Empire came to an abrupt end when he fell at the battle of Durnkrütt on 26 August 1278, against the closest he had to a German rival, Rudolf of Habsburg.

The petty rulers of the disintegrating Piast lands looked abroad for protection: one such focus of attraction was the Přemyslid court of Bohemia; the other was its rival, the Arpad court of Hungary. After the death of Henry Probus, Vaclav's own ambition to acquire Kraków was abetted by the local barons and patricians. In terms of security, prestige and economic prospects, he offered far more than either Przemysł or Łokietek. Vaclav secured the crucial support of Małopolska by the Privilege of Litomyšl of 1291. He promised its clergy, knights, lords and towns the preservation of all their existing rights, immunities and jurisdictions; he would impose no new taxes on them and fill all existing offices from their ranks. Łokietek's position collapsed. His unruly soldiery and knightly followers spread alienation everywhere they went. By 1294, he had not only to sue for peace but to receive his own remaining lands back from Vaclav as a fief. It may have been to pre-empt the almost certain coronation of Vaclav that Archbishop Świnka persuaded the pope to consent to Przemysł II's coronation in Gniezno cathedral on 26 June 1295. The machinations behind this decision are as obscure as anything in Polish history; nor is it clear whether Przemysł regarded himself as ruler of the whole of Poland, or just of Wielkopolska and eastern Pomerania. He did not survive long enough to test his real support. In February 1296 he was murdered, almost certainly on the orders of the margraves of Brandenburg, whose territorial ambitions were blocked by the new king's lands. He left Poland one enduring bequest, in the shape of the crowned eagle which he adopted as the emblem of his new state.

The nobles of Wielkopolska opted at first for Łokietek as his successor – but his continued inability to control his own men, his readiness to carve up Przemysł's kingdom with other petty dukes, and a military offensive from Brandenburg drastically eroded his support. In 1299, he once again acknowledged Vaclav as overlord. Even Archbishop Świnka, conscious that the Kraków clergy were behind Vaclav, accepted the inevitable. In September 1300 he crowned him king – although he could not refrain from complaining at the 'doghead' of a priest who delivered the coronation sermon in German. Unity, of a kind, was restored. Łokietek was forced into exile. His quest for support took him as far as Rome, where he won the backing of Pope Boniface VIII, hostile to the Přemyslids. Vaclav's last serious opponent, Henry, duke of Głogów/Glogau (1273–1309), nephew of Henry Probus, recognized his suzerainty in 1303. Much of Poland, however, continued to remain under the immediate rule of territorial dukes. Vaclav's direct authority covered mainly Kraków-Sandomierz, Wielkopolska and eastern Pomerania. He left an enduring administrative legacy in the office of *starosta* (literally 'elder'). Its holders acted as viceroys in his different Polish provinces, although his preference for Czechs in this role provoked growing resentment. To Vaclav, of course, the Polish lands were simply a subordinate part of a greater Přemyslid monarchy. Polish reunification for its own sake was of little interest to him.

In January 1301, King Andrew III of Hungary died, leaving no male heirs. Vaclav found the temptation irresistible. His attempts to impose his 11-year-old son, another Vaclav, on Hungary and, in the process, massively expand Přemyslid power, were too much for the Hungarians, the papacy, Albrecht of Habsburg and the rulers of south Germany. By 1304 a Hungarian–German coalition had been formed. To gain the support of the margraves of Brandenburg, Vaclav promised to hand over to them eastern Pomerania and the port city of Gdańsk. His supporters in Wielkopolska, already seething at the harsh rule of Czech *starostowie*, could not accept this. Early in 1305, revolt shook the southern part of the province. Those not reconciled to Czech rule would have preferred to turn to Henry, duke of Głogów. Vaclav's Hungarian and German enemies declared for his exiled rival, Łokietek. Hungarian forces supporting Charles Robert of Anjou's bid for their throne helped Łokietek seize control of almost all the territories of Małopolska, except for Kraków itself. Vaclav II made peace with the coalition, just before he died on 21 June 1305. He agreed to withdraw from Hungary. But to keep the margraves of Brandenburg on his side, the young

Vaclav III renewed his father's undertaking to cede Gdańsk and Pomerania and prepared to enter Poland at the head of an army. If Vaclav had not been murdered at the instigation of discontented Czech lords on 4 August 1306, he and Łokietek might well have divided the Polish territories between themselves. Instead, Bohemia was plunged into rivalries over the succession, until the election of John of Luxemburg in 1310. In Poland, although the townsmen of Kraków reconciled themselves to Łokietek, most of Wielkopolska preferred to recognize Henry of Głogów.

In 1307, disaster struck Łokietek in Pomerania. The German patriciates of the two chief towns, Tczew and Gdańsk, gravitated towards the margraves of Brandenburg; the Polish knighthood of the countryside remained loyal to Łokietek. In August 1308, the castle of Gdańsk was besieged by the troops of margraves Otto and Waldemar. Łokietek called on the help of the Teutonic Knights. The arrival of their forces lifted the siege of the castle – which on the night of 14 November they proceeded to seize for themselves, massacring Łokietek's men in the process. By the end of 1311, most of Polish Pomerania was in the Knights' hands.

Founded in the late twelfth century as an offshoot of the Order of St John of Jerusalem, just in time to be forced out by Islam's counter-attack against the Crusader states of the Middle East, the Teutonic Knights had relocated their military-proselytizing operations to Hungary and Transylvania. King Andrew II threw them out once their ambitions to carve out their own independent state revealed themselves. In 1227, Conrad I, duke of Masovia, settled them in the county of Chełmno on the Vistula in order to defend his eastern borders against the pagan tribes of Prussia, while he devoted himself to feuding with his Piast relatives. Backed by emperors and popes (the Knights proved adept at playing one off against the other), patronized by the rulers and knighthood of Christian Europe (not least by individual Piast princes), they built up a a *de facto* independence. Their most enthusiastic supporters included Přemysl Otakar II (in whose honour they named the new port of Königsberg in 1255), Vaclav II and John of Bohemia. By the late 1270s, they had subdued the Prussian tribes; they could embark on the process of colonisation which gave the area its Germanic character for over 600 years. The Order was also able –

precisely because it was a religious organization, bound by a rule, dedicated to the higher goal of the spread of the Catholic faith and the conversion of the heathen – to organize its territories on lines very different from those of contemporary medieval territories. The Order represented the impersonal state – something higher than a dynastic or patrimonial entity. The command structures of what has come to be known as the *Ordensstaat* were less subject to the whims and favouritisms of individual monarchs. Its Grand Masters were elected from the tried and the tested by an inner circle of superiors who had shown how to combine prayer and aggression, faith and brutality. They and their fellow northern-Crusaders, the Knights of the Sword further along the Baltic coast, in what are now Latvia and Estonia, could suffer setbacks, but, constantly renewed by fresh recruits and enthusiastic part-timers, they could always rise above them. The actual fighting monks, the German Knights of the Blessed Virgin, were, however, few in numbers – this was their weakness. Control of Gdańsk and its hinterland permitted a steady flow of settlers, soldiers, recruits and allies from the German lands. In 1309 the Grand Master, Conrad von Feuchtwangen, moved his principal headquarters from Venice to Marienburg (now Malbork) on the lower Vistula. This was the *Ordensstaat*'s new capital, rapidly built up into one of the most formidable fortified complexes of medieval Europe, a mirror of the Knights' power and pride. The fragile entity ruled by Łokietek and his successors could do little more than rail and complain at the Order's perfidy and brutality – but its rulers could not subdue what they had nurtured.

Łokietek had no realistic hopes of recovering Pomerania. Most of Wielkopolska remained alienated. The dukes of Masovia mistrusted him. In May 1311, only Hungarian help enabled him to subdue a major revolt of German townsfolk in Kraków. Poles replaced Germans in key positions on the town council, Latin replaced German as the official language of town records. True, it was not many years before German burghers and merchants regained their old influence, but the town itself ceased to be the political force it once had been. The repression did little to enhance Łokietek's appeal to townsmen elsewhere.

In 1309, his rival in Wielkopolska, Duke Henry of Głogów died,

2   The Teutonic Knights' castle and principal administrative seat, at
Malbork (Marienburg). Fourteenth century. The castle underwent
extensive restoration in the 1820s by the Prussian authorities, who used it
as a showcase for the Teutonic Knights' (and, by extension, Prussia's)
'historic mission' in the east.

leaving five young sons, all more German than Polish. The region's
knights preferred Łokietek to fragmentation and German rule, but
it was not until the submission of the town of Poznań in November
1314 that serious opposition was eliminated. In control of Wielkopolska and Kraków, Łokietek could realistically aspire to the
royal dignity – were it not for the rival claims of the new king of
Bohemia, John of Luxemburg, who had cheerfully taken over the
claims of his Přemyslid predecessors. Most of the Silesian and
Masovian dukes looked to him. Brandenburg and the Teutonic
Knights endorsed him, in the expectation of satisfying their own
titles and claims. Pope John XXII, whose consent was necessary to
a coronation in what was technically a papal fief, was reluctant to
offend either party. He gave his consent in terms so ambiguous as
to suggest that he considered both men to have a legitimate royal
title. When Łokietek's coronation did finally take place on 20
January 1320, it was not in Gniezno but, for the first time, in

Kraków. The new venue was dictated not only by a recognition of the greater economic importance of the southern provinces but by a tacit acknowledgement of the still limited extent of Łokietek's territorial support. He controlled less than half of the territory which Bolesław Wrymouth had ruled: Wielkopolska in the west, Kraków and Sandomierz in the south, the two regions linked in the central Polish lands by his own duchies of Łęczyca and Sieradz. Łokietek was more king of Kraków than king of Poland. He was fortunate that John of Bohemia had his own difficulties with the Czech nobility.

Łokietek sought security through marriage alliances: in 1320, he cemented his long-standing alliance with the Angevins of Hungary when his daughter Elizabeth (1305–80) married King Charles Robert (1308–42). In 1325, the king secured his son's marriage to Aldona (d. 1339), daughter of the Lithuanian prince Gediminas – at the cost of driving the Masovian dukes, perpetually feuding over their eastern borderlands with the Lithuanians, into an alliance with the *Ordensstaat*. His only recourse against the Knights lay in persuading the papacy to issue legal pronouncements enjoining them to restore Pomerania. Such pronouncements (never definitive) were indeed made, but the Knights paid no attention. John of Bohemia prepared, in 1327, to attack Kraków – and had he not been kept in check by Charles Robert from Hungary, Łokietek's monarchy might not have survived. Most of the dukes of southern Silesia declared themselves John's vassals. Łokietek's offensive against Duke Wacław (1313–36) of Płock only precipitated incursions by his allies, Brandenburg and the Knights. Łokietek bought Brandenburg off in 1329 with the county of Lubusz (Lebus), at the confluence of the Warta and the Oder. In the winter of 1328–9, John of Luxemburg and the Knights undertook a 'crusade' against Łokietek's Lithuanian allies. The Polish military diversion into the county of Chełmno backfired: John and the Knights conquered the northern Polish territory of Dobrzyń, which John, by virtue of his claims to the Polish throne, generously awarded to the Knights. Duke Wacław of Płock declared himself to be his vassal. So did most of the remaining Silesian dukes. The Knights followed up with an offensive into Wielkopolska in July 1331. They comprehensively sacked Gniezno, although, as a religious order, they felt it politic to spare the cathedral. On 27 September, the Polish and Teutonic armies met at Płowce. The battle lasted most of the day; if, on balance, this pyrrhic encounter was a Polish victory, it resolved nothing. It marked the limit of Łokietek's military endeavour. The king could raid, but not reconquer; above all, he lacked the resources and the organization to take on the Knights' strongholds. Had John of Luxemburg also invaded – as he had promised the Knights – Płowce might have been even more irrelevant than it was. In 1332, the Knights more than made up for Płowce by occupying Łokietek's old patrimonial duchy of Kujawy. In August, he had to agree to a truce which left them in possession of all their recent gains. Through sheer, murderous persistence, he had semi-reunited Poland. But at his death, on 2 March 1333, he left an even smaller kingdom than the one which had acknowledged him at his coronation in 1320. His successor, Casimir III, began his reign by renewing the truce with the Teutonic Knights.

Domestically, Poland needed stability, which could only come about by strengthening royal authority. Externally, the new king had not only to resolve relations with the *Ordensstaat* and the House of Luxemburg, he had to deal with a power vacuum on Poland's south-east borders, which threatened to embroil him with the Tatars and with Lithuania. Poland continued to lie in the shadow of the Hungarian Angevins, first, of Casimir's brother-in-law, Charles I Robert, and then his nephew Louis the Great (1342–82), both of whom had their own designs on the Polish throne. The realm, the 'Crown' as it was styled by his jurists – Corona Regni Poloniae – that Casimir ruled, a narrow and irregular lozenge of territory, spilled from north-west to south-east on either side of the Vistula; with probably fewer than 800,000 inhabitants, it contained less than half the territories and population that might plausibly have been called Polish. Against the Knights, Casimir was largely on his own. The Angevins wanted good relations with them in their own struggles against the Wittelsbachs and the Luxemburgs. Poland was to be kept in its subordinate place. The treaty of Kalisz of 8 July 1343 was a 'compromise' which benefited the Knights. They restored the vulnerable border territories of Dobrzyń and Kujawy lost by Łokietek, but kept what they really wanted – Gdańsk and Pomerania. Casimir also had to

Map 2   Poland under Casimir the Great (1333–70).

face up to the loss of Silesia. In 1348, John of Bohemia's successor
and heir-elect to the Empire (he was to succeed Louis the Bavarian
in 1349), Charles IV, decreed its incorporation into the kingdom of
Bohemia. He even contemplated the incorporation of the duchies
of Płock and Masovia, by virtue of the claims he had inherited from
the Vaclavs and his father. With only faltering support from Louis
of Hungary and with a storm brewing in the south-east, Casimir
resigned himself. By the treaty of Namysłów (Namslau) of 22
November 1348, he abandoned his claims to the Silesian principalities. There was some consolation in the north-east, where in 1355,
Duke Ziemowit III (1341–70), who succeeded in reuniting (albeit
briefly) most of the Masovian lands, acknowledged Casimir's overlordship. He stipulated, however, that the preservation of the
relationship after Casimir's death was contingent on the king's
siring a legitimate male heir.

The troubled situation in the south-east, in the lands of Rus',
helps explain Casimir's retreat in the west. After the reign of
Yaroslav I the Wise (1019–54), the once-great principality of Kiev
had undergone its own dynastic fragmentation. The Mongol onslaughts of 1237–40 had savaged these lands even more viciously
than Poland. The successor-states of Kievan Rus' were largely
reduced to tributaries of the Golden Horde, established in the
Eurasian steppes. The continued raids of the Mongols, or Tatars as
they were widely known, carried them periodically into Polish
territory. In 1338, Bolesław-Iurii, the childless ruler of the two
westernmost principalities of Halych and Vladimir, and a scion of
the Masovian Piasts, recognized Casimir as his heir; two years later
his chief nobles poisoned him.

After Bolesław-Iurii's death, Casimir set out to assure himself of
what he regarded as his legitimate inheritance. The fertile Rus'
principalities, straddling the great east–west overland trade route
from Germany to the Black Sea, offered pleasing prospects of
enriching both the nobility of southern Poland and the merchants
of Kraków. They could serve as a buffer zone against Tatar raids.
They offered some compensation for the lands renounced in the
west and north. They also aroused the appetite of Lithuania and
the Hungarian Angevins. If Casimir did not annex them, others
would. His invasion of 1340 may have been prompted by the very

real fear that the Tatars would impose their direct rule in the 'regnum Galiciae et Lodomeriae', the 'kingdom of Halych and Vladimir'.

It took twenty years of intermittent struggle to impose even partial Polish authority. The Lithuanians established themselves in the north. Casimir satisfied himself with acknowledgement of his suzerainty by Lithuanian princelings. Casimir held the south, centred on the town of L'viv (Lwów/Lvov/Lemberg). But even here he owed his position to Hungarian support. Poland's Rus' lands remained separate from the rest of the Crown: in return for Louis of Hungary's assistance in their subjugation, Casimir agreed in 1350 that they would pass to him on his demise. Divisions in Lithuania, where Duke Gediminas' seven sons quarrelled among themselves after his death in 1341, worked to Casimir's advantage. Even the Black Death helped: it left a sparsely populated Poland largely unscathed, but in 1346 it devastated the Golden Horde. Despite all this, the venture cost Casimir dear. In 1352, to raise money for his war effort, he plundered the archiepiscopal treasury in Gniezno. He borrowed from all and sundry, even from the Teutonic Knights, to whom he allocated the county of Dobrzyń as security. Casimir was playing a risky game.

Casimir's principal achievement was to restore strong monarchic rule at home, within the narrow limits open to any medieval ruler. His deliberate patronage of talented lay and ecclesiastical advisers from southern Poland, the advancement of their careers by service on the royal council, created a generation of new men, ready to aid and abet fresh fiscal and administrative initiatives. The king was more aware than his predecessors of the value of more formal means of government. In 1364, he set up, in Kraków, a partial university or *studium generale*, teaching mainly law, with some medicine and astronomy (the papacy would not agree to instruction in theology). The new institution above all aimed at producing the jurists and lawyers increasingly indispensable to the government of a self-respecting monarchy. Casimir introduced written regulation of judicial procedure and criminal law. In the 1360s, he began to widen the bases of his support to Wielkopolska. He never sought to put an end to the established divisions and differences between his two chief provinces, but instead played their elites off against each other. An extensive programme of revindication of usurped royal lands, often by arbitrary royal fiat, recovered hundreds of properties, though it led to revolt in Wielkopolska in 1352. Casimir made some tactical concessions. In 1360, after the troubles had died down, he had the revolt's leader, Maćko Borkowic, arrested, chained in a dungeon and starved to death. It may be that Casimir wished to build up new elements on which he could base royal power. For the first time, the non-knightly administrators of peasant villages, the *wójtowie* and *sołtysi*, were expected to turn out in their own right on military campaigns. His confiscational programme was matched by an extensive settlement of peasants under 'German law' on royal domain. The king encouraged Jewish immigration, mainly from the Empire, to a greater extent than his predecessors. Whatever reservations his Christian subjects had about them (and there were occasional anti-Jewish riots), Casimir appreciated that they represented an invaluable asset. The 1338 coinage reform helped boost the circulation of small-denominational silver monies. All this, combined with a flourishing north–south and west–east trade, with Kraków at its crossroads, enabled Casimir successfully to pursue a harsh fiscality. He subjected peasant holdings on lay and ecclesiastical estates to an annual land ('plough', *poradlne*) tax of 12 *groszy* per *łan* (about 18.5 hectares). Only land worked directly for the lords was exempt. Such taxation, combined with a reform of the administration of the lucrative royal salt-mines at Bochnia and Wieliczka, first exploited in 1251, enabled him to finance a major defence and reconstruction programme. He built some fifty castles across Poland, and provided twenty-seven towns with new curtain walls (or, rather, they did so on his orders). It was enough to contain the incursions of the Tatars and the ever more frequent raids of the Lithuanians; but none of Casimir's new fortresses could match the Teutonic Knights' defensive marvel at Marienburg. The Kraków patriciate was kept sweet by Casimir's successful commercial policies and by the enhanced prestige it enjoyed from his ban on all municipal appeals to Magdeburg: two appellate urban courts were set up in the capital.

Casimir's greatest failing was dynastic. He had four wives: the first, Aldona-Anna of Lithuania, produced two daughters. The second, Adelaide of Hesse, was pious, unexciting and possibly barren. Casimir despised her and ensured that she spent a miserable marriage confined in remote castles until a divorce came through around 1356 – in scandalous circumstances. The king's lust for Krystyna, the widow of a patrician of Prague, got the better of him. He contracted a bigamous marriage with her even before his divorce from poor Adelaide. No children were produced. In a race against time, he put Krystyna aside to marry, in 1363, Jadwiga, daughter of Duke Henry of Żagań. Four children followed – all girls. Casimir could not produce legitimate sons. He may, nevertheless, have had second thoughts about letting the Angevins get their hands on his lands. In 1368 he adopted as his heir his grandson Kaźko, heir to the duchy of Słupsk in Pomerania. Days before his death on 5 November 1370, he bequeathed his patrimony of Łęczyca, Sieradz and Kujawy to Kaźko. The Rus' lands, Wielkopolska and the territories around Kraków and Sandomierz were to pass to Louis of Hungary. The will threatened to undo at least two generations of progress towards reunifying the old Polish lands. The leading clergy and nobility would not have it. The county court of Sandomierz ruled the will invalid. Kaźko settled for compensation in the shape of the county of Dobrzyń, to be redeemed from the Knights, as a fief to be held of Louis of Hungary, who was to inherit the Crown.

Even in his own lifetime, Casimir III's attainment of a relative peace and prosperity, his legal and administrative reforms earned him the title 'the Great' (the only Polish monarch so honoured). Yet Poland remained a lesser power, too weak to assert its claims to its old territories in the west and north. Casimir probably did as much as could be done with some unpromising materials. For better or worse, he paved the way for a new course of eastwards expansion. He restored strong monarchic rule, although nothing that he did could compensate for the lack of a legitimate son. The kingdom remained desperately vulnerable to personal, dynastic interests.

Whatever the vagaries of Casimir's policies, he had been a strong, at times even brutal, ruler. The nobility had good reasons for welcoming Louis' accession. An absentee king (he ruled in Poland largely through his mother, Casimir's sister, Elizabeth) would almost inevitably be less demanding. He had made promising concessions in return for acceptance of his succession. In 1355, by the Privilege

3　Interior view of the cathedral at Gniezno, as rebuilt after 1342 in the gothic style, replacing the earlier romanesque building. This can be seen as part of a general programme of renovation which contributed much to the reputation of Casimir III.

of Buda, Louis had solemnly assured the nobility and clergy that he would exempt them from any new taxation. His uncertain health, and the gratifying inability he shared with Casimir to father sons, opened up even more favourable prospects. In 1374, the nobility agreed that he could designate one of his three daughters as successor in Poland. In return, from Košice in northern Hungary, Louis promulgated a Privilege, reducing in perpetuity the *poradlne* tax paid by peasants on noble and knightly estates from 12 to 2 *groszy* per *łan*. He went on to promise that he would pay his knights for any military service beyond Poland's borders. In 1381, he extended these provisions to the clergy.

In retrospect, these concessions can be viewed as the beginning of a linear process which was to give the nobility a dominant and domineering position within the state. At the time, they were more an attempt to secure protection against royal fiscal arbitrariness. The 'nobility' were the beneficiaries because they held a near-monopoly of military force. But the Polish 'nobles' at this time were simply all those who held land carrying the obligation – even if it was in many cases notional, rather than real – of performing military, or knight, service. Those affected ranged from lords of the royal council to backwoods squires barely able to afford a horse and military accoutrement. The driving force consisted of a core of some twenty families, most of whom had risen under Casimir III and were determined not to lose their standing in the state. These were the primary beneficiaries of the Privileges of Buda and Košice. That their lesser fellow-*rycerze* also gained was a useful bonus which enabled the great families to build up followings and clienteles – it was to be at least another century before these junior knights/nobles became a serious political force in their own right. Louis' Privileges also applied to the townsmen – their existing rights were confirmed – but they enjoyed only local and *ad hoc* concessions, grants and favours. The towns, divided by commercial rivalries, failed to show a common front. Members of the Kraków patriciate, who might even sit on the royal council, were concerned only with the well-being of their own city, not that of other towns; in any case, they could reasonably aspire to a niche among the aristocratic core. The clergy followed on the coat-tails of the 'communitas nobilium'.

While Louis accepted that he had to make concessions in order
to secure the throne for his daughters, like Vaclav II barely two
generations previously, he felt no compunction at truncating Polish
territory. In 1377 he incorporated Polish Rus' into Hungary. He
confirmed the cession of Silesia to the Luxemburgs. He transferred
disputed border territories to Brandenburg. These measures and the
behaviour of Hungarian officials caused immense resentment,
culminating in the massacre of dozens of Hungarian courtiers
during riots in Kraków in 1376. In 1380, Louis judged it prudent to
relinquish rule in Poland to a caucus of Małopolska potentates,
which did nothing for his wavering support in Wielkopolska. When
he died, in September 1382, the question of the succession was
almost as vexed as ever. The Polish elites had promised to accept his
daughter, Maria – but jibbed when Louis, in an attempt to unite the
Angevin and Luxemburg houses, insisted that she should marry the
unpopular Sigismund of Luxemburg. The Hungarians compro-
mised and suggested that a younger daughter, Jadwiga (she was
barely 10-years-old), could be substituted. Małopolska agreed, but
Wielkopolska wanted Duke Ziemowit IV of Płock as king. Angevin
support in the south proved too strong for him. The entry of pro-
Jadwiga troops obliged Ziemowit to withdraw. Wielkopolska's
leaders were prepared to accept Jadwiga if her long-standing
betrothal to Wilhelm of Habsburg could be broken off in favour of
Ziemowit. She was crowned 'king' (this was not an age which
discarded law and custom lightly) in Kraków on 15 October 1384.
The southern lords had little truck with Wielkopolska's provinc-
ialism. They, too, could play the dynastic card as well as any
Luxemburg or Angevin. Jadwiga's engagement was broken off –
not in favour of Ziemowit, but of the illiterate heathen, Jogaila,
ruler of Lithuania. At Krėva, in Lithuania, on 14 August 1385,
Jogaila promised to convert to Catholicism, to marry Jadwiga –
and to annex to Poland his vast principality, stretching from the
Baltic to the Black Sea. Małopolska's elite had embarked on a
spectacular exercise in corporate dynasticism, well worth the price
of a 12-year-old's feelings. Former Piast Poland stood on the
threshold of a bizarre and unexpected new career.

2

Jagiellonian Poland, 1386–1572

Jogaila of Lithuania was received into the Catholic Church in Kraków cathedral on 15 February 1386. His baptismal name, Władysław, harked back to Łokietek, re-unifier of the 'Crown', the kingdom of Poland – reason enough for Ernst von Zöllner, Grand Master of the Teutonic Knights, to decline the invitation to stand as godfather. In the autumn of 1387, Peter I Mushat, *hospodar* of Moldavia, transferred allegiance and homage for his lands from the rulers of Hungary to Władysław and Jadwiga of Poland. He and Zöllner recognized that a new power had arrived. Barely a hundred years later, not only Poland and Lithuania, but Hungary and Bohemia had come under Jagiellonian rule. It was the greatest dynastic concatenation of territory Europe had yet seen.

Appearances flattered to deceive. In 1386, it was the Teutonic Knights who menaced the existence of Lithuania. Only three years before, they had capped over a century of bloody, unremitting effort by sacking much of the Lithuanian capital of Vilnius and destroying the great stronghold of Trakai. Lithuania was riven by civil war; western, 'lower' Lithuania, Žemaitija, had been ceded to the Teutonic Order by Jogaila's cousin and rival, Vytautas, in return for its support. The union with Poland and the acceptance of Latin Christianity were a desperate gamble by Jogaila to avert a seemingly inevitable subjugation.

Lithuania, stretching from the Baltic in the north to the Black Sea in the south, to the upper Volga and beyond the Dnieper in the east, was a highly unstable political entity. Its rulers had imposed themselves on these vast lands in the the wake of the Mongol invasions of the 1230s. In the late fourteenth century, the Lithuanians proper are unlikely to have numbered more than 300,000. Mainly pagan, they would have been outnumbered sevenfold by the Christian Orthodox inhabitants. Many of the descendants of the ruling house of Gediminas had converted to Orthodoxy. What linguists call 'Middle Belorussian' prevailed in the government's chancelleries, albeit with admixtures of native Lithuanian and Latin. Lithuanian began to receive written form only in the mid-sixteenth century. To the majority of his subjects, Lithuania's 'Grand Duke' was *hospodar* rather than *didysis kunigaikštis*. The formally untrammelled powers of the ruling house allowed for enormous bursts of political and military energy before the inevitable blood rivalries erupted. Jogaila himself had come to power in 1382 with the murder of his uncle Kestutis. When, in February 1387, Jagiełło (to use the polonized form) instituted the bishopric of Vilnius and ordered his armed followers, his 'boyari sive armigeri', to convert to Catholicism, he aimed to deny the Knights any further justification for their onslaught on his homeland. As co-monarch with Jadwiga of Poland, he hoped for Polish support against both them and Kestutis' dangerous son, Vytautas.

The decision by the barons of Małopolska to offer the throne to a pagan ruler was one of the most remarkable in the annals of medieval Europe. While the Union of Krèva of 14 August 1385 obliged Jagiełło, in very general terms, to undertake the recovery of 'all the lands stolen from . . . the kingdom of Poland', the territories annexed by the *Ordensstaat* were a secondary issue. The lords of Małopolska were more concerned to neutralise the dangers from Lithuania itself. As recently as 1376, Jogaila had participated in a savage raid which had laid waste the rich lands between the San and the Vistula. The Krèva Act specifically promised that he would incorporate Lithuania into Poland. For over a hundred and fifty years the Poles were to insist on this. A series of further acts of 'union' (Vilnius, 1401; Horodło, 1413; Grodno, 1432; Vilnius, 1499) continued to stress Lithuania's incorporation or subordination. The term used for 'incorporate' in 1385 – 'applicare' – has given rise to much acrimonious discussion between Polish and Lithuanian historians, but the Poles had no doubt of what it meant at the time. On the other hand, Jagiełło and his successors had no intention of implementing these purely tactical promises. For in the Crown (Poland), they remained elected monarchs, tightly constrained by grants of privilege to the nobility; in the 'Grand Duchy' (Lithuania), their hereditary status was their guarantee that they would remain rulers in Poland.

With Lithuania, Poland meant much; without it, little. It remained perilously fragile. To the suspicious nobility of Wielkopolska, Jagiełło's elevation was a bid for political dominance by the the baronage of Małopolska. The two provinces were physically separated by a belt of fiefs granted by Louis the Great to his helpmate, the Silesian Piast, Władysław of Opole, who, in 1392, floated a scheme to divide the Crown between the *Ordensstaat* and Sigismund of Hungary. Only in 1396 were his lands forcibly annexed by Jadwiga and her husband. In 1387 disorders in Hungary helped Jadwiga to recover the Rus' territories transferred by her father from Poland. The Crown's narrow lands were painfully slowly bulked out with the extinction of the ruling lines of minor Piast branches, especially those associated with the duchy of Masovia. The final incorporation of Masovia and its capital, Warsaw, came only in 1526. Silesia and, even more so, western Pomerania, remained out of reach. The Crown lacked the strength to enforce its annexationist claims on the Grand Duchy, whose leading lords remained wary of such aspirations, even after the extinction of the Jagiellonian dynasty. After 1422, Poland and Lithuania pursued different, if often complementary, foreign policies, with Poland looking to the north and south and Lithuania to the east. Chronic strains dogged their relationship, not least over the possession of the southern Rus' territories of Podole and Volhynia. In 1492, the separate, independent accessions of Jagiełło's grandsons, John Albert (Jan Olbracht) in Poland and Alexander in Lithuania, represented, strictly speaking, a sundering of the dynastic union, stitched together once more in 1501, when Alexander succeeded his childless elder brother in Poland.

The Union survived its early years because Jagiełło and Vytautas were able to compose their differences in what was, in effect, a partnership of equals. In 1392, Jagiełło acknowledged his cousin as 'dux' of Lithuania, while maintaining a formal overlordship as

Map 3   Poland under Jagiellonian rule, 1386–1572.

Royal Prussia, incorporated into the Crown, 1454/66

Boundary between the Crown and the Grand Duchy of Lithuania (before 1569)

Boundary between the Crown and the Grand Duchy of Lithuania (after 1569)

Lithuania's eastern border, *c.* 1454

Lithuania's eastern border, 1503
n.b. 1514, loss of Smolensk to Muscovy

Narva

Novgorod

Pskov

Moscow

Dvina

Viazma

Polotsk

ina

Ulla

Vitebsk

Smolensk

Orsha

SCALE

0   50   100   150   200   250   300   350 km

0   50   100   150   200 miles

Minsk

Briansk

M U S C O V Y

U A N I A

Gomel

N

YNIA

Vorskla

k

Kiev

Dnieper

PODOLE

ieniec Podolski

Boh

Azov

Dniester

(under Turkish–Tatar control from the 1480s)

MOLDAVIA

Ochakov

CRIMEAN

Belgorod

TATARS

Kaffa

Kilia

WALLACHIA

'supremus dux'. Each clung to the hope of siring legitimate sons who would succeed to both Crown and Grand Duchy. It was Jagiełło who finally scored, at the impressive age of 72 and on his fourth marriage (Jadwiga died in 1399). In 1424, Władysław was born, in 1426 Casimir. The latter's unilateral acclamation as hereditary *hospodar* by the great families of Lithuania in 1440 put an end to a decade of strife between rival, stop-gap successors nominated by Jagiełło after Vytautas' death in October 1430. Casimir IV's accession to the Polish throne in 1447 restored a measure of stability in relations between the two states.

Vytautas' grandiose hopes of securing mastery of the whole of old Rus' ended in disaster in 1399 when the Mongols of the Golden Horde destroyed his army on the Vorskla river. In the previous year, he had had to recognize the consequences of his own folly in dallying with the *Ordensstaat* when, by the peace of Salin, he had been obliged to confirm its possession of Žemaitija. The Teutonic Knights and their associated Order, the Knights of the Sword in Livonia, now had a perfect springboard against Vilnius. Vytautas began to scheme for Žemaitija's recovery almost as soon as he had surrendered it. He could count on Jagiełło's support. Officially, neither the king nor his Polish subjects were involved in Vytautas' wars. Yet many Poles served him in their private capacities: on the Vorskla in 1399, in the uprisings which he fomented in Žemaitija between 1401 and 1404 and again in 1409. They helped garrison Lithuanian strongholds. But it was only in July 1409 that Jagiełło was able to persuade an assembly of Polish nobles openly to oppose any attack by the Knights on Lithuania. In August, Grand Master Ulrich von Jungingen responded with an attack on northern Poland.

So began a long conflict which Poland eventually 'won' but never truly resolved. Not until 1466 were the territories the Order had seized during Łokietek's reign recovered. The stunning victory which the forces of the Polish-Lithuanian lands won over the Knights on 15 July 1410, near the villages of Grunwald and Tannenberg, failed to deliver the capital, Marienburg. Behind their fortifications, the Knights were impregnable, for their enemies lacked the resources for sustained siege warfare. A series of debilitating wars (1409–11, 1414, 1422, 1431–5) gave the Crown almost nothing in territorial terms. Lithuania at least secured the unconditional restoration of Žemaitija at the peace of Melno in September 1422. Vytautas and his successors concentrated their attention on Rus'. Their co-operation with Poland against the Knights largely ceased.

The inconclusive, periodic fighting caused immense devastation in and around the Teutonic Knights' Prussian lands. Germany's parallel political and demographic crisis led to severe recruitment shortages for the Order, which tried to compensate by increasingly brutal fiscal policies. When, on 6 March 1454, the Crown chancellery issued an act of incorporation of Prussia, it did so in response to growing agitation and rebellion among the Order's own subjects, with the nobility and the great towns of Danzig, Thorn and Elbing in the van. Such was the massive scale of initial defections that it might have seemed the Order would be swept away almost without a fight. Its nerve held. The Polish treasury was empty. To begin with, Casimir IV was barely able to afford the services of 2,000 mercenaries. The Polish *levée en masse*, the *pospolite ruszenie*, was routed at Chojnice on 18 September 1454. The war dragged on for thirteen years. Though Poland taxed itself heavily (Piotr Świdwa, castellan of Poznań, complained that 'the war cost the king more than all of Prussia is worth'), the chief burden was borne by the Prussian lands themselves. But the Knights had their own financial problems. Marienburg castle was delivered into Polish hands in June 1457 by their Czech mercenaries in return for payment of their wage arrears. The peace of Thorn of 19 October 1466 showed just how badly hit the Order was. Its rich, western territories along the lower Vistula passed under Polish suzerainty as 'Royal Prussia'. The rich see of Warmia (Ermeland) was detached from the Order as a separate *dominium* under the Polish Crown. The Order retained the hinterland of the port of Königsberg, poorer lands for which its Grand Masters now had to perform homage to the kings of Poland.

The success came at a price. Despite the incorporation of 1454, Royal Prussia received, in law, enough autonomy for its elites to regard it as a distinct political unit. Successive Grand Masters did their utmost to ditch their vassal status or even to reverse the peace of Thorn altogether. Their support for the fractious bishops of Warmia brought about the short-lived conflict of 1478–9 known as

4   The town hall of Danzig/Gdańsk, 1379–80. Note the sixteenth-century Flemish-style buildings, much influenced by Danzig's commercial contacts. Extensive post-1945 restorations.

'the padres' war', *wojna popia*. Open conflict resumed in 1519, to end in inconclusive truce in April 1521. That *Deus ex machina*, Martin Luther, helped resolve the situation. In March 1525, Grand Master Albrecht of Hohenzollern-Ansbach proposed to King Sigismund I the secularization of the Order in its Prussian lands. He had been openly backing the Reformation in Königsberg since at least 1523. He was also bankrupt: the secularization of the Order's lands would enable him to claw his way out of a financial hole. The few remaining members of the Order were content to share in the spoils. The treaty of Kraków on 8 April 1525 reaffirmed that of Thorn of 1466, but delivered eastern, now 'Ducal', Prussia to the Grand Master as his hereditary possession and a fief of the Polish Crown. Two days later, outside the Kraków cloth-hall, Albrecht of Hohenzollern, the first territorial Lutheran ruler, swore his oath of fealty. The duchy was to revert to Poland on the extinction of his line. Contemporaries criticized Sigismund for not embarking on outright annexation. Experience showed, however, that such a course might well have led to more prolonged warfare. A secularized, Lutheran Ducal Prussia would be utterly reliant on the Crown and might yet revert to it.

The difficulties in the north seemed to be counterbalanced by advances in the south. In Hungary and Bohemia at the turn of the fourteenth and fifteenth centuries, royal authority crumbled. The Jagiellonians sought to acquire these lands because that was what kings were supposed to do, and because they wished to prevent them from falling into the hands of hostile rulers. But the regency council which ruled Poland after Jagiełło's death in 1434 gravely miscalculated in trying to foist young Władysław III on Hungary in 1440. The civil war which erupted between his supporters and opponents was provisionally resolved in a misguided crusade against the Turks. At the battle of Varna in November 1444, Władysław was among the dead. Only John Hunyadi's generalship prevented the total destruction of the Christian army.

The tortuous road to Hungary turned out to lie through Bohemia. There, the chronic feuds between nobles and magnates, between Hussites and Catholics, their jockeyings for outside support, led, in 1469, to the election of Casimir IV's eldest son, Władysław, as king-designate. He ascended the throne two years later, on the death of George of Poděbrad. However, his elevation brought him into conflict with the energetic king Matthias Corvinus of Hungary, who, by 1474, succeeded in wresting Moravia, Silesia and Lusatia from him. Casimir IV's efforts to support his son foundered on lack of money.

Matthias died without a legitimate heir in April 1490. Władysław/Vladislav/Ulászló, the notoriously easy-going King 'Bene', King 'Fine' (reputedly, his stock response to any request) was just what the Hungarian nobility wanted after the late king's harsh rule. They chose him as king in February 1491. Casimir IV had hoped they would choose his second, favourite son, John Albert. He even undertook a disastrous military intervention, which ended in John's defeat at Eperyes in January 1492. But it was John Albert, not Władysław, who secured election to the Polish throne on Casimir's death in June of that year. A younger brother, Alexander, was recognized as separate *hospodar* by the Lithuanian nobility: partly in deference to the old king's wishes to provide for his youngest son; partly out of concern to block Polish annexationist hopes.

The Jagiellonian family firm had made its greatest gains, but emphatically by invitation only. The separate successions of John Albert in the Crown and Alexander in the Grand Duchy showed that it was a highly fractured dynastic enterprise. The only major military expedition undertaken by the Jagiellonians across their southern borders brought home the limitations. John Albert's attempt in 1497 to provide a throne for his youngest brother, Sigismund, in Moldavia, ended in a humiliating reversal. The uncertain loyalty of Moldavia had long given cause for concern. John also harboured utterly unrealistic hopes of blocking further Ottoman advances in the eastern Balkans, advances which threatened Poland's southern trade routes to the ports of the Black Sea. The siege of the Moldavian capital of Suçeava was a dismal failure. The *pospolite ruszenie* suffered heavy losses in the retreat. The debacle encouraged the designs of Moldavia's rulers on the rich marcher territory of Pokucie. They were a thorn in Poland's side for decades, until Suleiman the Magnificent asserted much closer control over his wayward Moldavian vassals in 1538.

The last Jagiellonian kings, Alexander (1501–6), Sigismund

(Zygmunt) I (1506–48) and Sigismund II (1548–72) all sought good relations with the Turks. Although the Sultans were generally content to conclude non-aggression pacts, they had no objections to reminding the Poles and Lithuanians of their power by turning a blind eye to the depredations of their vassals, be it from Moldavia or, more damagingly, from the Crimea. Conscious of dynastic over-stretch, the Jagiellonians resigned themselves to letting the Habsburgs take over their position in southern Europe. When Louis II, Władysław/Vladislav/Uláiszló's son and successor, was killed at Mohacs in February 1526 and the Hungarian army annihilated, it was the Habsburgs who scooped up the Jagiellonian inheritance south of the Carpathians. Under the terms of the treaty of Prague of 1515, Louis' sister, Anna, married to the emperor Charles V's brother, Ferdinand, was to inherit Louis' lands if, as he did, he remained childless. The Czechs duly elected Ferdinand, the Hungarians split between him and a native contender, John Zápolya. Though Sigismund kept up a residual interest in Hungary – in 1529 his daughter, Isabella, married Zápolya – the once ambitious Jagiellonian policy was reduced to a delicate balancing act between the Zápolyas, the Habsburgs and the Turks. It was Turkish protection, not Polish influence, which allowed John Zápolya's and Isabella's son, John Sigismund, to hang on in Transylvania as an Ottoman client after 1547.

As the fifteenth century ebbed, a threat from the east assumed more pressing form. After 1422, Vytautas had returned to his hopes of subordinating the lands of Rus' to his rule. As the Tatars of the Golden Horde squabbled among themselves, the principality of Moscow emerged as the greatest obstacle to his ambitions. The adoption of Latin Christianity drove a wedge between native Lithuanians – who gravitated towards Catholicism – and the majority of their Rus' subjects. The gradual percolation of Polish-style rights and privileges ought to have had its own attractions for the Rus' nobility; however, the Union of Horodło of 1413 had barred non-Catholics from the leading dignities of state. To Orthodox nobles, taking service with Moscow often seemed to offer a more promising path of advancement. To the grand princes of Moscow, Catholic rule in Lithuania provided the perfect pretext for seeking to 'recover' the Rus' lands ruled from Vilnius. Casimir IV

5 The battle of Orsha, 1514: view by an unknown painter, but almost certainly a participant in the battle, fought on the north-eastern marches of Lithuania. A feigned cavalry retreat brought the Russian forces onto the Polish and Lithuanian artillery. The victory, however, was not enough to recover over two decades' territorial losses (including the town of Smolensk) to Muscovy.

managed, by and large, to preserve good relations with Muscovy, but, towards the end of his reign, this was only by turning a blind eye to repeated border violations. On his death in 1492, Ivan III unleashed open war.

The comparatively loose military organization of the Grand Duchy, composed of the retinues of great magnates and princes, the *pospolite ruszenie* and all too few mercenaries, could not cope with the forces the much more centralized Muscovite state could mobilize. A series of dogged conflicts (1492–4; 1498–1503; 1507–8; 1534–7) left Lithuania on the ropes. Its eastern border in 1492 was less than a hundred miles from Moscow, but some four hundred from Vilnius; after the catastrophic loss of Smolensk in July 1514, it was pushed back to around half that distance. While Polish volunteers fought in the Lithuanian ranks, it was not until 1508 that King Sigismund I was able to persuade the Polish parliament to vote any funding for the nebulously remote fighting in the east. Polish troops and funding helped the Lithuanians to victory at Orsha in September 1514, but they could not recover Smolensk. The lands around Homel, restored by Moscow in March 1537, were little more than a fleabite in Lithuania's losses. Respite came largely as a result of Ivan IV's internal preoccupations and his distractions against the Tatar Khanates of Kazan and Astrakhan.

It was on Lithuania's northern and eastern borders that the most ambitious and most fateful of Jagiellonian foreign policy initiatives was to unfold. The enfeoffment of Ducal Prussia in 1525 had settled, at least for the time being, the Crown's most vexatious problem. To the north of Lithuania lay the Livonian lands controlled by the Teutonic Order's sister organization, the Knights of the Sword. By the 1550s, these territories were largely Lutheran and the Knights virtually a secular institution, acknowledging a vestigial allegiance to the Holy Roman Emperors. Though Livonia grew rich on trade and tolls from Lithuania and Muscovy, the Knights' endless quarrels with the archbishop of Riga made for political weakness. It was all very tempting for Ivan IV, who regarded Livonia as part of his Rurikid inheritance. Should it fall into his grasp, he would have a boulevard to the Baltic and be placed to threaten Lithuania from the north as well as the east. Sigismund Augustus showed great interest in Livonia, not just for its strategic importance, but because its wealthy cities might provide new resources for his chronically hard-up monarchy.

Sigismund initially hoped to impose some form of vassal relationship, which would secure him what he called 'dominium maris Baltici' – 'mastery of the Baltic Sea'. Yet his Polish and Lithuanian lands were ill prepared for the sustained, large-scale warfare that conflict in the region was to demand. By massive alienations of royal domain, loans, by occasional, inadequate tax grants from the Polish and Lithuanian parliaments, by calling on the retinues of individual magnates or even the *pospolite ruszenie*, he was able to put together an impressive artillery park and to mass substantial numbers of troops for individual campaigns, but never to keep them on the constant war-footing required (though his enemies had the same problems). A series of understandings between the Livonian Masters, the archbishop of Riga and Sigismund between September 1557 and November 1561 progressed from an agreement on mutual assistance to the outright incorporation of Livonia into the Polish Crown. The Order was secularized. Its last Grand Master, Gotthard Kettler, received the territory of Courland, running along the southern bank of the Dvina river, as a hereditary duchy and fief of Poland.

Sigismund was powerless to deflect the ferocious invasions which were Ivan IV's response. In 1558, the Russians captured Narva and Dorpat, in 1560 the strategically central town of Fehlin. Distractions against the Crimean Tatars and Ivan's decision in 1563 to switch his main war effort directly against Lithuania helped stave off outright conquest. Ivan was also wary of the involvement of other parties. Denmark showed a close interest in the area. In 1561, the port of Reval submitted to the ambitious Erik XIV of Sweden, whose forces began to extend Swedish rule throughout Estonia.

Ivan's diversion against Lithuania eased the pressure on the luckless Livonian lands, but it cost the Grand Duchy the fortress of Polotsk, which fell in February 1563. It was not, however, the Lithuanian victory over the Russians on the river Ula in 1565 which led to a prolonged lull in the fighting. Rather it was renewed Tatar onslaughts (which, in 1570, saw much of Moscow destroyed by fire), and Ivan's disastrous inauguration of the *Oprichnina*, the reign of terror against his domestic enemies, real and imagined, in

January 1565. From July 1566, a kind of truce prevailed between Moscow and its Polish-Lithuanian protagonists. Sigismund Augustus' forward policy had foundered: more Lithuanian territory than ever was under Russian occupation; Livonia was torn between chaos, Swedish occupation in the north, Polish and Lithuanian garrisons in the south and west and Russian forces in the centre. The repercussions went further: fishing for support in the Empire, Sigismund had, in March 1563, agreed that, should Albrecht of Prussia's line fail, Ducal Prussia could revert to the electoral, Brandenburg branch of the Hohenzollerns. Thus did the 1525 treaty of Kraków begin to be jeopardized by the Jagiellonians' own brand of imperial overstretch.

The problems facing the dynasty were on a physical scale scarcely to be found elsewhere in Latin Christendom. In 1490, Poland and Lithuania covered vast expanses, getting on for twice the size of France, yet numbering fewer than 8 million people. From Kraków or Poznań to Viazma or Briansk on Lithuania's eastern marches was over 700 miles – almost as far as to Paris. East of the Vistula, agriculture scarcely rose above subsistence level in a landscape dominated by forest, swamp and steppe. The preservation of the link between the Polish Crown and the Grand Duchy of Lithuania was an achievement in itself. Only the Ottoman Porte and Muscovy faced comparable difficulties. Their solutions – sustained, brutal centralism with little or no regard, nor even conception of, their subjects' rights and privileges – were utterly impracticable in Poland.

Władysław II Jagiełło was made king not just to bring territory, but to consolidate the dominance of an elite of 'prelates et barones'. In 1426, when Jagiełło refused a fresh confirmation of privileges, his leading nobles slashed their document of assent to the succession of his baby son to pieces in front of him. He relented and issued the confirmation four years later. His successors were never allowed to forget their elective position. His second son, Casimir IV, had to wait almost three years after the death of his elder brother, Władysław III 'of Varna', before he was accepted as king and had to be threatened with deposition before he would confirm his subjects' privileges in 1453.

The 'prelates et barones' or 'proceres' were, in the first instance, members of the royal council, which, in the early sixteenth century, assumed the name of Senate: the Catholic bishops and great officers (chancellor, treasurer, marshal); the palatines (*wojewodowie*) and castellans, heading the hierarchy of counties (*terrae*) and palatinates (*palatinatus*) which had coalesced out of the old Piast duchies. Of these approximately seventy dignitaries, those who took key decisions of state with the king numbered some half-a-dozen. Membership of the council depended on talent and patronage (especially through the royal chancellery). Its members took further royal favour for granted – and could be relied upon to cause trouble if they did not receive it. Once made, appointments were regarded as irrevocable.

Lower down the scale, participation in the feudal levy, the *pospolite ruszenie*, might be enough to ensure acceptance as a knight/gentleman/noble – a *szlachcic*. Even this was not always necessary. To ease the incorporation into the Crown of the duchies of Płock and Masovia in 1495 and 1526, John Albert and Sigismund I confirmed the supposedly noble status of thousands of impoverished smallholders – illiterate, uncouth and eager to be distinguished from what were, in reality, other peasants. The result, by the second quarter of the sixteenth century, was social inflation, with a 'noble' estate making up as much as 10 per cent of the 5 million or so inhabitants of the Crown – a proportion largely maintained until the end of the eighteenth century.

The *szlachta* of the wider 'communitas nobilium' voiced their hopes and fears at the local assemblies, *sejmiki*, which had their roots in the judicial and administrative activities of the Piast era. During the fifteenth century, the practice grew for the holding of larger, regional assemblies, a development which nurtured the emergence of representatives or 'envoys' – *nuntii terrarum*. The nobility were largely free to attend in person more important sessions of the royal council. Their attendance converted its sessions into a 'conventio generalis' or 'Sejm Walny'. Those present tended to be drawn from the ranks of councillors' clienteles. During the 1490s, these *nuntii* gained their own separate chamber at the Sejm, probably as a deliberate move by John Albert to keep a check on over-mighty councillors. The Sejm was never able to disencumber itself of its original character of an outgrowth of the faction-ridden royal council, mistrusted by the *szlachta* at large. Envoys rarely felt confident of being able to speak for their electors on matters not directly put to them. Tax grants were often accompanied with the rider that their payment depended on final approval by individual constituencies. *Sejmiki* felt able to advise, enjoin or even restrain their envoys' activities. The growing number of envoys, from around forty in 1500 to almost eighty by midcentury, brought the Sejm, at best, only increased moral authority. The Chamber of Envoys regarded itself as a forum for local emissaries, rather than as part of a sovereign legislative body in its own right.

Poland's cash-strapped monarchs had no alternative but to look to the *szlachta* for support. In 1422 and 1454, the *pospolite ruszenie* refused to move against the *Ordensstaat* until its grievances were addressed. In 1496, John Albert, in return for backing for his expedition to Moldavia, not only confirmed all existing privileges but went on to grant the nobility exemption from customs duties on all commodities of domestic production and consumption. He even agreed that townsmen should be barred from owning land and to making it almost impossible for peasants to leave their seigneurial estates. Yet this was not just constitutional extortion – the monarchs, too, were bidding for wider support against their over-mighty subjects – usually members of the royal council who sought, unavailingly, to distance themselves from their lesser fellow-nobles. The Chojnice–Nieszawa Privileges of 1454, binding the king not to levy taxes, enact new laws or even call the *pospolite ruszenie* without the prior consent of the *sejmiki*, were designed to enable Casimir IV to appeal over more powerful magnates to the nobility at large.

To begin with, the nobility did not seek to share power with the monarchy, but protection against oppression. The bulk of the 1454 Privilege addressed *szlachta* concerns at judicial abuses and arbitrariness by councillors and royal officials, or the monarchy itself. The post of justiciar, with its virtually unlimited powers of arrest, which Jagiełło had promised to abolish in 1386, was wound up by John Albert only in 1496. The Privileges of 1422 (Czerwińsk) and 1430 (Jedlnia) had supposedly safeguarded the nobility from confiscation of property and arrest, save after due process – *Neminem captivabimus nisi iure victum.* Yet complaints against the abuse of power by royal officialdom continued to increase.

Royal councillors seized the opportunity of John Albert's death to secure a whip-hand. At Mielnik, in November 1501, they warned his brother, Alexander, ruling in Lithuania, that they would elect him king only if they themselves received the right to determine the Senate's membership and appoint to lesser offices of state. Should the king refuse to follow policies which they were to propose, he would forfeit their obedience. Alexander, distracted by war with Muscovy, agreed – only to turn the tables at the Sejm which met in Radom in 1505. He used the resentments generated by the senators' self-seeking misrule to rally the *szlachta* behind the statute known as 'Nihil Novi', 'Nothing New': 'We have hereby affirmed for all time to come that nothing new may be enacted by Us and our Successors save by the common consent of the senators and the envoys of the constituencies.' The place of the gentry within the parliamentary system was confirmed, as a check on the Senate. 'Nihil Novi' laid the cornerstone of *szlachta* freedoms for almost three centuries. The Mielnik concessions became a dead letter. Even so, it was not until the 1550s that the open nomination by great lords and royal dignitaries of envoys supposedly mandated by the *sejmiki* ceased.

The king had to work within the limitations imposed by the *szlachta*. Sigismund I was able to resume much alienated royal domain by more careful administration. He extended the range of customs duties, albeit at the cost of extensive *szlachta* exemptions. In the late 1520s, he was able to reform the currency. His actions lay within the acknowledged royal prerogative and could rely on wider noble support. It was otherwise when kings attempted policies which threatened noble interests directly. Sigismund I's hopes of commuting the obligation to serve in the *pospolite ruszenie* to a regular cash levy were rebuffed. The election by the Senate-dominated Sejm of 1529–30 of his 9-year-old son, Sigismund Augustus, provoked such an outcry among the *szlachta* that the Sejm of February 1530 banned future royal elections *vivente rege* – during the reigning monarch's lifetime. Sigismund I's second wife, Bona, daughter of Gian Galeazzo Sforza of Milan, was widely suspected to be behind Sigismund Augustus' premature elevation. As a foreigner, a woman, and a representative of a wholly different political tradition, she attracted much suspicion during the reigns of her husband and son. Their clear preference for working with the lords of the Senate only heightened fears of kingly absolutism. The scandalously damaging affront to royal authority in 1537, when the *pospolite ruszenie*, assembled near Lwów for a punitive expedition into Moldavia, went on strike, threatened royal ministers and had to be sent home, demonstrated just what monarchs could expect if they failed to show due regard for noble sensibilities (or failed to control mischief-making senators behind the scenes). In pursuing his ambitious Baltic policies, Sigismund II Augustus had to rely on the dangerous expedient of creating facts and then hoping that the Sejm would vote the funds. It did not always do so.

Their organization and military muscle gave the lesser nobility, or 'ordo equester' as its more learned members styled themselves, a major advantage over other social groupings. In the course of the fifteenth century, most of the *szlachta*'s privileges were extended to the clergy. Senior church positions were largely reserved for the nobility. A community of interest was produced which constant quarrels over tithe and jurisdiction shook, but could not undermine. The periodic alignments of king and *szlachta* prevented the emergence of a legally distinct higher nobility (lay places in the Senate came only through specific offices) and, instead, helped give birth to a fiction of equality among all nobles – but which more canny overmighty subjects learned to manipulate to their own advantage. Kings could, at best, manoeuvre between noble groupings.

There were no other sources of effective support. Major towns were pitifully few. Kraków, Lwów or Poznań were content with their individual privileges. Their town halls, markets and churches (most spectacularly, Veit Stoss of Nuremberg's dazzling altar-piece in Kraków's Lady-Church) bespeak a real prosperity, founded mainly on overland transit trade and raw material exports. But there were no centres of manufacture capable of competing with the Rhine valley, Flanders or northern Italy. Even the capital, Kraków, at the end of the sixteenth century, numbered around 14,000 inhabitants – barely the size of a secondary provincial centre in France. Piotrków, the usual venue for the Sejm Walny,

6   The church of the Blessed Virgin Mary, Kraków. Completed, 1397.
Kraków was unique among the major cities within the post-1945 borders
of Poland in suffering only minimal structural damage during the Second
World War.

7 The great altarpiece by Veit Stoss (Polish, Wit Stwosz) of Nuremberg (died, 1533) in the church of the Blessed Virgin Mary, Kraków. Stoss lived in Kraków between 1477 and 1496. He spent many years, between 1477 and 1489, working on his masterpiece. In 1484, he was granted full citizen rights in Kraków. In 1939, the Germans removed Stoss' triptych to Nuremberg. It was recovered by the Poles in 1946, but prolonged restoration work meant that it was reinstated in its rightful place only in 1957.

numbered only some 3,000 inhabitants. The fastest-expanding group within the towns were the Jews, who, by 1600, may have numbered over 200,000, through immigration and natural increase. Of course, they played no direct political role (though isolated individuals might rise high in the royal or magnate administration) and many towns legally excluded them from permanent residence. For that reason they were much favoured by the nobility whose 'protection' was bought by creaming off the profits of their trading and banking activities.

The one concentration of urban wealth allied to real political power lay in Royal Prussia. Danzig in 1500 counted over 35,000 inhabitants; Thorn and Elbing over 10,000 each; their commercial wealth allowed them to dominate the local nobility. Yet although the 1454 'Letters of Incorporation' proclaimed Royal Prussia's return 'to the body of the realm', they simultaneously conceded such extensive autonomy that the province regarded itself as virtually distinct from the Crown proper. Before 1569, the Prussian estates sent only observers to the Sejm and rarely, if ever, were prepared to vote tax monies unless their own immediate interests were served. The Jagiellonians courted individual towns (although Sigismund II, unlike his father, loathed Kraków and never visited it after 1559) for their goodwill and money. Towns sent representatives to assist in royal elections throughout the fifteenth century; leading patricians might even take a seat on the royal council. Wealthy townsmen and merchants had little difficulty in obtaining ennoblement, either by royal favour or by securing court judgements 'confirming' their new status. In 1492, Kraków took this to its logical extreme when it secured noble status and the right to send its own representatives to the Sejm, to exercise their influence on Kraków's behalf.

The nobility extended their advantages into the economic sphere. Under the Statute of Warka of 1423, noble landlords were permitted to buy out, against independently assessed valuations, the rich hereditary holdings (*sołectwa*) of negligent or recalcitrant village administrators (often *szlachta* themselves). Price controls were imposed on towns; guilds were declared abolished; peasants were forbidden to migrate to towns without their seigneurs' consent. Most of these provisions were unenforceable. They were reaffirmed and sharpened in 1496 and 1520. It was only from then that the restrictions on the peasantry began to take on real force, as an agrarian boom, fuelled by grain exports through Danzig, brought about a shift from cash rentals to revenues derived from the direct exploitation of peasant labour services. Free peasants became enserfed because there was no way of stopping the process, although for much of the sixteenth century, agrarian prosperity cushioned the worst effects of the restrictions on their freedom. Save for its Baltic rim, Poland remained overwhelmingly agrarian, even by contemporary European standards. The price revolution made manufactured imports much cheaper relative to raw material exports. If artisanal activity in Poland's own towns suffered, most nobles were unconcerned.

During the reign of Sigismund I, the tensions within the noble estate took on more definite contours with demands by the lesser nobility for 'Executio Legum', the 'Execution of the Laws', or full implementation of old laws supposedly designed to protect the *szlachta*. As a bonus, the same laws allowed them to strengthen their own position *vis-à-vis* non-nobles. The movement waxed and waned throughout the sixteenth century, to reach a sustained crescendo during the 1550s and 1560s. Prominent among its demands was the insistence that the king should provide for the defence of the realm out of his own resources, if necessary by resuming royal demesne alienated primarily to great magnates and royal creditors. Notionally, as much as one-fifth of the Crown and Lithuania counted as the Jagiellonians' direct patrimony. Jagiełło, almost from the moment he was chosen king, began alienations on a huge scale, to win political support and to raise cash for his wars. The Executionists' demands were not just motivated by a reluctance to accept taxation (although that was a powerful motive, even though the peasantry paid it): they rightly suspected that their grants of the extraordinary land tax, the *pobór*, were actually spent on ends other than military (barely 10 per cent of the 1485–6 military subsidy was spent on troops; most of the rest went on court and administrative outlays).

The nobility's capacity to be obstructive was stoked by the cultural efflorescence of the sixteenth century. The way was well paved. In 1400, Jagiełło had re-founded Kraków University with a

8 View of the Royal Palace on the Wawel hill in Kraków, dating mainly from the fifteenth and sixteenth centuries. In 1596 Sigismund III decided to transfer the court to Warsaw (the move was only completed in 1611), much more favourably placed for communications with Lithuania and the Baltic region. Polish kings continued to be crowned in the small cathedral attached to the Wawel palace until 1764, when the last king of Poland, Stanisław August Poniatowski, concerned at its ruinous condition, chose to have his coronation ceremony in Warsaw.

9   Sigismund I's Renaissance courtyard in the Wawel palace, Kraków
(early sixteenth century). Sigismund enjoyed the benefit of a humanistic
education. His second wife, the Milanese princess Bona Sforza,
contributed to the deepening of Italian cultural influences.

Theology Faculty to assist in the conversion of Lithuania. It was,
however, during the Council of Constance that the university's
jurists, especially Paweł Włodkowic (Paulus Vladimiri), came to the
attention of an international audience with their views on the rights
of nations and international relations. Their rejection of the validity
of Christian rule imposed by force sought to refute the propaganda
of the *Ordensstaat*. The presence of humanists such as Filippo
Buonaccorsi (1437–96) and Conrad Celtis (1459–1508) at the
turn of the fifteenth and sixteenth centuries made the university, if
briefly, one of the most exciting in Europe. Nicholas Copernicus
(1473–1543) represented the apogee of a well-established astro-
nomical tradition at the university, critically respectful of Aristotle.
Polish developed into a sophisticated literary medium through the
works of writers and poets such as Mikołaj Rej (1505–69), Łukasz
Górnicki (1527–1603) and, above all, Jan Kochanowski
(1530–84). Much of the literature of this 'Golden Age' was

produced in Latin – but it was very rapidly translated into Polish and disseminated throughout literate *szlachta* and urban society. The first printing-press had been set up in Kraków in 1476; the very first Cyrillic printed texts were published there in 1491; and the first Polish work aimed for wider circulation, the *Paradise of souls*, appeared in 1513. The earliest vernacular versions of the Sejm's statutes were published, to meet *szlachta* demand, in 1543 (the same year as the posthumous publication in Nuremberg of Copernicus' *De revolutionibus orbium coelestium*). Increasingly strong contacts with Italy helped the *szlachta* elite create a culture modelled (at least in their own minds) on the values of Republican Rome. Sigismund I and Queen Bona transformed the royal castle on Kraków's Wawel hill into a Renaissance showpiece. In the north, Königsberg formed a centre of Polish learning and humanism second only to Kraków. It was in the interests of its Lutheran rulers to produce bibles, books and Protestant literature both in Latin and Polish to cultivate support in the Crown and Lithuania. It was in Königsberg that Martynas Mažvydas' reformed catechism, the first printed text in the Lithuanian vernacular, was published in 1547, followed, four years later, by the first Polish translation of the New Testament. The first complete Polish translation of the Bible was printed in Kraków in 1561. The whirlpool of foreign and national influences found concrete expression in the welter of different dress styles adopted by the nobility, with native, western and oriental influences (the latter arriving largely through Hungary) combining to produce a distinctive couture of caftan, boots, belts and breeches around the mid-century.

In this bubbling cultural atmosphere, a combination of prosperous, ambitious, educated gentry and great lords drove the Execution movement. It had no single leader, although by the 1550s, its most distinctive personalities were closely associated with the Reformation; the disgorging of ecclesiastical wealth and land would reduce the need for extraordinary taxation and consolidate the nobility's pre-eminence in the realm. Since Lithuania increasingly called on the support of the Crown against Moscow, the Execution movement took up old calls for its full incorporation. All parts of the body politic, including Royal Prussia, were to contribute towards its defence. It was not a programme bereft of positive

10   The great cloth-hall ('Sukiennice') in the main square of Kraków, rebuilt after a fire in 1555. The architect was Giovanni Il Mosca of Padua (hence his sobriquet, 'Padovano'). Kraków owed its original prosperity to its situation at the junction of two major trade routes: east–west, between the Black Sea hinterland and Germany; and north–south between the Baltic and Bohemia/Hungary. Kraków's importance declined with the departure of the royal court for Warsaw and the wars and recessions of the seventeenth century.

aspects, but torchbearers such as Andrzej Frycz Modrzewski, who sought to extend its scope beyond sectional self-interest, were few and far between. In 1538, the 1496 law barring townsmen from acquiring landed property was reaffirmed; in 1550 guilds were again banned. Such restrictions, notwithstanding their ineffectiveness, also belonged to the old laws which the *szlachta*'s virtuous forebears had secured.

Sigismund I and Sigismund II Augustus were sceptical. Both felt that matters of state were not for debate with 'ploughmen', as they were ready to call *szlachta* agitators. They summoned their Sejmy almost annually, even in time of peace: for Poland (and Lithuania) were perpetually menaced by the raids of the Crimean Tatars, whom even their supposed overlords in Constantinople could barely control. Most Sejmy did vote funds for the *obrona potoczna*,

the 'general defence' force based around the fortress of Kamieniec
Podolski on the Crown's south-eastern border. But the monies
rarely sufficed to maintain this force at above some 2,000 men.
Kings had to resort to a variety of expedients to keep their troops in
being – negotiating with local *sejmiki*, calling on the local *pospolite
ruszenie* or magnate retinues, alienating royal demesne or even
establishing quasi-military colonists in the border areas – lawless
settlements of Cossacks, who gave the Tatars as good as they
received. The Sejm of 1508 agreed, for the first time, to financial
help for Lithuania against Moscow. For a few months, the Crown
and the Grand Duchy put some 25,000 troops into the field. Such
ad hoc efforts were no substitute for regular taxation which alone
would have permitted the long-term maintenance of large armies –
but then of course, these were still the exception, rather than the
rule, throughout most of Europe.

Agitation for the Execution of the Laws (Egzekucja) reached a
noisy height soon after Sigismund II's accession in 1548. Inevitably,
it fused with religious passions. Poland's western borders lay only a
day's ride from Saxony across Silesia. Reformed ideas and writings
began to circulate immediately after Luther's first protests, finding
their strongest support in the towns of Royal Prussia. Sigismund I's
one serious attempt at a crackdown took place in Danzig in 1525,
occasioned mainly by his fears of the unruly pretensions of the
lower orders. Once a few ringleaders had been executed and the
authority of the city council restored, Sigismund did not interfere:
Lutheranism, shorn of social radicalism, won over the German-
speaking patriciates. His son confirmed their confessional freedoms
in 1557 and 1558. If anything, it was Catholicism which was on
the defensive in Prussia.

Among the *szlachta*, reformed ideas – not only Lutheran but,
increasingly, Calvinist and even antitrinitarian – fused with long-
standing disputes over tithe with the Church and with the drive for
political dominance. The core of reformed support came from
wealthy families in Wielkopolska, such as the Górkas, Leszczyńskis
and Sienickis – all of them, by the mid-century, highly active in the
Egzekucja programme. The Reformation had to insinuate itself
into the movement, for there was never any other possibility of its
attracting mass political support. Freedom of religion was seen as

an extension of political liberties. But the decision by the Sejm of 1562–3, forbidding royal *starostowie* from using their police powers to carry out the judgements of ecclesiastical courts, was as much a triumph for *szlachta* anticlericalism as a success for the reformers. Once Egzekucja had run its course, the Polish Reformation found itself reliant on the uncertain protection and attitudes of individual noble patrons.

Exponents of Reformation could be found virtually anywhere from the Silesian border to the depths of the Ukraine. Attempts to form a common front foundered on doctrinal differences between Calvinists and Lutherans on the one side and the antitrinitarians, or Aryans, as they came to be called, on the other. The last two Jagiellonians tolerated religious diversity (which, after all, sprang from the very bones of the lands they ruled) out of necessity and good sense. The alternative, Sigismund II recognized, was probably internal disintegration, as in France or Germany. While he showed a proper humanist interest in the new doctrines, he had no intention of abandoning Catholicism.

By the late 1550s, Sigismund II had to face up to the real prospect that he might be the last of his line. He married three times, to no avail. In May 1543, it was Ferdinand of Habsburg's daughter, Elizabeth. She died two years later. In July 1547, in Vilnius, he secretly married a young widow, Barbara, born into the powerful Radziwiłł family, a love-match which fuelled paranoid fears among the Crown nobility of Lithuanian domination. Their relations with the king were blighted for years. Barbara died in May 1551. Two years later, Sigismund reluctantly married his first wife's younger sister, Catherine. He loathed both his Habsburg consorts. The last marriage petered out in a humiliating separation and Catherine's return to Austria in 1566 (she died at Linz in February 1572). Sigismund's failure to sire an heir and the manifest incapacity of Lithuania alone to withstand Muscovy undermined the rationale for maintaining the separation of the Crown and the Grand Duchy. The Executionists' calls for the resumption of royal demesne, restrictions on officials' abuses, and even for the annual summons of the Sejm offered scope for a platform of constructive reform. Their demands for the subordination of Lithuania and Royal Prussia to the Crown promised the chance of creating a new and formidable polity. In September 1562, Sigismund embraced their cause.

The Sejm which met at Piotrków from November 1562 to March 1563 attempted to secure peacetime revenues by the resumption and closer regulation of alienated royal demesne. The audits and surveys which the Sejm instituted were to be repeated at five-yearly intervals. The king could make land grants, but recipients were to enjoy only one-fifth of the income, while the remaining four-fifths were to cover the expenses of court and government. One-quarter (*kwarta*) of the monarch's share was specifically earmarked for the upkeep of the defence of the south-east against Tatar incursions. It could not, nor was it meant to, pay for the war with Muscovy. The *szlachta* voted an increased *pobór* (land tax), paid mainly by their peasants. They were, however, allowed to make up half of their amount from tithes due to the Church. The new *pobór* thus permitted indirect ecclesiastical taxation.

The *kwarta* eventually made available a regular source of monies for the defence of the south-eastern borders, but did little to increase the size of what was now known as the '*kwarta* army'. The survey commissions which completed their work by 1565 increased the returns from royal demesne to almost half a million zloties – an eightfold increase on the 1540s. Yet the commissions were so inadequately staffed, the task facing them was so enormous, that the new returns could scarcely have represented more than a fraction of the revenue potential. Certainly, individual magnate families lost extensive properties. The Executionists even succeeded in imposing the surveys and resumptions on Royal Prussia, on the grounds that royal demesne was involved. Once it became clear, however, that lesser *szlachta* were being drawn into the net of resumptions, interest rapidly diminished. After 1569–70, there was to be no full survey until 1660. Sigismund II himself connived at evading or softening the losses of some of the most badly affected senators. The returns of the new *pobór* proved disappointing because many *szlachta* simply did not want to pay. If it was true, as the historian Antoni Mączak has suggested, that in its supposed golden age, the Crown's economy was retarded by such shortages of specie that the nobility simply could not afford taxes on the scale necessary to meet Poland's needs, those needs remained. The Sejm of 1565 had to sanction the raising of fresh loans against the security of royal properties.

Sigismund II Augustus felt that only a new Union, on terms acceptable to both the Crown and Lithuania, would give the nobility of both a real stake in the survival of a reconstructed polity. The outright annexationism of the Executionists would not do. Convergence of a kind had long been under way. The Polish written and spoken word was, by the late fifteenth century, making rapid progress among Lithuania's elites, to produce a fascinating written and spoken linguistic hybrid of Belorussian, Lithuanian, Latin and Polish. Cultural polonization was certainly not opposed by Lithuanian elites: many, not least Rus' Orthodox, positively embraced it as a channel to a more sophisticated western European culture. The Radziwiłłs' conversion to and enthusiastic patronage of Calvinism was a means of combining integration with distinctiveness. But political polonization was a very different matter. The importation of distinct Polish-style courts, *sejmiki* and genuine elections to a central Sejm and to local offices threatened to overturn the patrimonial dominance of the members of the *hospodar's* council. The resumption of grand-ducal domain threatened them with economic catastrophe. But irresistible pressures were building up. The constant presence during the Muscovite wars of Polish troops, drawn mainly from the *szlachta*, served to familiarize their Lithuanian counterparts with Polish ideas and institutions. Sigismund Augustus' Privilege of Vilnius of July 1563 aimed to win round Orthodox nobles by restoring their access to offices on the *hospodar's* council. The Lithuanian magnates, led by the Radziwiłłs, offered concessions. The Vilnius Sejm of November 1565 to March 1566 sanctioned the introduction of distinct courts on the Polish model. A hierarchy of local officials patterned on Poland's followed in 1566 as part of a new codification of common law (the so-called Second Lithuanian Statute). The Lithuanian Sejm, hitherto largely a magnate mouthpiece, formally assumed the same legislative powers and procedures as the Crown's. Union was being administratively engineered from within.

The climax came at the Sejm which met in Lublin in January 1569. Sigismund insisted that the Lithuanian lords and envoys should attend. Prompted by Sigismund, the Poles declared their readiness to accept a separate hierarchy of great offices of state for Lithuania – but there would have to be a common Sejm; the Poles' right to settle and own land in the Grand Duchy would have to be conceded. This last demand led to fears that the generally wealthier Poles would swamp the Grand Duchy. When most of the Lithuanian representation walked out on 1 March, Sigismund angrily announced the incorporation of Volhynia and Podlasie, part of Lithuania's Rus' lands, into the Crown. The local *szlachta* proclaimed their assent *en masse*. On 16 March, the king ordered the senators and envoys from Royal Prussia, attending as observers, to take their seats in the assembly – their separate status, too, would end. They caved in. On 6 June, the royal chancellery announced the incorporation of the sprawling palatinate of Kiev, with the overwhelming approval of the local nobility. If the Lithuanian objectors persisted, there was every likelihood that the original annexationist demands of the Executionists would be carried. Sigismund still believed that 'voluntary' union was better: he even promised that the resumption of royal demesne would not apply to Lithuania. The Poles agreed that Lithuanians could enjoy reciprocal rights of settlement in the Crown. On 28 June the last objections were overcome. The new Union was confirmed by the king on 4 July. A new entity, the Rzeczpospolita Obojga Narodów, Polskiego i Litewskiego, 'The Commonwealth of the Two Nations, the Polish and Lithuanian' had come into being.

The Union was Sigismund Augustus' greatest achievement and greatest failure. Hard experience had taught him to make compromises whenever possible, perhaps too much so. Through the Union of Lublin he hoped to establish a realm based on partnership between the *szlachta* and a future monarchy. But the aftermath demonstrated what he must have always feared. To the overwhelming majority of the *szlachta*, 'Executio' was a means of securing their rights and privileges. Nothing was done to improve the workings of the Sejm. The balance between Sejm and *sejmiki* remained unsteady and, if anything, in favour of the latter. The Union probably made the problems worse. Magnates and *szlachta* may have been theoretically equal in law, but in practice, the former could and did use their sheer wealth to dominate their 'lesser brethren'; the mutual opening up of the Crown and

Lithuania meant that magnates on both sides could now acquire landed estates and the influence that went with them throughout the new Rzeczpospolita. Mikołaj Radziwiłł 'the Red' complained that a 'free' Lithuania had been buried 'for all time'. He need not have worried. His idea of freedom had a long career before it. Despite formal unification and supposed closer integration of the Crown, Royal Prussia and the Grand Duchy, in practice the forces of local particularism remained strong. Danzig remained *sui generis*. Right up to Sigismund's death it continued to sabotage his plans to build a Baltic navy, which it saw as a threat to its own position.

The Lublin Sejm itself and the Sejmy of 1570 and 1572 refused to discuss machinery for the regulation of royal elections after Sigismund's death. The *szlachta* feared a *rapprochement* between Sigismund and the magnates and, from that, a Habsburg succession. The Habsburgs could always count on considerable support among the senators, who felt their rule could only strengthen their own position. But among the wider masses of the *szlachta*, Habsburg rule in Hungary and Bohemia had secured them a bizarre reputation, brokered largely by anti-magnate demagogues, as enemies of freedom second only to the tsars of Muscovy. The Executionist leaders were content to protect the gains of 1569. Some, rewarded with royal demesne and new offices by the king, went over to the senatorial side; others shared the fears that a strengthened monarchy might ultimately pave the way to Habsburg tyranny. Rather than vote extraordinary subsidies for the Russian war, the *szlachta* settled for a three-year truce with Muscovy in June 1570. Polotsk remained in Ivan IV's hands.

Sigismund consoled his last years with a string of sexual liaisons, which did nothing to enhance his reputation. A daughter born to his mistress, Barbara Giżanka, in 1571, provoked grumbling that her mother was a whore and the king was not her father. The last Sejm of his reign had to be abandoned in May 1572 because of his poor health, broken by gout, gallstones, tuberculosis and frustration. At six o'clock in the afternoon on 7 July 1572, Sigismund II Augustus, Poland's last Jagiellonian king, died at the royal hunting-lodge at Knyszyn, where he had sequestered Giżanka, fearing his nobles might abduct her. The *szlachta* were on their own.

3

The Commonwealth of the Two Nations, 1572–1795

In a field outside Warsaw on 10 May 1573, Henri, duke of Anjou, was elected king of Poland. His elder brother, King Charles IX of France, appreciated that a Valois-ruled Poland, bordering on Austria, could prove very useful. As for the *szlachta*, so confident were they in their constitutional defences that even Protestants welcomed a ruler widely deemed responsible for the previous year's St Bartholomew's massacre.

At the 'Convocation' Sejm in January 1573, the gentry's leaders had blustered the senatorial elite into conceding that all nobles were entitled to vote for their king *viritim* – in person. The Sejm formed an association, the 'Confederacy of Warsaw', which drew up constitutional ground rules. The ruler would not secure a successor *vivente rege*, during his own lifetime; he would have to preserve interdenominational peace; he would decide matters of peace and war in conjunction with the Senate and the Sejm; parliament was to be called every two years for a six-week term, or as necessary; its consent would be required for all extraordinary taxation. The nobility's jurisdiction over their peasants would remain untouched. If a ruler failed to observe his sworn commitments, he would forfeit his subjects' obedience. These 'Henrician articles' were complemented by the *pacta conventa*, obligations crafted for individual kings. King Henri's ranged from the provision of scholarships at the Sorbonne for young nobles to extravagant promises of financial and military support for Poland-Lithuania in the Muscovite war.

The 1573 settlement remained basic to the structure of the Commonwealth of the Two Nations for most of its existence. Interregnums and 'free' royal elections were essential to correct the abuses and infractions of the previous reign. Warsaw's central location made it much more convenient as the election venue than Kraków (for the same reason Sigismund III made it his permanent place of residence from 1611). The formal procedures evolved during the first interregnum remained in place for two centuries. The archbishop-primate of Gniezno stood in for the king, as *interrex*. The Election Sejm heard representations from candidates' agents (would-be monarchs were not allowed into the country before the election). The attendant *szlachta*, organized by palatinates and counties, camped around the huge barn-like structure in which the senators and gentry leaders debated before proposing a candidate for general acclamation.

As many as 40,000 nobles may have attended Henri of Anjou's election. Only some 4,000 turned up for Władysław IV's election in 1632, because no one seriously doubted he would succeed his father, Sigismund III. Most elections saw several 'Piast' (native Polish) candidates, but a nation of supposedly equal noblemen could hardly stomach seeing one of its fellows elevated above the rest. When electors divided, as in 1576, 1587 or 1697, then readiness to move quickly and use force carried the day.

At his coronation, Henri refused final confirmation of the articles bearing his name. Monarchy in the French tradition was incompatible with Polish legalism. The extent of privilege, and its dissemination among as much as 10 per cent of the population, gave so many an immediate, vested interest in the status quo as to make change enormously difficult. Wealthier, better-educated and more widely travelled nobles might be sufficiently mature (or cynical) to appreciate that their kind could do very well under strong monarchs, but even they were predisposed, by custom and outlook, to the preservation of extensive constitutional checks. On the night of 18 June 1574, four days after hearing of the death of his elder brother, Charles IX, a frustrated Henri III of France slipped out of Kraków's Wawel palace and made for the nearby frontier as fast as his horse could carry him.

The *szlachta* nation ran its own affairs: the *sejmiki* performed a huge range of tasks and gave men of even moderate wealth (even those who owned only a fraction of a village, if they had the education) an opportunity to engage in local government and self-advancement. The creation, in 1578 and 1581, of independent, annually elected supreme courts, the Crown and Lithuanian Tribunals, placed the bulk of judicial business affecting the nobility in its own hands. The Sejm's enactments, particularly on taxation, continued to require the electorate's further approval, amendment or even rejection at the *sejmiki*. Direct royal appeals to the constituencies for monies usually received a sympathetic response, but did nothing to enhance parliament's authority. Nevertheless, the extensive network of local institutions which the *szlachta* built up provided them with a machinery for dealing with most of the public business they deemed important – there was therefore little purpose served in building up the elaborate, centralized bureaucracies developing elsewhere in Europe.

The reforms of the Execution movement proved inadequate. Kings felt they alone should decide what use they made of royal domain lands. The *szlachta* acknowledged that they (or their peasants) would pay extraordinary taxes to deal with emergencies: mainly the traditional land tax, the *pobór*; they were ready to pay them at higher rates; they were even prepared to accept wholly new imposts – even the highly 'demeaning' poll tax. But supply was rarely voted for more than twelve months at a time. In 1620, in anticipation of a Turkish invasion, the Sejm voted to increase the regular army from 12,000 to some 60,000 men – impressive by the standards of the time, but, in 1622 scaled back to under 12,000. Such fluctuations were all too characteristic. Recruitment and pay inevitably lagged. Signal victories such as Kircholm over the Swedes in 1605 or Cudnów over the Russians in 1660 went to waste as troops mutinied over arrears. A numerous *soldatesca* emerged, plundering its own taxpayers in order to survive. Kings, magnates, officers had to dig deep into their own pockets to keep troops in being and supplement them with their own private retinues. The feudal levy of the nobility, the *pospolite ruszenie*, usually a disastrous encumbrance, remained a significant feature of the military panoply well into the eighteenth century.

The Commonwealth was more a cumbersome federation than a

unified state. The great magnate families who dominated Lithuania built on the compromises of the 1569 Union of Lublin to preserve a distinct political identity, even as cultural and linguistic differences crumbled. The revised codification of common law of 1588, the 'Third Lithuanian Statute', even contravened the Union of Lublin in barring those born outside the Grand Duchy from office – although as wide-scale Polish settlement proceeded, and as 'Lithuanian'/ 'Polish' magnates acquired land and positions across the Commonwealth, such restrictions became meaningless. In 1673, the Lithuanian magnates secured approval for every third Sejm to meet in Grodno, in Lithuania. Yet at the Election Sejm of 1697, the mass of Lithuanian gentry dealt a blow to magnate hegemony by extending the Crown's restrictions on multiple office-holding to the Grand Duchy. The adoption by that Sejm of Polish, in place of a hybridized Belorussian, as the Grand Duchy's official chancery language marked the progress of cultural unification. The origin myth of a common, 'Sarmatian' ancestry, assiduously propagated by humanist writers, allowed very different groups to merge their identities into a wider whole – provided they were nobles. To the disgust of later nationalists, Lithuanians and Ruteni, Rusini (nowadays, Belorussians and Ukrainians) could regard themselves as 'Poles' because they were also 'Sarmatians'.

Integration had mixed success in the Ukraine. Pride in the traditions of Kievan Rus' could not always accommodate itself within the framework of the Rzeczpospolita. If the native nobility of these sparsely populated marches wished to get on, polonization and the adoption of 'Latin' faiths, Catholicism above all, offered the means. When, in 1608, his Catholic heirs closed Prince Konstanty Ostrogski's Academy at Ostróg, Orthodoxy lost its only school capable of competing with Jesuit colleges or Protestant gymnasia. The decision, in 1596, by a majority of the Orthodox bishops at Brest, in Lithuania, to unite with Rome, was prompted by more than Catholic pressure or fear of the increasingly hostile patriarchate of Constantinople or the new patriarchate of Moscow. To some, at least, of the 'Uniate' bishops, the only means of restoring spirituality and intellectual credibility to the Orthodox religious tradition, even, indeed, of the preservation of a distinct cultural identity, lay in borrowing from the Latin West. The Uniates kept their own liturgy and even their married parish clergy – but an obdurate Latin episcopate prevented their bishops from taking up the senatorial seats promised them. The Union provoked enormous hostility among the Orthodox laity and clergy. In 1620, the patriarch of Jersualem surreptitiously consecrated a number of Orthodox bishops. Sigismund III tactfully turned a blind eye and in 1632 Władysław IV officially acknowledged their reinstatement. Yet the survival of the Uniate Church, its often heavy-handed proselytizing and the continued readiness even of former opponents to convert to it kept religious frictions in the expansive eastern marches on the boil.

The late sixteenth and early seventeenth centuries saw the creation of massive complexes of estates in these lands. Intermarriage and royal favour allowed comparative newcomers such as the Potockis or Lubomirskis to measure up to the likes of established princely houses of Lithuania, the Radziwiłłs or the Wiśniowieckis. These great landowners soon learned to manipulate the values of 'Golden Liberty'. By the eighteenth century, Polish politics largely became centred on the acquisition of office and crown leaseholds. Kings rewarded for service – or because they had to. Their power to punish was increasingly limited. King Stefan Batory (1575–86) had Samuel Zborowski executed in May 1584 for plotting his overthrow. His successor, Sigismund III (1587–1632), won praise for pardoning those who, in 1606 and 1607, had fomented armed revolt and sought his deposition. But he dared not press matters too far: even the army which defeated the rebellious 'rokosz of Sandomierz' in July 1607 suspected that their opponents had some justification in claiming that they were resisting 'absolutum dominium'. Attempts by John II Casimir (1648–68) in the 1650s and 1660s to rid himself of prominent opponents backfired, even when proofs of their dealings with hostile powers were palpable.

The Sejm proved unable to cope with regional differences and magnate rivalries. It was these which underlay the emergence of the *liberum veto* – the right of a single individual to destroy the parliamentary session. Bills became law only after a final reading in the closing days of the Sejm: Władysław Siciński's protest in March 1652 against any prolongation of the normal six-week term terminated the proceedings. Though the detailed circumstances of this

first, formal disruption remain controversial, royalists and opposi-
tionists allowed it to happen because both feared that prolongation
would bring them political defeat. In November 1669, a Sejm was,
for the first time, disrupted before the end of its normal term. The
veto caught on at local level – *sejmiki* became liable to disruptions,
wreaking administrative and judicial havoc. The *szlachta*'s attitude
to the veto was ambivalent. It was the 'palladium of liberty', yet
individuals who wielded it (though no one man would do so unless
he was sure of strong support) were widely condemned. In the
eighteenth century it was as common to talk proceedings out as to
disrupt the Sejm outright. Three of the five Sejmy of Michael
Wiśniowiecki's reign (1669–74) were broken; under John III
Sobieski (1674–96), it was five out of eleven. Of thirty-seven Sejmy
between 1697 and 1762, only twelve enacted legislation. The
establishment of a Confederacy – a league with a common programme – was the only effective means of setting the veto aside, but
such leagues, formed during wars or interregnums, invariably
aimed to preserve cherished ancestral liberties – and for all the
opprobrium heaped on individuals who dared exercise the veto, it
had become one of those freedoms. Sejmy which met after 1763
were much more successful – but most met under the aegis of
confederacies imposed on the nobility.

And yet the Rzeczpospolita showed itself capable of bursts of
astonishing energy and resilience in the face of invasion and
rebellion. The campaigns of Stefan Batory between 1578 and 1582
reversed the territorial gains notched up by Ivan IV, securing
Livonia and Polotsk. Batory oversaw the emergence of a veteran
military cadre which was to render sterling service over the next
generation. Sigismund III's reign witnessed even more remarkable
successes. Intervention in Russia during the later reign of Boris
Godunov and the 'Time of Troubles' saw a Polish-backed pretender
briefly placed on the Muscovite throne in May 1606. In 1610,
Russian boyars elected Sigismund's 15-year-old son, Władysław, as
tsar. Though the prince never entered Moscow, the city received a
Polish garrison in September 1610, which, in the face of a massive
uprising, held out in the Kremlin until October 1611. The election
of Michael Romanov in March 1613 gave the Russians a ruler
around whom to unite, but it was years before Polish troops and

cossack freebooters were cleared from Russian soil. In 1618, Russia acknowledged Polish possession of Smolensk. Michael Romanov's attempt to recapture it during the 'Smolensk war' of 1632–4 ended in humiliation. The 'Perpetual' peace of Polanovo of June 1634 left Smolensk in Polish hands.

Some of these achievements pointed to shortcomings, as well as strengths, in the Polish-Lithuanian polity. The Russian adventure of 1606 was begun by irresponsible grandees seeking to exploit the disorders of Boris Godunov's reign. By the time the Sejm approved involvement in 1609, the opportunities seemed too good to ignore. Likewise, the semi-private initiatives of ambitious border magnates at the turn of the sixteenth and seventeenth centuries aimed to reassert Poland's dormant influence over Moldavia and Wallachia. This courted disaster, for such undertakings could only jeopardize the good relations established with the Porte by the Jagiellonians. Unofficial, destructive raids by Poland's Cossacks against Turkish possessions on the Black Sea aggravated matters. The 1620 expedition under Crown grand *hetman* (military commander) Stanisław Żółkiewski, to keep a friendly *hospodar* on the Moldavian throne, suffered a crushing defeat at Turkish hands at Cecora. Poland was fortunate that domestic troubles in Turkey weakened its ability to launch a full-scale counter-offensive and facilitated the defeat of the Turkish punitive expedition of 1621 at Khotin, just inside Moldavia.

Even in victory, the *szlachta* were divided over these foreign ventures. Stefan Batory did not fight just to repel Muscovite invasion. He viewed Poland through the prism of his native Transylvania and Hungary, which he wished to free from Turkish and Habsburg domination. The reduction of Muscovy to a dependency was a necessary step. His fantastic dreams to take on the Porte represented a major deviation from Jagiellonian prudence. The Sejm refused to endorse his plans for resuming the Russian war in 1584 and to many, his unexpected death in December 1586 was a relief. His Vasa successors, Sigismund III and Władysław IV (1632–48) preferred good relations with Austria rather than Turkey. Habsburg support, they hoped, would help clinch their aspirations for hereditary rule in Poland – and/or make good their claims against Sweden. Sigismund III, son of John III of Sweden and Sigismund Augustus' formidable sister Catherine, had been brought up a staunch Catholic in a Lutheran country. Elected king of Poland in 1587, he succeeded in Sweden as hereditary king in 1597, to be deposed within two years in favour of his uncle, the future Charles IX. Fishing for international support, the Vasas followed Batory in making concessions to the Hohenzollerns over Ducal Prussia, until in 1618 Sigismund III assigned the duchy's reversion to the collateral Brandenburg line.

The Vasas' Swedish preoccupations brought a chain of misfortunes on Poland-Lithuania. The Poles had elected Sigismund III partly with the expectation of 'recovering' Estonia, filched, as they saw it, by the Swedes during the wars with Ivan the Terrible. Sigismund only agreed to the transfer in 1600, after his dethronement in Sweden. Poland ground itself down in an unavailing effort to expel the Swedes. After 1626, Gustavus Adolphus carried the war into Polish Prussia. The six-year truce of Altmark of 1629 left Riga and the bulk of Livonia in Swedish hands and northern Poland devastated. Władysław IV modernized the army and then found the *szlachta* would not let him use it. In 1635 they insisted, over the king's objections, on extending the truce for another sixteen years.

A frustrated Władysław looked to the cossacks of the Ukraine. Sigismund Augustus had used these lawless frontiersmen as a counter-force to the perpetual Tatar raids. Batory had made use of their sterling infantry. In their stronghold of Sicz, on the lower Dnieper, they elected their own *hetman* and army council. They fought the Tatars; they raided the Black Sea littoral. In 1614 they attacked Trebizond and Sinope; in 1615, they burned the suburbs of Constantinople. The Sejm had agreed to 'register' and pay those in the Commonwealth's direct military service – but this accounted for only a fraction of those who regarded themselves as cossacks. The *szlachta* spurned the aspirations of those on the register to be counted as nobles. The drive to exploit the fertile soils of the Ukraine, 'Poland's Indies', and the systematic imposition of labour-services provoked a series of uprisings, suppressed with increasing difficulty. After the defeat of the 1637 rising, the Cossacks were formally degraded to 'a commonality of peasants', save for a register of 6,000.

11 The Royal Castle ('Zamek Królewski') in Warsaw; seventeenth and eighteenth centuries, destroyed during the Second World War: the present building has been reconstructed since 1971. The castle also provided accommodation for Poland's parliament (Sejm) when it met in Warsaw. To the right of the picture is the column first erected in 1643–4 by Władysław IV in honour of his father, Sigismund III, bearing a cross and a drawn sword, the symbols of the militant Counter-Reformation. The statue was raised despite the objections of the papel nuncio, Mario Filonardi, who felt that this kind of honour belonged to religious, rather than secular, figures.

Władysław IV saw his chance in the outbreak of war between Turkey and Venice in 1645. If he could engineer Poland's involvement, he would leave the Sejm with no choice but to vote campaign monies. Success would allow him to strengthen the monarchy and assure his son of the throne. Instead, the Sejm got wind of his plans and forced him to promise to disband the troops he was raising. Undeterred, Władysław cut a secret deal with the Cossacks. He would double their register to 12,000 and grant near-autonomy to the Ukraine if only they would help provoke a conflict with Turkey's vassals, the Crimean Tatars.

This fantastic exercise was rendered meaningless by the deaths, first of the king's only son, Sigismund Casimir, in August 1647, then, the following May, of the king himself. The powder-keg of the Ukraine had already exploded. A private feud between a Polish official and Bohdan Khmel'nytskyi, one of those party to the clandestine dealings with the king, escalated beyond all control. Much of the Crown army was wiped out in May 1648; hurriedly reconstituted, bolstered by private militias, placed under the orders of a demoralisingly divided committee of squabbling nobles, it fled in panic before a joint Tatar–Cossack force in September.

Khmel'nytskyi, far from provoking the Tatars, looked to their support – though they were not prepared to allow him to become too powerful. His periodic bids to impose control over Moldavia were bound to suck in the Turks. Whether he wanted an independent Ukraine, or a looser relationship with his more powerful neighbours, remains uncertain. He could scarcely control the forces he had unleashed. At its height, his rebellion numbered some 150,000 armed men, mainly peasants who loathed their Polish masters and the Jews who dominated much of Ukrainian commerce as the *szlachta*'s economic agents. The swing of the pendulum in the Poles' favour, marked by the victory of Władysław's successor and half-brother, John II Casimir, at Beresteczko, in June 1651, was nullified by the massacre of most of the Polish regular army at Batoh a year later.

The hitherto cautious Russians now seized their chance. In January 1654, by the Union of Pereiaslav, the Ukraine placed itself under Tsar Alexei's protection. An irresistible Russian invasion followed. By August 1655, most of Lithuania was overrun. The Russian advance precipitated an invasion by Charles X of Sweden, alarmed by its implications for his Baltic position. He also had a splendid opportunity to eliminate, once and for all, the Polish Vasas' claims on Sweden. With the fall of Warsaw in September to Charles; with mass defections among the Polish nobility; and with John Casimir's flight to Silesia, the Commonwealth seemed about to disintegrate. Indeed, at Radnot in Hungary, on 6 December 1656, Sweden and Transylvania agreed to carve up the Commonwealth between themselves, the Ukraine and Brandenburg. Brandenburg's ruler, Frederick William, the 'Great Elector', was awaiting his chance to cement Ducal Prussia to the Brandenburg heartland by acquiring Royal, Polish Prussia. All that would have remained would have been a small principality under Swedish protection, carved out of Lithuania for Bogusław Radziwiłł, protégé of Charles and the Elector.

Poland survived the 'Deluge' – Potop – of invasions. The brutality of the over-extended Swedish and Muscovite forces provoked a major national uprising, embracing every level of society. The successful defence of the fortified shrine of the Madonna at Częstochowa in December 1655 proved a legendary turning-point. The defections to Charles X went into reverse. His seemingly remorseless progress provoked Austrian, Danish and Russian attacks on him – though the 'help' the Austrian troops gave the Poles was almost as ruinous as their enemies' invasions. Polish and Tatar forces smashed a Transylvanian invasion in the summer of 1657. By the autumn, Polish troops were coming to the assistance of the hard-pressed Danes. Frederick William switched sides, but at a price: under the treaty of Wehlau of September 1657, the Commonwealth abandoned its suzerainty over Ducal Prussia – which, in 1701, was to be accorded the status of a kingdom in its own right by the Emperor Leopold I. The unexpected death of Charles X in February 1660 paved the way for the end of the Northern War. The peace treaty of Oliva in May 1660 was concluded on the basis of the *status quo ante bellum* – and the surrender by the (childless) John Casimir of his dynastic claims on Sweden. After all the rivers of blood shed in the Swedish wars, he was allowed to retain the courtesy title of king of Sweden.

The struggle with Russia had resumed. Khmel'nytskyi died in August 1657. His *de facto* successor, Ivan Vykhovskyi, himself of noble birth, judged that 'liberty' could have no future under the tsars' rule. The Accord of Hadziacz which he signed with Poland on 16 September 1658 would have created an autonomous principality of Rus', the equal of the Crown and Lithuania. But it came a good ten years too late. Popular venom against the Poles made it unworkable. Hadziacz, a direct challenge to the Union of Pereiaslav, made renewed war with Russia unavoidable. Inadequate taxation and renewed domestic unrest undercut the Poles' ability to exploit a string of military successes. At the little village of Andrusovo in 1667, the exhausted protagonists concluded an armistice, to run for thirteen years. Smolensk and its hinterland remained in

Russian hands. The Ukraine was partitioned: the territories east of the river Dnieper, with the addition of Kiev – which the Russians promised to restore within two years (they never did) – remained under Russian control; the 'right bank' Ukraine remained nominally Polish.

During the wars, John Casimir and his queen, Louise-Marie de Gonzague, made no secret of their hopes of strengthening royal power. Though they dallied with the thought of reforming the veto, their attention focused on securing the succession. The childless couple looked above all to Louis XIV of France. The Great Condé; his son, the duke of Enghien; the French client Philip Wilhelm, duke of Neuburg – all were seriously considered. Once the immediate pressures of the 'Deluge' eased, the king and queen pushed for election in the king's own lifetime. The Polish nobility and Poland's neighbours were equally alarmed. The court's efforts to destroy its chief opponent, Jerzy Lubomirski, provoked rebellion. The defeat at Mątwy on 12 July 1666 cost the royal army 4,000 casualties; the king barely escaped with his life. Only Lubomirski's own death the following year put an end to his plotting. The embattled John Casimir abdicated on 16 September 1668, to die in France in 1672.

Even at John Casimir's election, prognosticators saw in his Latin title 'Ioannes Casimirus Rex' the legend 'Initium Calamitatum Regni' – the beginning of the calamities of the realm. The wars devastated huge swaths of the Commonwealth, inflicting damage to match anything in the Germany of the Thirty Years War. The *szlachta* greeted with suspicion the king's vow in April 1656 to alleviate the oppressions of the common people – the peasantry and townsmen fighting so vigorously in the guerrilla war. Pressures on the peasantry intensified as landlords tried to reconstruct their devastated properties; the ruined towns became an even feebler political and economic force.

The *szlachta* had borne the brunt of Khmel'nytskyi's fury. So too had their protégés, the Jews, who dominated the commerce of Ukrainian settlements, in the wake of the *szlachta*'s colonization drives. Though the figures remain hotly disputed, up to 10,000 Jews may have perished during the Cossack rebellion; many more would have been massacred without the protection of magnate

Map 4   The Polish-Lithuanian Commonwealth in the later sixteenth and
seventeenth centuries.

Boundary between the Crown and the Grand Duchy of Lithuania after 1569

Border of Poland–Lithuania after 1629/34

Border of territories ceded to Russia in 1667

Territory under Turkish rule, 1672–99

Narva

Novgorod

Pskov

a, 1721)

vina   Polotsk

Vitebsk

Smolensk

Andrusovo

Minsk

MOSCOW

(to Russia, 1667)

R U S S I A

SCALE

| 0 | 50 | 100 | 150 | 200 | 250 | 300 | 350 km |

| 0 | | 50 | | 100 | | 150 | | 200 miles |

(to Russia, 1667)

Kiev   Hadziacz

Pereiaslav

o

róg   Cudnów   *Dnieper*   Poltava

(under Turkish rule, 1672–1699)

uczacz

Kamieniec Podolski   Batoh

Khotin   *Dniester*   Sicz

Cecora   Ochakov   (to Russia, 1667)

MOLDAVIA   *Prut*

OTTOMAN   **CRIMEAN TATARS**

NIA

LLACHIA   **EMPIRE**

N

militias. However, amid the decay of commercial and urban life, the Jews, unconstrained by medieval guild regulations, more entrepreneurial, and actively encouraged by their noble patrons, were able to consolidate and expand their already strong position in Polish commercial life, particularly in the smaller townships. Even in the many royal towns which forbade Jewish settlement, the Christian guilds found themselves frequently on the defensive, as Jewish traders settled in suburbs or noble-owned enclaves beyond municipal jurisdiction. Even in the Polish Ukraine, the Jews were rapidly restored. Nowhere in Europe were there so many Jews as in Poland-Lithuania (around a million by the 1770s). But their dominance of much of commercial and economic life, their distinctive faith and culture, also gave rise to resentment, envy and hatreds which have never fully been excised.

The wars diminished Poland's toleration, even if they did not destroy it. The Swedish Lutheran and Russian Orthodox invasions were seen as a religious war. Protestants were convenient scapegoats. Although the treaty of Oliva specified continued public Lutheran worship in Polish Prussia, elsewhere it was a different tale. Most great magnates had long converted to Catholicism – Bogusław Radziwiłł, the last great Calvinist patron, died in 1669. And although mainstream Protestantism was too deeply rooted to be eradicated, its lesser fringes could be picked off. After all, the Warsaw Confederacy of 1573 had been a compromise, a grudging safety valve to prevent civil collapse. The open-ended consensus to preserve peace 'among those who differ and dispute in religion and rite' had been matched by no specific commitments towards non-Catholics. The bishops remained overwhelmingly hostile to wider toleration; the vast majority of the *szlachta* remained catholic. The 1573 agreement had had only limited effect in preventing sporadic religious violence in the towns. As the network of Jesuit colleges thickened, as elected kings looked to the Church to provide them with support, so the Counter-Reformation began to take its toll. As early as 1638, the antitrinitarian school and printing-press at Raków in western Poland had been closed, following charges of blasphemy. Confessional war left little room for mutual tolerance. The 1658 Sejm ordered the exile of all antitrinitarians.

The Commonwealth's failure to reassert its position over the Ukraine combined with the opposition to the Vasas' supposedly absolutist intentions to break the back of Poland's aspirations to pre-eminence in eastern Europe. Domestic politics fused with the foreign policies of its neighbours. The treaty of Stockholm of 1667, between Sweden and Brandenburg, was the first in a long series of agreements between neighbour-states aiming specifically to block any political reform in the Commonwealth.

The effects appeared starkly under John Casimir's successors. The magnate families which had backed French or Austrian candidates would not forgive Michael Wiśniowiecki's elevation, forced on them by *szlachta* gathered in unprecedented numbers for the election (80,000 according to some observers). Disgusted by endless grandee rivalries, the nobility insisted on one of their own – the impoverished scion of a once great family, whose father had distinguished himself (more by brutality than effectiveness) in the wars against Khmel'nytskyi. A coterie centred around the primate, Nicholas Prażmowski, and the grand Crown *hetman*, John Sobieski, spent most of Wiśniowiecki's brief reign plotting his overthrow. When, in 1672, Poland was invaded by the Turks, it stood on the verge of civil war. Once Kamieniec Podolski fell and Lwów was besieged, Polish negotiators had little choice but to capitulate. Podole and Kamieniec were ceded outright to the Porte; the right-bank Ukraine was placed under its overlordship. The Rzeczpospolita agreed to pay an annual tribute to the Turks. The Sejm of February–April 1673 rejected the terms; it voted unprecedented sums for a new army; but it could not heal internal divisions. Sobieski's spectacular destruction, in November, of a Turkish army at Khotin could not be followed up, as Lithuanian forces, commanded by his rival, Michael Pac, refused co-operation; the unpaid Crown troops deserted in droves.

Yet the victory created a huge wave of euphoria, which secured the throne for Sobieski (King Michael died before news of the victory arrived). To Michael Pac, and to most magnate clans, every victory the new king gained would be one for Sobieski and his family (Wiśniowiecki at least had the good grace to be impotent) and promised to do nothing at all for the liberties that constituted the Commonwealth. Pac would not furnish the military support from Lithuania which Sobieski needed. At Żurawno in October 1676, the king had to settle for a renewal of the terms of 1672 – the Turks dropped only the demand for tribute.

Sobieski's plans for recovering Ducal Prussia for Poland (preferably as a hereditary Sobieski fief) were dashed by the same opposition. His hopes of building up support around the Sapieha family in Lithuania backfired as the Sapiehas exploited his patronage to tighten their own grip on the Grand Duchy and then turned against the king as virulently as had the Pac family. Monarchs would continue to be hamstrung by an opposition which elsewhere would have been viewed as treasonable but in Poland-Lithuania genuinely saw its mischief as a defence of ancestral liberty.

When the Turks finally attacked Austria and besieged Vienna in 1683, Sobieski appreciated that he could recover lost territories only by alliance with the Habsburgs. The victory which the combined Polish and Imperialist forces won under his command at Vienna, on 12 September 1683, was – for Poland and its king – a mirage. Crucified by domestic politics, Sobieski was always in a position of weakness – made only worse by relations with Muscovy. Between 1676 and 1681, Tsar Feodor's government actually went to war against the Turks in an unsuccessful bid to push them from the right-bank Ukraine and impose Russian suzerainty. The Russians even warned that, unless the Poles finally agreed to convert the Andrusovo armistice into a definitive peace, they would realign with the Turks. The treaty of Moscow of 6 May 1686 finally ratified Andrusovo. Kiev was definitively lost. Moreover, the Russians secured the role of protectors of the position of the Commonwealth's Orthodox – in effect, giving the tsars the right to intervene in Poland's domestic affairs. For Sobieski, it was one of the worst humiliations of his reign – but so dire was Poland's situation, that he had no option but to ratify the treaty. At least it obviated a Russian invasion, but Moscow's ineffectual campaigns against the Crimean Tatars brought Poland no direct benefits. Polish military efforts for the rest of the war were largely restricted to unhappy thrusts into Moldavia. Their expeditions helped weaken Turkish resistance in the Balkans, but it was primarily thanks to Imperialist successes that the Poles finally regained Kamieniec, Podole and the right-bank Ukraine at the peace of Carlowitz in January 1699 – after Sobieski's death.

Sobieski sought solace during his last years in accumulating a massive private fortune and beautifying his private residences. He died on 17 June 1696, in his beloved palace of Wilanów, outside Warsaw, almost as despised as his two predecessors. The rivalries and unpopularity of his sons doomed their bids for the throne. The energy of the Wettin elector, Frederick Augustus I of Saxony, his cynical conversion from Lutheranism to Catholicism and his paying off of the army's arrears, assured him of the throne over his dithering French rival, the prince of Bourbon-Conti.

The new king, hereditary ruler of the wealthiest state of the Holy Roman Empire, schemed to weld Saxony and Poland into a new northern power. Along with the young tsar Peter I, he envisaged relieving the teenage Charles XII of Sweden's Baltic empire. Swedish Livonia would become a Wettin principality. Augustus invaded Livonia in February 1700, using Saxon troops stationed in Lithuania supposedly to keep the peace between the Sapiehas and their opponents. In November 1700, the Sapiehas were resoundingly defeated by their rivals, but the hopes that Augustus had of exploiting their discomfiture were dashed by his own troops' miserable performance against the Swedes and the crushing rout of the Russian army at Narva by Charles XII in the same month. The Poles' attempts to persuade Charles that Augustus' attack was nothing to do with them found no sympathy. For five years, Charles pursued Augustus, hoping to terrorize the Poles onto his side. In January 1704, Charles even stage-managed the election, by a rump of a few hundred *szlachta*, of his own puppet king, Stanisław Leszczyński. Much of the time, Charles was fighting Saxon or Russian, rather than Polish troops, many of whom were kept waiting in the wings, living off the land, while their commanders, the *hetmani*, awaited the outcome of the conflict. Rival confederacies supported the two kings, and once more civil war took hold.

Only in 1706 did Charles judge the international situation right to strike Saxony itself and force Augustus to abdicate as king of Poland. He was reinstated by grace and favour of Peter the Great, following the Swedish disaster at Poltava in July 1709. While Charles had bogged himself down in Poland, Peter had rebuilt

Russia's army. After Poltava, he used it to impose his protectorate over Poland, which was to remain a liberty-addicted, unreformed Commonwealth, a massive security buffer along Russia's western border. Peter was satisfied with what he extracted from Sweden at Nystad in 1721: Karelia, Ingria, Estonia and, most valuable of all, Livonia – once Poland's own. The Rzeczpospolita counted for so little that it did not even participate in the peace talks.

Throughout the war, extra-parliamentary assemblies struggled to maintain some kind of army and raise some kind of taxation. The 'General Assembly' of 1710 optimistically voted an army 64,000 strong. In fact, supply depended on a combination of looting and *ad hoc* decisions by local *sejmiki*. The *hetmani* acted as regional warlords, regarding the troops as their own private armies. The exactions of Swedish, Saxon and Russian forces, famine and plague compounded the miseries – as bad as anything suffered during the 'Deluge'. The devastation of the towns, the destruction of schools and churches plunged literary and cultural life into a frozen torpor.

Augustus' quartering of Saxon troops in Poland provoked the *szlachta* in November 1715 to form the Confederacy of Tarnogród in defence of its liberties. The more disciplined Saxons might have crushed the movement, had Russian diplomats, backed by Russian arms, not brokered a settlement profitable to Peter. The treaty of Warsaw of November 1716 gave Poland new constitutional and fiscal machinery. Most Saxon troops were to be evacuated. The army was fixed at 24,000 units of pay (in real terms, perhaps half that number of men) drawn from specified, permanent revenues – no longer under the control of the *sejmiki*. The troops themselves were dislocated across specific crown estates. A permanent budget was thus established – to support a pitifully small force utterly incapable of resisting any invader. The so-called 'Silent Sejm' of 1 February 1717 confirmed the deal, without debate, in a single day. The Commonwealth had been reduced to a *de facto* Russian protectorate. The threat of armed Russian intervention, encouraged by Peter's many clients in Poland, frustrated all attempts which Augustus was to make to restore his freedom of action. That his son was to succeed him would owe nothing to the king's efforts – it, too, would owe everything to Russia.

Augustus II died in February 1733. An emotional reaction

12   A fat Polish noble (*szlachcic*); sketch (1776) by Jean-Pierre Norblin (1745–1830). Norblin was active in Poland in 1774–1804, benefiting especially from the patronage of the Czartoryski family.

1776 .W.

13   A thin Polish noble (*szlachcic*); sketch by Jean-Pierre Norblin, 1776.

against foreign rulers and their dubious designs swept the country. A 'Piast' was waiting in the wings – none other than the Stanisław Leszczyński pushed onto a temporary throne by Charles XII. In exile, his daughter, Marie, had in 1726 won the European marriage sweepstake by becoming bride to Louis XV of France. Some 13,000 nobles, confident of French support, enthusiastically elected Leszczyński in September 1733. But Russia and its Austrian ally had decided that continued Wettin rule in Poland was preferable to that of the king of France's father-in-law. Russia was anxious to maintain its new pre-eminence not only in Poland, but in fractious Sweden, a shadow of its old self. Leszczyński was too closely associated with the adventure of Charles XII to be acceptable in St Petersburg. Once Friedrich August III of Saxony promised to preserve the Polish constitution, Vienna and Petersburg went to war on his behalf. In December 1733, 4,000 nobles, 'protected' by Russian troops, elected him King Augustus III. Russian arms ensured his triumph. In Italy and on the Rhine, the French secured what they wanted from this War of the Polish Succession. In October 1735 the Preliminaries of Vienna delivered Austria's satellite duchy of Lorraine to France. Leszczyński would be allowed to rule over it as nominal duke; on his death, it would pass to France; and he could keep his title, king of Poland.

Amid the political degradation, Augustus III's reign saw a kind of healing. By the late 1740s, much of the worst damage after the Great Northern War had been repaired. Although Poland never regained its sixteenth-century pre-eminence as purveyor of grain to Europe, cereals and other commodity exports – timber, cattle, horses, naval stores – pump-primed prosperity for great and middling landowners. The Catholic Church, with its international connexions, was in the forefront of a cultural reconstruction. The two teaching orders, the Piarists and the Jesuits, began to compete from the 1740s and 1750s to provide the kind of elite education they were offering in Italy and France. Dresden was a second home to many Polish nobles – and a channel for new ideas. 'Enlightenment' became chic. The most effective exponent of reinvigorating old traditions through new philosophies was the Piarist Stanisław Konarski, whose Collegium Nobilium, established in Warsaw in 1740, served as a model school for the more fashionable nobility. In 1733, as an active Leszczyński supporter, he had tried to persuade his countrymen that liberty without sovereignty was unsustainable. His *On the means to efficacious councils* of 1761–3 was a blistering demolition of the *liberum veto* and its evils. It attracted mixed opinions, but broke the ice of political debate. Its recourse to new ideas, not least in its unprecedented exaltation of the English constitution, forced even conservative critics to look beyond their homespun sloganeering.

Konarski's ideas found favour with one powerful grouping – the

Czartoryski family. Of ancient, princely Lithuanian stock, they had long languished in obscurity, until, under Augustus II, a combination of royal patronage and useful marriages built them up into a formidable political force. The Czartoryskis appreciated that if Poland were to be anything other than a passive victim of international circumstances, the whole shape of its politics had to be recast. Even under Augustus II they cautiously advocated restrictions on the *liberum veto*. They believed that they could both preserve liberty in the Commonwealth and run it themselves – in the manner of the Whig grandees of Britain, whom they so admired. The cultured, ruthless brothers August and Michael looked to Russia to break the impasse of domestic politics. To them, the worst danger came from Frederick II of Prussia. His conquest of Habsburg Silesia between 1740 and 1742 made Polish Prussia, that traditional object of Hohenzollern appetite, even more enticing. Ties with Russia, the Czartoryskis felt, would offer some protection.

Under Augustus III, Poland periodically served as transit route for the warring armies of Prussia, Russia and Austria, even the Ottoman Porte. At least the full horrors of the past were not repeated. Exactions were localized, on occasion even orderly. To large landowners, insulated from the incidental damage which foreign armies caused, their custom furnished useful market opportunities. For most of the Seven Years War of 1756–63, Austria's client, Saxony, was under Prussian occupation. Augustus III, who, like his father, always preferred the delights of Dresden, was forced into a prolonged residence in Warsaw. He returned to a devastated Saxony only in March 1763, to die that October. Russia again settled the Polish succession – this time, single-handedly. Its troops had been stationed in Poland during the Seven Years War – topping them up to ensure the return of the preferred choice of the new empress, Catherine II, was an easy matter.

The man elected king in September 1764 was Stanisław Poniatowski, nephew to Michael and August Czartoryski. In St Petersburg on diplomatic business in 1754–5, he had become the grand duchess Catherine's lover. He desperately wanted to reform Poland – he even adopted the coronation name of 'August' as a sign of his wish to be his country's renovator, just as Augustus had been of the

14 A view of Polish political life: Jean-Pierre Norblin's sketch of a *sejmik* (local parliamentary assembly) meeting outside a church. Eighteenth-century English electors might have felt almost at home.

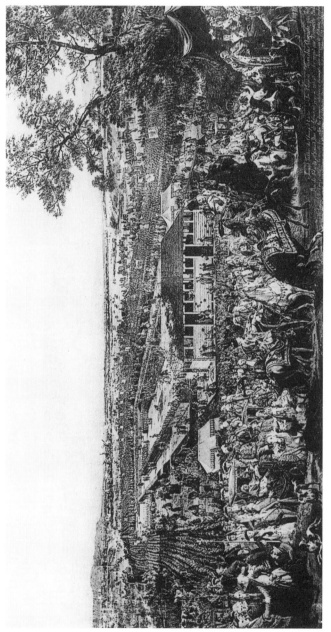

15   Another view of Polish political life: Canaletto the Younger's (Antonio Eugenio Bellotto, 1721–80) painting of the election of King Stanislaw August Poniatowski in 1764 (painted 1778). Canaletto was court painter to Augustus III and Stanislaw August Poniatowski

Roman world. Catherine saw in him, however, not a reformer, but a pliant, accommodating puppet. Her ambitious plans to succeed where Peter the Great had failed – to thrust back the frontiers of the Ottoman Porte and to project Russian influence into the Holy Roman Empire – posited a manageable, not merely anarchic, Poland. A soft intellectual reliant on her financial bounty (she even paid for Stanisław August's coronation) seemed ideal.

The empress sought to further her control by reversing the disadvantaged position of Poland's Protestants. The 1733 Convocation parliament had barred them from the Sejm. But Protestants continued to be the recipients of crown estates, local offices, even army officerships, up to and including general rank. They played a key role in the public life of Royal Prussia and its towns. The execution of ten leading burghers in the aftermath of a religious riot in Thorn in 1724 barely dented the dominance of the town's Lutheran elite. That the overwhelming majority of the Polish nobility were hostile to the Protestants is unquestionable – yet at a time when Catholic nobles constantly complained at the lack of offices and rewards open to them, their Protestant counterparts continued to play a role in public life far more prominent than that enjoyed by religious minorities in countries such as Britain or the Netherlands which regarded themselves as the van of European civilization. Catherine counted on them to form a dependent, reliable agency. In a Europe whose intellectuals despised the backwardness of the Catholic Church, her supposedly enlightened intervention might even help cleanse the stigma of her murderous way to the Romanov throne. Of course, she went through the motions of improving the position of Poland's Orthodox – but Orthodox nobles of any standing had almost disappeared. Her real energies centred on the Protestants.

No Polish politician seriously dared endorse a massive, sudden restoration of the old Protestant position. The empress' efforts in this respect collided with those of Stanisław August to implement his own reform agenda. Catherine could accept the shackling of hitherto irresponsible ministers such as the *hetmani* or the treasurers by collegiate boards; she could not accept major restrictions on, let alone the abolition of, the *liberum veto* – precisely what the king hoped to secure at the 1766 Sejm. The Russian ambassador warned that his troops would tear Warsaw down 'stone by stone' unless the assembly reaffirmed the veto in full. The *szlachta* could accept even the imposition of a king from Russia. They had so far swallowed transit marches and occasional military intervention. But Catherine's systematic, sustained application of force to bend their constitution to her plans was something new. The last straw was the Russian treatment of the confederated Sejm of 1767–8. It was only by the use of force, terror and even the deportation of opponents to the Russian interior that Catherine secured her aims: the opening up of the Sejm and Senate to dissenters; a senatorial seat for the Orthodox bishop of Mohylew (a Russian subject, imposed on the Poles); a restructuring of parliamentary procedures, obviating its total disruption, but retaining the veto for all but the most insignificant legislation. To cap it all, the Poles were made to accept a Russian guarantee of their laws and constitution, even their territory, binding them hand and foot to their seemingly irresistible neighbour.

Even before the Sejm ended, a group of nobles gathered at Bar, in Podole, in late February 1768, to set up a confederacy aiming explicitly to reverse the new religious settlement. Their further, as yet unstated, plans called for the overthrow of Poniatowski and a restoration of the Saxon Wettins. The Russians easily crushed the initial outbreak; but the Confederacy of Bar opened the way to four years of civil and guerrilla warfare, with uncontrollable international repercussions.

In October 1768, the exasperated Ottoman Porte declared war. It had long feared that Russia was set on reducing the Commonwealth to a supply base for a future reckoning with Turkey. The conflict brought Russia an almost unending string of military and naval victories. The peace of Kuchuk Kainardji of June 1774 was a dreadful humiliation for the Turks, not only costing them territory, but forcing them to abandon their lordship over the Crimea. Conducted over distances almost unimaginable in western Europe, the triumphant campaigning imposed a massive strain on Russia. It was to provoke the great Pugachev revolt. The resources to crush the guerrillas of Bar were not there. Neither Poniatowski nor the Czartoryskis were willing to assist the Russians; on the contrary, they hoped to use the Confederacy to secure, at the very least, a reversal of Russia's guarantee; even to escape its clutches altogether.

Russia's thrusts into the Danube basin alarmed Austria. Austria's ally and Turkey's friend, France, was equally anxious to roll back the Russian advance. France, Austria and Turkey each gave greater or lesser degrees of support to the Barists. The resulting tensions were brilliantly exploited by Frederick of Prussia. Russian power, which had so nearly destroyed him during the Seven Years War, had come as a shock. In April 1764, he had formed an alliance with Catherine and had seconded her activities in Poland. He appreciated that Russia's was the dominant role in Poland. He loyally (if querulously) supported Catherine's Turkish war with financial subsidies. Wary of direct military involvement, he realized that he could yet draw profit from the war. He constantly warned Russia that immoderate expansionism would provoke the Habsburgs. And, in the end, he was able to persuade Russia that a wider European conflict could be averted only by desisting from outright gains in the Balkans. Instead, Russia should seek 'compensation' from the original cause of the trouble, the Rzeczpospolita. Of course, Austria, too, had to be pacified – by taking matching territory from Poland; the disadvantage that Habsburg expansion would confer on Prussia could be met only by allowing Prussia to take its 'share of the cake'.

Russia had had its eyes on the Lithuanian lands west of the Smolensk area since the 1740s. Catherine's territorial guarantee of 1768 was elastically worded. And while the empress had never intended to share Poland with anyone (least of all Frederick), many in St Petersburg were persuaded that the road of all-round compensation offered the best exit from the imbroglio. Russia would, after all, still control what remained of Poland.

The precipitating factor was Austrian annexation of small strips of Polish highlands along the rugged Carpathian border. Frederick remorselessly played up the extent of this petty territorial larceny, warned of (non-existent) French preparations for war and, by 1772, had persuaded the Russians that a deal had to be cut. On 5 August, three bilateral conventions signed between Russia, Austria and Prussia in St Petersburg gave Catherine the territories along the headwaters of the Dvina and Dnieper; the Austrians received

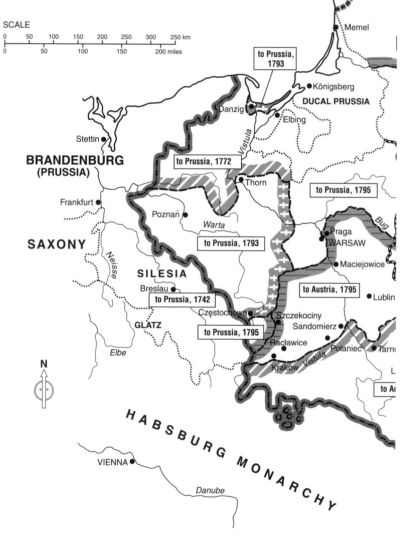

Map 5　The Polish-Lithuanian Commonwealth in the eighteenth century.

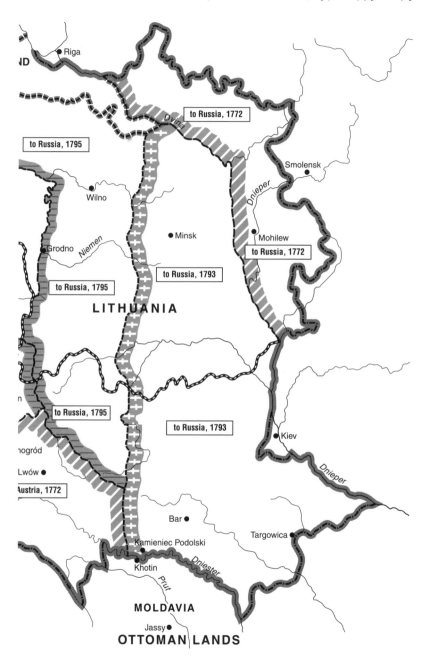

extensive lands along the upper Vistula and San rivers; and Frederick finally obtained Polish Prussia – without Danzig, deemed too valuable by Catherine to deliver to her all-too-clever friend. Even so, in economic terms, he was the biggest gainer, seizing Poland's most valuable lands and the economic jugular of the Vistula (which he proceeded to squeeze for all he could for the rest of his reign). Practical measures of occupation began in April 1772, in anticipation of the final agreements. Most Poles were astonished – rumours of Partition had circulated for years; their own kings had warned them of their likely fate. The protection so long afforded them by God and the European balance had finally run its course.

The humiliation was compounded by a prolonged Sejm, insisted on by the partitioning powers. It was bludgeoned into giving formal approval for the whole partition. Stanisław August's hopes, that in return for loss of territory the monarchy's powers might be strengthened or the *liberum veto* rescinded, were dashed. The 1768 constitutional settlement was reaffirmed, though the concessions to the dissenters were drastically scaled back – the great bulk of Protestants were, in any case, now under Prussian rule. The bishopric of Mohylew, the last Orthodox see, had passed to Russia. A new administrative body, the 'Permanent Council', was set up to provide a minimum of day-to-day administrative continuity and co-ordination. The major innovation was the creation of a Commission for National Education, aimed at supervising and modernizing the curriculum in the secondary colleges and the two 'Principal Schools' (universities) of Kraków and Wilno. It was made possible by the papal abolition (under French and Spanish pressure) of the Jesuits in 1773: the Order's schools and properties furnished the backbone of the new educational regime. But it took a decade for the Commission to extricate itself from its teething troubles – longer still to overcome noble suspicions of its new-fangled ideas.

The Commonwealth was too weak to resist dismemberment. The most spectacular act of defiance, attaining near-mythological status in folk memory, occurred in April 1773, when Tadeusz Rejtan blocked access to the Sejm's debating-chamber in a vain protest against the inevitable. Although the demographic estimates can be only tentative, Poland may have lost getting on for 5 million of its 14 million inhabitants, with Austria taking the largest

16 Rejtan at the Sejm of 1773; an iconic painting of an emotional protest against the First Partition by Jan Matejko (1838–93). Painted 1866. The painting infuriated a number of Polish aristocrats who objected to this close identification of their ancestors with a less than happy turning-point in Polish history. One complained: 'The exploitation of an historical scandal for mere popularity's sake has never been the task of artistic masters.' On the other hand, the Emperor Franz Joseph was sufficiently taken with it to purchase it for 50,000 francs after its exhibition in the Paris salon of 1867.

number, over 2.5 million. Poland was deprived of about a third of
its territory, including its richest provinces. The frontiers of Austria
and Prussia advanced towards the old Polish heartlands. Russia's
gains were the most extensive, Prussia's the least, but they were
economically and strategically the most valuable. The Austrians
rued the day they had allowed themselves to be manoeuvred into a
settlement which disproportionately strengthened their hated rival.
All three powers extended their guarantees, as solemn as they were
worthless, of the new constitutional and territorial order.

The king hoped against hope that the new educational reforms
and his generous cultural patronage would eventually permit the
emergence of a more mature and responsible citizenry. His reign
did indeed see a cultural efflorescence. The poetry of Ignacy
Krasicki (1735–1801) or Stanisław Trembecki (1740–1812)
matched anything produced during the Renaissance. The output
of major political and social commentators such as Józef Wybicki
(1747–1822) or Hugon Kołłątaj (1750–1812) deliberately eschewed the latinisms of their predecessors and gave the Polish
language a new force and sophistication. The king saw in the
Warsaw theatre a means of propagating new ideas. The press was
as free and exuberant as any in Europe. Yet all this was not
enough. The sole means of survival lay, Stanisław August was
convinced, in keeping with Russia in the hope of persuading
Catherine to countenance further reform. But the last thing
Russia wanted was any form of Polish revival. St Petersburg
confirmed itself as Poland's unofficial capital. Magnate coteries
appealed to the Russian court to put them in positions of profit
and power. The king was seen, even by his erstwhile allies, the
Czartoryskis, as a Russian cipher, to be used, abused and circum-
vented. This was what Catherine wanted. So dependent did
Poland seem that by 1780, she felt sufficiently confident to withdraw the great majority of her troops.

Some hoped the European diplomatic conjuncture might yet
bring salvation. In 1781, Catherine effectively ditched her Prussian alliance, to realign with Joseph II of Austria. Only the
Habsburgs, not the Hohenzollerns, could offer effective support
for her grandiose ambitions of throwing the Turks out of Europe
and establishing her grandson, Constantine, as ruler of a new

Greek Empire. Russia's outright annexation of the Crimea in 1783 ultimately brought about a fresh Turkish declaration of war in August 1787.

The Russo-Turkish war of 1787–92 furnished a final interval for the reassertion of Polish sovereignty. Catherine's conviction that her interests were best served by preserving a tried, if not entirely trusted, Poniatowski on the throne led a frustrated opposition to cast about elsewhere for support – Prussia. At the same time, Prussia's new king, Frederick William II, and his chief minister, Friedrich von Hertzberg, hoped to round off earlier gains with the acquisition of Danzig, Thorn and whatever other territories they could: their chosen means was to encourage Polish 'patriotic' indignation against Russia, to foment internal disorders, which they would exploit to secure their aims. When, in October 1788, a new Sejm met, it gloried in an orgy of virulent russophobia. The appalled king, who had a good inkling of the Prussian game, was unable to prevent emotions from running amok. In what amounted to a constitutional coup, the Sejm took over the running of the country. Egged on by Prussia, it repudiated the 1773–5 settlement and guarantees.

Russia's distractions – the Turkish war, combined with a war with Sweden between July 1788 and August 1790 – allowed the Poles to conduct a prolonged debate as to how the state should be reformed. Within months, much of the constitutional machinery set up after 1773 had been dismantled; the Sejm voted to increase the army from around 18,000 to 100,000 – only too late did it give serious consideration to paying for it. Patriotic fervour, not political calculation, carried all before it. Events in France, of which the uncensorable press kept the public fully informed, added to the general excitement. Even the hitherto largely passive townsfolk of Warsaw – whose population during the Sejm exceeded 100,000 – began actively joining in the politics. The offer of an alliance from Prussia (designed to reassure the Poles as to Prussian intentions), and successful insistence that the Russians should desist from using Polish territory as a transit route to the Balkan front, helped convince the 'Four Years Sejm' that the era of humiliations was over.

The most important achievement of the dizzy years of 1788–92 was the experience of unprecedented rule-by-parliament. Poniatowski's reign had been a harsh political school. For all the brutality which accompanied them, the Sejmy of 1764, 1766, 1767–8, 1773–5 and 1776 hammered home a new principle: that parliament could and should legislate; and that it was for the rest of the country to follow. For two centuries or more, the *szlachta* had been unwilling to learn these lessons themselves. Now, others inculcated them. The Four Years Sejm was the culmination of this process of forced political education, as a political elite discovered that it could create new administrative bodies, vote new taxation, take diplomatic and political initiatives – that it could do more than simply defend old privileges, that it could govern.

The sense of freedom provided by the temporary lifting of the Russian protectorate was not always well used. Garrulity ruled in the debates, as individuals showered the assembly with pet projects and the Sejm and its sub-committees tried vainly to cover all aspects of government activity. So matters might have gone on, had not the opposition to Stanisław August split: between those who wanted genuine reform, even enlightened social policies, and those who merely wanted a return to the status quo of Augustus III's reign. It was the former who mended their fences to the king; and it was in collaboration with him that, on 3 May 1791, in a legitimist *coup d'état*, they sprang a new constitution on Poland: a curious hybrid of royal hopes for a more vigorous monarchy and a more effective parliament, with checks and balances to curb any despotic tendencies. The two sacred cows of the Rzeczpospolita's history were slaughtered: the *liberum veto* was abolished and, even more remarkably, elective monarchy was rejected. A dynastic throne was offered to Augustus III's grandson, Frederick Augustus III of Saxony. The English principles of ministerial accountability and monarchic irresponsibility were adopted. New central commissions, reflecting an obsession with a Montesquieu-inspired conception of the separation of legislative, executive and judicial branches, were introduced. Townsmen were given limited rights of participation in the Sejm in matters directly affecting commerce. Poland's politically active 'bourgeoisie' was still very weak and largely confined to Warsaw. More thoughtful souls among the *szlachta* were keen to play up its potential role for the future. Townsmen settled gratefully for what they were given. The Sejm

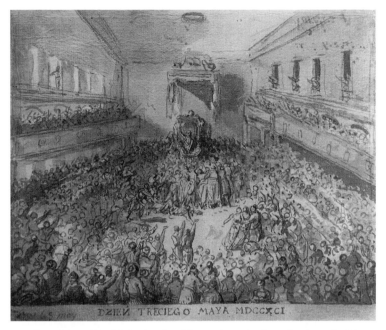

DZIEN TRECIEGO MAYA MDCCXCI.

17   Jean-Pierre Norblin's sketch of the oath to the Constitution of 3 May
1791.

never got around to proper consideration of the place of Poland's
many Jews, despite their prominent commercial role. They had a
vibrant culture of their own, but they continued to remain outside
the political framework. Peasants were given little, beyond a vague
commitment to the state's legal protection – but even this was a
major turning-point after almost three centuries of letting noble
landowners have their way over their serfs. On the other hand,
peasants migrating to Poland were assured of their personal
freedom. The changes promised far more than was delivered – but
they were radical enough to alarm both Russia and Prussia: only
struggling Austria welcomed the Third of May Constitution, for its
policy-makers hoped that a revived Poland might be turned into an
ally against Prussia.

   The new constitution was fêted throughout Europe: in Paris,
because it carried the promise of even backward Poland joining the
revolutionary bandwagon; in London, because it was not French

and the Polish minister produced a nicely honed translation which made it appear almost English. Of course, the constitution sealed Poland's fate. The Saxon Elector did not dare take up the offer of the throne. Russia could not tolerate such a show of defiance in its vassal. As soon as the Turkish war was over, in May 1792, over 90,000 troops poured across the frontier, overwhelming the untried Polish army. The Prussians refused to honour their defensive alliance on the grounds that they had not been consulted over the new constitution. In St Petersburg, half a dozen Polish malcontents proclaimed that they had set up a confederacy in the border village of Targowica, in defence of Polish liberty. It was true – 'Targowica' (a political insult which has lost none of its venom even in a new millennium) was the last gasp of the 'Liberty' that the Third of May Constitution tried to redefine. Even the many for whom the Third of May was a step too far could not but despise the diehards who invoked the empress' protection.

Targowica's leadership embarked on an orgy of score-settling and self-enrichment. Poniatowski's accession to the Confederacy, in the hope that he could restrain its excesses, brought him only an opprobrium from which his memory has not yet recovered. It was clear within weeks that, even backed by Russian troops, the Targowica confederates were utterly incapable of providing effective rule in Poland-Lithuania.

The solution was simple: another Partition. Catherine's latest lover, Platon Zubov, and his friends were all too eager to enrich themselves with the Polish Ukraine. The empress herself had gone fully native and decided that it was her historic mission to reunify the old Rus' lands, so many of which still lay inside the Rzeczpospolita's borders. Prussia could scarcely wait for a deal: since April 1792, it had been supporting Austria in the war against revolutionary France, in the belief that the rabble who had taken over would provide easy pickings. Instead, in September, the democratic rabble turned back the Prussians at Valmy. A humiliated Frederick William looked to Poland for 'compensation' for his trouble. Behind the back of the Austrians, who were committed to defending their possessions in the Netherlands against the French, the Prussians and the Russians signed a second treaty of Partition in St Petersburg on 23 January 1793. Catherine would take an enormous slab of land between the Dvina in the north and the Dniester in the south. Frederick William would acquire a triangle of territory between Silesia and East Prussia. A little buffer-state would be left – for how long? Prussian troops began to enter Poland on 24 January, without even waiting for news of the agreement to be confirmed.

The brutal pantomime of the 1773–5 Sejm was repeated at the parliament summoned to the Lithuanian town of Grodno (Warsaw was deemed too subversive) in June 1793. Consent to the cessions and a new constitutional package, formally reducing Poland to the status of a subservient Russian ally, was extracted from the assembly by the end of September. The rump state of some 4 million inhabitants remained under a Russian occupation which few doubted could be anything other than a prelude to final partition. In desperation, some Poles looked to revolutionary France for support; some even dreamed of a genuinely national uprising. General Tadeusz Kościuszko, who had played a distinguished role in the war of American Independence (on the colonists' side), had good connexions in France and had given sterling service against the Russians in the unhappy war of 1792, was chosen to head the insurrection. The rising itself was precipitated by a wave of Russian arrests and proposals to scale back the Polish army – demobilized men were to be pressed into Russian service. It began in Kraków on 25 March 1794. Even after Kościuszko's tactical victory over a small Russian force at Racławice on 4 April, it should have been rapidly snuffed out by the more numerous Russian veterans. But the news of the victory electrified Poland – not since Sobieski had the Poles won a set-piece encounter against a foreign army. Warsaw rose in bloody revolt and expelled the Russian occupiers. Wilno followed suit. Frederick William II, scenting easy victory, joined the Russians. Their combined forces defeated Kościuszko at Szczekociny in June. The Prussians went on to take Kraków but the siege of Warsaw which they undertook with the Russians ended in failure. Lack of heavy artillery, mutual mistrust and an uprising in his newly annexed Polish lands caused Frederick William to break off his operations in early September.

Kościuszko hoped that if the peasantry could be rallied to the cause of independence, revolutionary France might be persuaded to lend its assistance. But unless centuries of serfdom were overturned, the peasantry would never furnish enthusiastic support. Equally, Kościuszko could not fight without the *szlachta* and few of these were prepared to welcome the overturning of the only social and economic system that they knew. They wanted an independent Poland, but very few could imagine a free peasantry. Peasant support did, indeed, play a key role at the battle of Racławice – but Kościuszko could at best only admonish, cajole and plead with landowners to reduce peasant obligations. His Proclamation of Połaniec of 7 May 1794, declaring all peasants personally free and cutting back their labour services, was largely a dead letter. As for revolutionary France, it offered revolutionary rhetoric, but nothing else.

It was to anticipate the arrival of Russian reinforcements under General Suvorov that, on 10 October, a badly outnumbered Kościuszko attacked General Fersen's corps at Maciejowice, south-east of Warsaw. Kościuszko's army was defeated; he was captured. On 4 November, Suvorov's troops stormed the poorly fortified suburb of Praga, across the Vistula from Warsaw. Around 10,000 people were massacred. Warsaw capitulated the following day. The Rising was over.

This time, Vienna would not miss out. It had begun to send troops across the Polish border in June. Catherine was now ready to favour the Austrians. On 3 January 1795, Austrian and Russian diplomats signed a fresh treaty of Partition in St Petersburg, carving up what remained, and assigning a share to Prussia. Russia, once again, took the greatest share. The Austrian portion, smaller than Prussia's, was economically far more valuable. Prussia's would include Warsaw – which would now become a frontier town – but it would have to disgorge Kraków. Catherine was determined to make it quite clear to her allies that it was by her grace and favour that scraps of Poland were being thrown to them. Not that the Prussians were grateful – their relations with Austria had deteriorated so much during their joint offensive against France that the two powers were on the verge of war. It was not until 24 October that a furious Frederick William agreed to accept what he had been given and to hand Kraków over to the Austrians. Prussia was too exhausted to do otherwise.

Since the Rzeczpospolita no longer existed, parliamentary ratification of the recent proceedings was irrelevant. On 25 November 1795, Stanisław August Poniatowski signed an act of abdication. He died in St Petersburg on 12 February 1798. On 12 January 1796, a tripartite convention between Russia, Austria and Prussia in St Petersburg insisted on 'the need to abolish everything which can recall the memory of the existence of the kingdom of Poland'. The experiment in noble-democracy was over, a resounding failure. What lived on was the resentment of a noble-nation which, despite being torn apart, still felt itself a coherent unity and which, in its final years, had experienced a new pride in cultural and political resurrection.

II

POLAND, AFTER 1795

4

Challenging the partitions, 1795–1864

Poland's cultural and civic revival during the reign of Stanisław August Poniatowski, impressive as it was, was unable to save the Polish state from annihilation in 1795. If anything, by challenging Russia's domination, the Polish reformers had precipitated the very disaster they were desperate to avoid. One can only speculate whether greater patience would have enabled a compliant Poland to survive intact into the nineteenth century under the watchful eye of Empress Catherine's successors, or whether the Napoleonic wars would have dragged Poland, in any case, into some disastrous international quagmire. One way or the other, it is difficult to imagine the Poles escaping unscathed from the upheavals of the Napoleonic period.

Be that as it may, from 1795 until the end of the First World War the extensive lands of the former Polish-Lithuanian Commonwealth remained politically divided and under foreign rule. This long period of partition, punctuated with several heroic but unsuccessful bids for independence, did not destroy Polish high culture or many of the traditions and values of the *szlachta*, out of whose ranks was to emerge the modern Polish intelligentsia, or indeed the Roman Catholicism which distinguished most Polish-speakers from Protestant Prussians and Orthodox Russians, if not Catholic Austrians. Nevertheless, the different patterns of political, economic and social development of the separate parts of historic Poland were to accentuate regional differences, while the emergence of several mutually exclusive ethnic and linguistic nationalisms was to add a further twist to the complex issue of national identity. The answers to the questions 'Who is a Pole?' or 'What is Poland?' would be very different in 1918 from those given in the last decades of the eighteenth century. Not surprisingly, the re-creation of a Polish state after 1918 was to be no easy task.

As things stood in the mid-1790s, Poland's prospects were very bleak indeed. For many of its political and intellectual elite their once free and glorious republic, like the great polities of the ancient world, had disappeared for ever; many educated Poles doubted at first whether their nation could survive without a state. The Austro-Prussian-Russian convention of January 1797, removing the very name of Poland from official usage, seemed only to confirm such a pessimistic verdict. The leaders of the movement of national regeneration of 1788–94 had to flee abroad or languished in prison: Kościuszko in St Petersburg until 1796, and Kołłątaj in the Austrian fortress of Olmütz until 1803. All attempts to renew armed resistance within Poland between 1796 and 1798 were likewise brutally crushed. At the same time, many men of property felt that to save their fortunes they had little choice but to adapt to the new political realities and to swear fealty to their new masters. Two young Czartoryski princes were sent as supplicants to the Russian court in the hope of recovering their family's sequestrated estates; the court of Berlin succeeded in winning over Prince Antoni Radziwiłł, who even married a Hohenzollern princess, and Prince Józef Poniatowski, the nephew of Poland's last king, who settled down to a life of revelry in Prussian-occupied Warsaw. By the same token, many Galician aristocrats established fine residences in Vienna.

While delighted to receive such submissions from the Polish aristocracy, the three partitioning powers pursued contrasting policies towards their vast ex-Polish territories in the immediate post-1795 period. Although in her propaganda Catherine II had claimed that she was recovering the lost lands of old Kievan Rus', Russia lacked the more sophisticated bureaucratic machinery of her Germanic neighbours to embark on a thorough policy of russi-fication. Much of the distinct social order of the western *gubernii* (governorships) of the Russian Empire was to remain unchanged for many decades: the local Polish-Lithuanian landed gentry retained many of its social and legal privileges, and some vestiges of local self-government. Polish schools continued to function, as well as the Lithuanian legal system which had been in operation in the eastern part of the Commonwealth since the sixteenth century. Nor did the Russian authorities do anything to alleviate the conditions of the serfs, whose labour exactions were even increased. This suited many landowners, especially in the southern (Ukrainian) districts, who looked with glee at the attractive prospects of exporting their grain through Odessa, the newly founded Russian emporium on the Black Sea. Only in the area of religion did Catherine attempt to strengthen the 'Russian' character of these lands: most of the Greek Catholic Ukrainian peasants were obliged to return to the Orthodox fold. In the former Grand Duchy of Lithuania, where Catholicism had struck deeper roots, this policy was abandoned by Tsar Paul. The resulting contrast between the Catholicism (both Roman and Uniate) of the Lithuanian-Belorussian north and the Orthodoxy of the Ukrainian south, where social tensions were also more acute, was to contribute markedly to the shaping of very different regional attitudes to the Polish national movement in the Russian Empire in the nineteenth century.

In the Polish lands acquired by Prussia in 1793 and 1795 the Hohenzollerns introduced a centralized and highly staffed system of administration and the Prussian legal system (*Landrecht*); consequently, many noble privileges were respected but the serfs did acquire a degree of protection against seigneurial exploitation. The Polish secondary school system was largely dismantled and German-language education was promoted. Easy credits in Berlin banks and the prospect of handsome profits from grain exports via the Baltic ports helped to mollify the local Polish landowners' feelings of national resentment, although in the long run many estates would be ruined by high mortgages and would fall into German hands. In Austrian Poland the centralized Josephinist system of administration which had been introduced in 'Old' Galicia in the 1780s was now extended to 'New' Galicia acquired in 1795. The amorphous Polish noble estate was reclassified on the Austrian model into a titled hierarchy, the Polish school system was abandoned, and censorship introduced. The Polish university in Kraków was turned into a German-Latin institution. On the other

hand, sentiments of loyalty to the Habsburg emperors were encouraged among the peasants of the two Galicias by the easing of
labour burdens and the granting to the serfs of some property
rights. Although all three partitioning powers imposed a twenty-
year period of military service on their serf conscripts (a burden
that had not existed in the largely demilitarized Polish-Lithuanian
Commonwealth), Austrian military discipline was the least harsh.

The three partitioning governments placed the Roman Catholic
Church under tight state supervision. Nor did they spare the large
Jewish population from heavy taxation and bureaucratic controls:
in Galicia, for instance, the Jews were obliged to adopt German
surnames, while in Russia (which had acquired half of the Commonwealth's Jewry) they were confined to their area of settlement
and were later subject to a misguided and ultimately unsuccessful
physiocratic policy to force them out of their artisanal and inn-
keeping trades into farming. Many of Poland's towns were also
afflicted by the economic dislocation brought about by arbitrary
frontier changes; after a period of vibrant growth in the 1770s and
1780s, when its population reached 100,000, Warsaw now found
itself reduced to a half-deserted Prussian frontier town.

Despite the shock of the final Partition and the resignation of
many aristocrats and notables in favour of a quiet life, 1795 proved
not to be the end of Polish yearnings for independence. The long
legacy of nobiliary republicanism contrasted starkly with the absolutism of Poland's conquerors, and the national awakening of the
reign of Stanisław August Poniatowski could not simply be obliterated from the minds of Poland's elite. The presence across the
length and breadth of the former Commonwealth of hundreds of
thousands of petty noblemen, many unsophisticated yet fiercely
proud of their former status as free citizens, was also to provide a
reservoir of future freedom fighters – soon to be exposed to the
intoxicating message of Romantic nationalism. The long period of
continuous international instability generated by the French Revolution and the Napoleonic wars also provided many Polish patriots
with opportunities to challenge the post-partition status quo in
their homeland.

Initially Polish national aspirations were kept alive mainly by
exiled patriots, many radically minded, who sought the assistance

of the French Republic for their cause. About 20,000 Poles, many of them Austrian conscripts taken prisoner by the French, were to serve in the Polish legions formed in Italy under French aegis and commanded in a spirit of egalitarianism by Generals Henryk Dąbrowski and Karol Kniaziewicz. The legend of their exploits against the Austrians and Russians between 1797 and 1800 was to inspire many future Polish generations, while their hymn 'Poland has not perished while we live', a mazurka with Józef Wybicki's words of defiance against Poland's oppressors, eventually established itself as the modern Polish national anthem. The radicals also launched several clandestine organizations in Poland itself, such as the Society of Polish Republicans, which linked the cause of national independence with that of serf emancipation and dreamt of introducing a French-style constitution in a restored Poland.

In the immediate term the radical patriotic cause was a failure. The Polish exiles in Paris were divided, the conspirators at home lacked wide support, while the French Republic under the Directorate lost its initial revolutionary ardour. Bonaparte's rise to power dismayed Kościuszko and other Polish democrats. The Polish legionaries' dream of marching through Austria to liberate Poland was finally shattered when France concluded peace with Austria and Russia in 1801, and when Bonaparte cynically dispatched 5,000 Polish legionaries to reconquer Haiti. The freedom fighters had been transformed into an instrument of colonial repression; few of them were ever to see Europe again. Kościuszko's proposal of 1800 for waging a peasant-backed guerrilla war in Poland, without any foreign aid, against the armies of Austria, Prussia and Russia was, in the circumstances, sheer quixotic fantasy.

The disenchantment with Republican France and the consequent return to Poland of many exiles (although not of Kościuszko) only strengthened the hand of those who saw better prospects for preserving Polish national identity through legal cultural activity. The Warsaw Society of the Friends of Learning, established in 1800, gathered some of Poland's leading scholars and writers; it aimed at making Polish a major language of scholarship and one of its leading lights, the lexicographer Samuel Bogumił Linde, was to publish between 1807 and 1814 the first modern dictionary of the Polish language. At the same time in Puławy Princess Izabela

Czartoryska founded a museum devoted to the glorification of Poland's past.

The greatest Polish hopes, however, came to be associated with Alexander I, Russia's tsar since March 1801, who privately condemned his grandmother's treatment of Poland, and professed 'liberal' political views. At Alexander's side was his close friend Prince Adam Czartoryski who had been sent to Russia to recover his family's estates. Confident that an honourable Russo-Polish reconciliation, underpinned ideologically by sentiments of Slavonic solidarity, was possible under Alexander, Czartoryski accepted high office from his imperial friend. As curator of the Wilno (Vilnius) educational district from 1803, Czartoryski presided over the reform of the university of Wilno which stood at the apex of an extensive network of Polish-language secondary schools in Russia's ex-Polish *gubernii*. Tsar Alexander's recognition of the supremacy of Polish nobiliary culture in his western territories militated against the russification of this area but also of course did nothing to promote the literary development of the local non-Polish tongues. The university of Wilno became a beacon of Polish academic life and by far the largest university in the Russian Empire. Within its walls were to study many eminent figures in Polish culture, such as the Romantic poet Adam Mickiewicz and the historian Joachim Lelewel. Little wonder that for many Polish noblemen Russia appeared the most tolerant of the three partitioning powers.

More controversial was Czartoryski's record as director of Russia's foreign policy from 1804 to 1806. His vision of Alexander as a crusader for a new just and moral European order, in which Poland would be restored in dynastic association with Russia, appealed to the young tsar's vanity and idealism, but collapsed in the face of harsh political realities and the tsar's own indecisiveness. Russia's attempt in 1804–5 to draw Austria and Prussia into an anti-Napoleonic coalition could hardly be reconciled with Czartoryski's scheme of despoiling those states of their Polish provinces. The defeat of the Russian and Austrian armies at Austerlitz in December 1805 undermined Czartoryski's influence in St Petersburg and brought about the end of his ministerial career. And by the end of 1806 the situation in the Polish lands was dramatically reversed by another twist of fate: Napoleon's victorious campaign in 1806 against Prussia which brought the French army into Prussian Poland.

As the Hohenzollern state collapsed under Napoleon's blows, Berlin's Polish provinces erupted in a widespread national uprising. The appearance of the former legionaries Dąbrowski and Wybicki in the van of Napoleon's army revived earlier hopes of French assistance that had been so cruelly dashed in 1801. Tsar Alexander joined the the fray on Prussia's side, and the war dragged on. Napoleon therefore authorized the creation in Prussian Poland of an administration run by local Poles that would maintain social order and provide him with additional fighting men and supplies. After much soul-searching, Prince Józef Poniatowski was persuaded by Murat to accept the command of a resurrected Polish army to fight alongside the French. Prince 'Pepi', the playboy of Warsaw, had taken the first step that would turn him into a national hero and the most chivalrous symbol of Polish military valour in the Napoleonic period.

The creation of a *de facto* Polish government with a regular conscripted army (numbering over 30,000 men by June 1807) in western Poland was an accomplished fact, but its future prospects depended entirely on the outcome of the war. The battle of Friedland on 14 June 1807 finally established French superiority and obliged Alexander I to sign a compromise peace treaty with Napoleon at Tilsit on 7 July. Most of Prussia's Polish lands went to form the so-called 'duchy of Warsaw'; Russia annexed the district of Białystok and undertook to join the Continental System against Britain; and Danzig was restored as a free city. In October 1809, following a brief war between France and Austria, in which the Polish army gave a good account of itself, the duchy was enlarged at Austria's expense: Vienna had to surrender about half of its gains in the partitions, including Kraków and Lublin.

The duchy of Warsaw was undeniably a French satellite, harnessed to and exploited by the Napoleonic war machine; 20,000 of its troops participated in Napoleon's inglorious attempt to subjugate Spain, and nearly 100,000 Polish soldiers accompanied the Grande Armée into Russia in 1812. The duchy had to accept a constitution dictated by Napoleon, a French-style centralized ad-

18 Napoleon bestowing a constitution on the duchy of Warsaw. This
allegorical painting by Marceli Bacciarelli (1731–1818) depicts the event
which occurred on 22 July 1807 in Dresden where the emperor had
summoned leading Polish notables, including the venerable Stanisław
Małachowski (6th from the left), the former speaker of the Great Sejm of
1788–92. Napoleon ignored the proposals brought by the Polish
delegation and proceeded to dictate his own version in one hour. The
constitution was nonetheless an effective adaptation of the French model
to Polish realities. Bacciarelli was court painter to Stanisław August
Poniatowski and remained active in Polish cultural life to his death.

ministrative system staffed by professional bureaucrats, and the Napoleonic legal code. On the other hand the duchy's creation shattered the mould of the partition treaties and reawakened hopes of national revival. Although it comprised a mere fifth of old Poland and only 30 per cent of its population, the duchy did contain within its post-1809 borders the Polish heartland: Poznania, the cradle of Poland's medieval statehood with the ecclesiastical centre of Gniezno, and the two historic capitals of Warsaw and Kraków. The elevation to the ducal title of King Frederick Augustus of Saxony, the nephew of Augustus III of Poland, and the restoration of a bicameral Sejm and provincial dietines (*sejmiki*) represented a gesture to Polish tradition. The duchy's large army instilled civic virtues in its officers and soldiers, while its exploits revived military values in Polish society and inspired a cult of Napoleon that would survive in Poland into the twentieth century. The duchy's uhlans, with their distinctive square caps (the *czapka*) and their red and white pennants, became a model for the lancer regiments of many European armies; and despite its appalling human losses in 1812, the duchy's army had the satisfaction of returning from Russia with all its standards and artillery pieces intact.

The Napoleonic regime, backed by the duchy's rationalist aristocracy, also injected modern elements into Polish society. The Napoleonic Code abolished serfdom, introduced legal equality and personal liberty for all inhabitants, and permitted civil marriage and divorce, to the horror of the episcopate. Some non-nobles could now vote, sit in the Sejm, and hold office, while the Voltairean education minister Stanisław Kostka Potocki expanded elementary schooling. All this contributed to the growth of a professional intelligentsia and the narrowing of the gap between the *szlachta* and the urban middle class. But there were also compromises with Polish 'feudal' traditions: the landed nobility obtained full property rights to all manorial land and all former serf allotments, while the now 'free' peasants were reduced to a landless class of tenants still obliged to perform the corvée. The Jews were barred from buying land and had their political rights suspended for ten years, on the grounds that they were not yet fully assimilated into Polish society.

Map 6   The duchy of Warsaw, 1807–15.

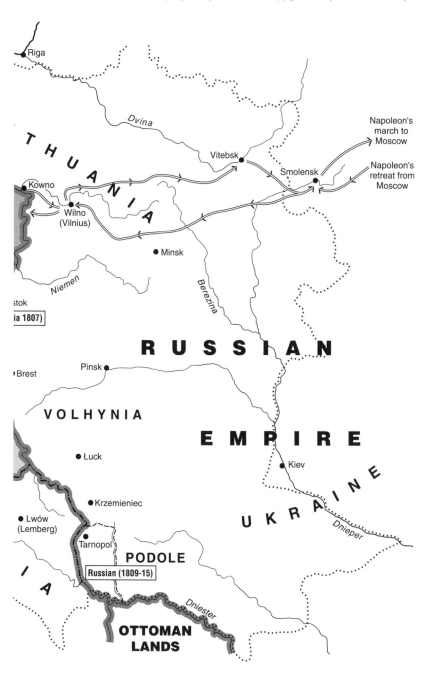

Polish traditionalists and republicans resented Napoleon's authoritarianism, and the Continental System accentuated further the structural weakness of Polish agriculture. Nevertheless, in contrast to Spain or Germany, the national movement in Poland became associated with Napoleon, who by 1809 had forced two of the partitioning powers to relinquish a large proportion of their Polish possessions. Tsar Alexander's belated attempts to lure the Polish leadership in Warsaw away from the Napoleonic alliance with tempting political and territorial offers failed; his half-baked schemes to restore a Grand Duchy of Lithuania as a rival to Napoleonic Poland fared no better. The Polish imbroglio inevitably contributed to the rapid deterioration of Franco-Russian relations between 1810 and 1812. The duchy's leaders welcomed the war of 1812: the restoration of the Kingdom of Poland was solemnly proclaimed on 28 June and the recovery of Russia's ex-Polish lands was regarded as certain, although in Lithuania there was a cautious rather than an enthusiastic response to the French invasion.

Napoleon's disaster in Russia shattered Polish hopes and illusions. It was now Tsar Alexander's turn to be the arbiter of Poland's future, although to avoid weakening the new anti-Napoleonic coalition he initially refrained from making public his ambition to restore a Polish kingdom under his rule. In these ambiguous circumstances Prince Józef Poniatowski felt he had no choice but to stay at Napoleon's side; he died a hero's death while covering the French retreat with his troops at the decisive battle of Leipzig (16–19 October 1813). Immediately after Napoleon's abdication on 6 April 1814, Alexander openly laid claim to the duchy of Warsaw, took the remnants of the Polish army under his protection, and authorized a reform committee in Warsaw to prepare the ground for a Romanov kingdom of Poland to which, he intimated to the Poles, he was willing in due course to add the western *gubernii*. Although pro-Napoleonic sentiments remained strong in the duchy, many of its notables, actively encouraged by Czartoryski, accepted the tsar's professed magnanimity as their country's only hope. Even Kościuszko, that paragon of patriotic virtue, briefly left his Swiss exile to offer his services to Alexander.

The final outcome of the Congress of Vienna (1814–15) fell dramatically short of what had been Polish hopes and expectations.

However, it was simply not possible in 1815 to restore an independent Poland with the frontiers of 1772. It was the Poles' misfortune that the continental powers that had finally toppled Napoleon happened to be the same states that had partitioned Poland. It was also plainly unrealistic to expect Russia to surrender the conquered duchy of Warsaw as well as all its gains in the partitions of Poland on the very morrow of its greatest military triumph since Peter the Great. At the same time, the Napoleonic presence in eastern Europe had revived Polish national aspirations to such an extent that it would have been difficult to restore stability in this region without some concessions to the Poles. Among the peacemakers it was Tsar Alexander who appreciated this most, and recognized that Russia's security in the west would be increased by winning over the distraught Poles to his side. A constitutional Poland under his sceptre could also provide a pilot project for the reforms he still contemplated for the Russian Empire. On the other hand, Alexander's insistence on having a free hand in arranging the future of a Polish state under his control met with strong international opposition and dominated the diplomatic struggles at the Congress.

Metternich and Castlereagh, the Austrian and British foreign ministers respectively, both feared the extension of Russian power in central Europe under whatever guise and would have preferred a simple partition of the duchy of Warsaw. In the end they had to accept most of Alexander's Polish demands, although the tsar had to compromise by relinquishing his claims to Poznania, Toruń (Thorn) and Kraków. As a result the so-called Congress Kingdom of Poland emerged 30 per cent smaller than the duchy of Warsaw. Indeed the lands of the former Polish-Lithuanian Commonwealth remained fragmented after 1815 in a complex mosaic of six political-administrative units: Austria retained 'Old' Galicia; the contested city of Kraków became a republic under the protection of the three eastern powers; Prussia held on to West Prussia (its original gain of 1772) and received Poznania as the quasi-autonomous duchy of Posen; Russia's Polish lands also consisted of two regions with a different status, the western *gubernii* of the Russian Empire and an integral part thereof, and now the new autonomous Congress Kingdom of Poland. Little did the Polish patriots appreciate that, unlike the short-lived arrangements of 1795, the inter-

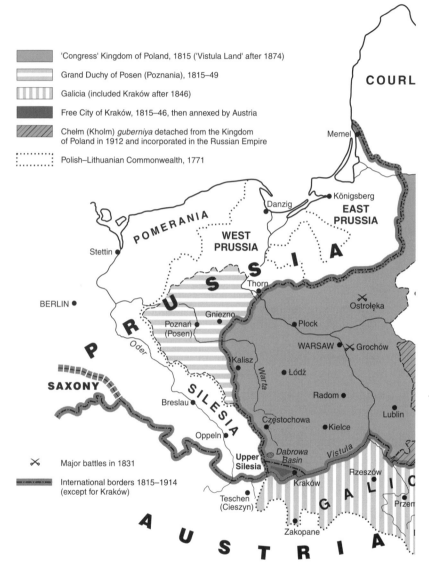

'Congress' Kingdom of Poland, 1815 ('Vistula Land' after 1874)

Grand Duchy of Posen (Poznania), 1815–49

Galicia (included Kraków after 1846)

Free City of Kraków, 1815–46, then annexed by Austria

Chełm (Kholm) *guberniya* detached from the Kingdom
of Poland in 1912 and incorporated in the Russian Empire

Polish–Lithuanian Commonwealth, 1771

✕ Major battles in 1831

International borders 1815–1914
(except for Kraków)

(AUSTRIA-HUNGARY AFTER 1867)

Map 7   Partitioned Poland, 1815–1914.

national frontiers established across Poland in 1815 were to last for a century, with the minor exception of Kraków.

Alexander must take most credit for salvaging a Polish state out of the ashes of Napoleonic Europe, yet his Polish kingdom owed much to its Napoleonic origins in terms of its size, its institutions and its legal system; Alexander retained the Napoleonic Code. Exhausted and war-weary, the Polish leaders accepted the new order and slipped easily into positions of authority under their new ruler. Indeed, all that Alexander had told them in 1814–15 led them to expect further acts of generosity from their tsar-king in whose exclusive gift remained both the new kingdom's constitution and its envisaged eastward extension. Intellectuals such as Stanisław Staszic and politicians like Czartoryski and the former radical Horodyski saw in Russia a defender of Polish national interests, and openly espoused sentiments of Slavonic solidarity. For all its limitations the settlement of 1815 was a marked improvement on that of 1795. In respect of their national rights, the Polish elite under Russian domination were to enjoy more favourable conditions between 1815 and 1830 than at any other time of the long partition period. No amount of Romantic nostalgia for the Napoleonic era could obscure the fact that the duchy of Warsaw, groaning under military exactions, stood on the shifting and ultimately perilous sands of the Napoleonic order. In 1815 the Great Powers explicitly recognized the Polish nationality throughout the area of the former Commonwealth, and took a number of steps to give an institutional expression of these rights not only in Alexander's share of Poland but also in Prussia's duchy of Posen, and even, although heavily watered down, in Austrian Galicia. In many areas Polish education was maintained, and scholarship and cultural life in general flourished. The decade and a half after 1815 also witnessed some economic development.

In 1815 Tsar Alexander was still the darling of many liberals and patriots. In November he granted to his Polish kingdom what appeared in the context of Restoration Europe an advanced liberal constitution. With its elected Sejm, wide franchise and extensive civil rights, the Congress Kingdom represented a stark contrast with the autocracy of the Russian Empire to which the Kingdom was united 'for ever'. Yet the deficiencies of the new constitutional order reflected well Alexander's narrow interpretation of 'liberalism'. The Sejm was denied all control over the budget and over the army, which became a major drain on state finances, and rarely met in the 1820s. Other mechanisms for the supervision and control of Alexander's Polish kingdom were created. The post of viceroy went to the obedient ex-Napoleonic general Józef Zajączek and not to the independent-minded Czartoryski; the erstwhile liberal and now cynical toady Nikolai Novosiltsev became the tsar's personal extra-constitutional overseer of the Kingdom, while Alexander's ill-tempered and brutal brother Grand Duke Constantine was given command of the Polish army and of the large Russian force stationed in the Kingdom. In 1819 preventive censorship was introduced. Disappointing also were Alexander's tantalizing but ultimately unfulfilled earlier promises to attach the western *gubernii* to the Congress Kingdom, one of the main attractions for the Polish elite of the Russian connection. Likewise, the treaty provisions for a free trade zone across the Polish lands proved unworkable; a customs barrier was established between Russia and the Kingdom, which also had to contend with high Prussian and Austrian tariffs.

The reactionary trend after 1819 in the internal and external policies of the so-called 'Holy Alliance' of the three eastern powers was to press heavily on their respective Polish provinces. The resulting restrictions were primarily of a political nature and were not aimed at 'denationalizing' the Poles; indeed, by twentieth-century standards they were very mild. Nevertheless, they were perceived by many contemporaries as inimical to the Polish national cause. The most vivid public expression of discontent in the Congress Kingdom came from a small group of enterprising gentry liberals led by the Niemojowski brothers from the western province of Kalisz. Their campaign in defence of the constitution prompted Alexander to warn the Polish Sejm in 1820 against the 'abuse' of liberty, and to authorize Constantine to use any means to maintain order in the Kingdom. The Sejm was not convened until 1825, when its debates were also closed to the public. The reactionary trend was supported by the Kingdom's episcopate and its native conservative champions of 'Altar and Throne'. The remaining representatives of the ideals of the Enlightenment came under direct attack; in December 1820 the anticlerical S. K. Potocki was replaced as education minister by the obscurantist Stanisław Grabowski. Decrees against secret societies led to the dissolution of masonic lodges which Alexander had himself once encouraged to promote ideas of social and cultural improvement and Russo-Polish reconciliation. Now also outside the law were clandestine patriotic societies committed to education and national reunification, which had grown since 1817 under the cover of masonic forms, and which attracted Napoleonic veterans, young officers and university students, many of poor *szlachta* backgrounds. Their first martyr was Walery Łukasiński, an army major, who was arrested in 1822 and who eventually spent most of his remaining forty-four years in a fortress dungeon outside St Petersburg. Reluctant to seek careers in the tsarist civil service and facing limited job prospects at home, the large student body in Wilno proved to be a particularly fertile ground for early Romantic ideas, but then faced the wrath of the authorities. Members of the Society of Philomats in Wilno, including Adam Mickiewicz, the most promising Romantic poet writing in Polish, were exiled into the Russian interior. In 1823 Czartoryski was replaced as curator of the Wilno educational district by Novosiltsev, nicknamed 'the Herod of Lithuania' for his brutal interrogation of the students.

Much of Polish public opinion took a dim view of the retreat from 'liberalism' during Alexander's last years. There was disappointment in many quarters when Alexander's successor in 1825, Nicholas I, further integrated the western *gubernii* with the rest of the Russian Empire, thereby dashing hopes that the Kingdom might be enlarged in the east. The trial in Warsaw, in 1828, of members of the revived National Patriotic Society for their contacts with the Russian Decembrists further damaged the already uneasy Polish–Russian relationship. Tsar Nicholas was furious when the Polish Senate, in its capacity as the Kingdom's High Tribunal, could not quite bring itself to condemn the conspirators' ideal of national reunification and acquitted the defendants of high treason. Only Russia's involvement in a new Turkish war in 1828–9 prevented the outraged Nicholas from over-riding the Senate's verdict and bringing about a major constitutional crisis.

To appease his Polish subjects, Nicholas attended a formal coronation ceremony in Warsaw in May 1829, presented Warsaw with Turkish guns from Varna (the place of death in 1444 of the crusading Polish king Władysław Jagiellon), and agreed to summon the practically defunct Polish Sejm in June 1830. Even so, Nicholas found the role of constitutional monarch not at all to his taste; it had to be politely explained to him that the rejection of a government bill (in this instance to abolish civil marriages) was not unusual in a parliamentary system and was not intended as an affront to majesty. Grand Duke Constantine's behaviour also improved in the late 1820s; he felt increasingly at home in Warsaw with his morganatic Polish wife, and even espoused Polish irredentist aspirations in the east.

Sober minds well appreciated that the Kingdom did not need irresponsible patriotic antics but a period of calm. Particularly conscious of the need for political stability and economic consolidation within the strict limits of autonomy prescribed by St Petersburg was Prince Ksawery Lubecki, a former civil governor of Wilno and from 1821 to 1830 the Kingdom's energetic and hard-headed finance minister. He balanced the Kingdom's chaotic budget through rigorous taxation, initiated the creation of a land credit society and of the Bank of Poland, and even launched a modest programme of state-encouraged industrial development. This period also witnessed the emergence of Łódź as the centre of the Polish cotton industry, while a favourable tariff treaty with Russia in 1822 opened Russia's vast markets to the Kingdom's manufactures. Lubecki's fiscal burdens were felt most keenly by the peasantry whose conditions did not improve in what continued to be a difficult period for agriculture. Little was done to endow peasants with leaseholdings on state lands and even less on privately owned estates, while the eviction of peasants by private landlords acquired alarming proportions, despite the examples set by Czartoryski, who introduced generous tenancy terms on his Końskowola estates, and by Staszic, who created a large peasant co-operative near Hrubieszów. Peasant discontent only grew as the number of landless peasants in the Congress Kingdom reached 800,000 by 1827, with obvious damage to the cause of national solidarity. There was likewise no Polish consensus for improving the status of the Kingdom's 300,000 Jews, who continued to be deprived of full civic rights.

The other region of historic Poland endowed with extensive autonomy in 1815 was the small republic of Kraków, which obtained a liberal-aristocratic constitution and also retained the Napoleonic legal system. The three Protecting Powers interfered in the 1820s in Kraków against liberal agitation and student conspiracies, but the republic managed to survive until 1846. The status of the republic's peasantry was to be for many years the most advanced in all of historic Poland. Electoral rights and security of tenancy holdings did much to encourage early political and national consciousness of the rural population, in stark contrast with the peasants of Austrian Galicia. As a free-trade entrepôt Kraków also benefited from commerce with Silesia and the Congress Kingdom and witnessed some early industrial activity on its territory; the first steam engine installed anywhere in Poland appeared here in 1817.

Prussia's ex-Polish lands presented a more complex picture. Roughly equivalent in size to modern Belgium, the duchy of Posen had a mixed population of nearly 800,000 in 1815, of whom the Poles represented about two-thirds; in the city of Poznań the Polish and German elements were roughly even. Although the Prussian *Landrecht* replaced the Napoleonic Code, Polish was recognized as the main language in the administration, the courts and the schools, and Prince Antoni Radziwiłł was appointed viceroy. In practice, Poznania's degree of autonomy remained limited but the Prussian authorities, well aware of the pull of the Congress Kingdom, avoided alienating the Poles and dealt leniently with illegal patriotic societies. In terms of rural property rights, the Prussian government brought Poznania in line with the land reform operational in the rest of the Prussian monarchy since 1811; the landed nobility retained most of the land, but the process of creating a substantial class of prosperous peasant farmers was now set in motion.

Unlike in Poznania, no significant institutional or administrative concessions were made to the Polish nationality in West Prussia (formerly Polish Pomerania held by Berlin continuously since 1772), to which were added Danzig and Thorn. In West Prussia,

Polish-speakers (including the Kashubians) equalled the Germans numerically, but the towns were predominantly German and the landed class was becoming increasingly so. In 1824 East and West Prussia were amalgamated into a single province, while the restoration of Marienburg (Malbork) castle, begun in the 1820s, was intended to express the 'idea' of the Teutonic Order and of German Prussia. There were even further intricacies on the linguistic and religious map of the eastern marches of the Hohenzollern state: the Protestant Masurians of East Prussia and much of the Roman Catholic country folk of Upper Silesia spoke Polish dialects yet their regions had never belonged to the Polish-Lithuanian Commonwealth. Both communities were to witness the gradual emergence of Polish national consciousness, of a highly distinct regional flavour, as the century wore on.

Of the three eastern powers it was Austria which made the fewest concessions to Polish nationality after the Congress of Vienna. Corresponding in size to three-fifths of the Congress Kingdom and with an almost identical population of 4.25 million (in 1830), Austrian Galicia continued to be administered by an imperial governor in Lwów (Lemberg) and a German-speaking bureaucracy. Austrian law continued to operate, while a strict censorship and a loyalist church hierarchy further reinforced the political status quo. Wealthy landowners dominated the largely ineffectual provincial assembly. The province was both economically underdeveloped and financially exploited by the imperial government. It was only Austria's concern with Russian successes against the Turks in 1828 and 1829 that prompted Vienna to woo Galicia's nobles with a series of linguistic and cultural concessions. And despite a degree of government protection, the serfs of Galicia, whether Roman Catholic Polish-speakers in the west or Uniate Ukrainian-speakers in the east, saw no further improvement in their condition.

It would be too one-sided to regard developments in Russia's share of Poland from 1815 to 1830 solely in terms of violations of Polish rights and a drift towards unavoidable conflict. Despite its many defects and lack of sovereignty, a Polish state in the form of the Congress Kingdom was able to function in relative stability for fifteen years, twice as long as the Napoleonic duchy of Warsaw.

Warsaw's status as a capital was enhanced by the construction of several imposing neo-classical buildings, such as the Great Theatre and the Bank of Poland, and of new palaces, churches, squares and avenues. The unveiling of Thordwaldsen's statue of Copernicus in 1830 served as a reminder of Poland's contribution to science and universal civilization. Three Polish universities functioned in this period: in Wilno, in Warsaw (founded by Alexander I in 1816) and in Kraków. Warsaw also acquired an Institute of Music (1821), a Polytechnical Institute (1828) and other specialist centres of professional training. Despite various restrictions imposed in the elementary sector in the 1820s, the Polish-language schools of the Congress Kingdom and of the Wilno educational district remained an impressive phenomenon by the standards of eastern Europe. In the realm of literary and philosophical ideas there was also much cross-fertilization across the borders, despite the irritating interference of censors.

At the same time the intellectual ferment generated by the influence of western Romanticism and of German idealistic philosophy encouraged the younger generation in the Kingdom and in the western *gubernii* to challenge the essentially rationalist political and ethical values of the old Polish elite. The appeal to heroic action and defiance against all odds, so vividly expressed in Mickiewicz's 'Ode to Youth' (1820), was given a further subversive twist in his poetic drama *Konrad Wallenrod* (1828), set in medieval Lithuania during the wars with the Teutonic Knights, in which duplicity was justified in the name of patriotism. The Romantic concept of the nation as a moral community yearning towards its self-fulfilment was advocated by the radical literary critic Maurycy Mochnacki. Democratic ideas too were fomented at the university of Warsaw by the popular history lecturer Joachim Lelewel, who had been expelled from Wilno in 1824 for his radicalism. The myth of Napoleonic military glory and the advent of Romantic nationalism made the vision of a reunited Poland even more painfully at variance with the narrow confines of the post-1815 settlement. Thoughts soon turned into action.

On 29 November 1830 in Warsaw a conspiratorial group of junior officers, fired by Romantic dreams of Polish independence and inspired by the political upheavals of that year in western

19   Portrait of Poland's greatest Romantic and poet, Adam Mickiewicz
(1798–1855), painted in 1828 by Walenty Wańkowicz (1799–1842).
Born near Nowogródek (Navahrudak in modern Belarus) in historic
Lithuania and educated at the university of Wilno (Vilnius), Mickiewicz
spent most of his life in exile, first in Russia and later in France. His poetry,
as well as his lifelong commitment to the cause of liberty, profoundly
shaped the Polish Romantic mind. With his fellow Romantic poet Juliusz
Słowacki he lies buried next to the kings of Poland in the cathedral of
Wawel in Kraków. He is also highly regarded in Lithuania and Belarus.

Europe, launched an armed insurrection against Russian domination. It was a reckless and inept affair. The attempted assassination of Grand Duke Constantine was bungled and only some units joined the rebels. However, the seizure of the arsenal and the distribution of 30,000 rifles among the city's population transformed the situation. All Poles in positions of higher authority in Warsaw condemned the revolt, while Lubecki and Czartoryski, two very different political temperaments but now acting together to save Poland's limited gains of 1815, even urged Constantine to use force against the rebels. To their dismay he refused, and left the restoration of order to the Polish authorities. Desperate to avoid a breach with Nicholas and to tame the fires of the insurrection, the government co-opted the respected Czartoryski and the popular Napoleonic veteran General Józef Chłopicki. Against it arose a new self-styled Patriotic Society, led by the radical Lelewel and the fiery orator Mochnacki, committed to widening the insurrection. In Warsaw the situation was getting out of control while more units outside the city joined the rebels. Further government reshuffles and Constantine's departure from Warsaw failed to restore order, and the government felt obliged to summon the Sejm.

Any hope that the Sejm would restrain public opinion failed; moved by a wave of patriotism, it endorsed the insurrection as 'an act of the Nation' and on 20 December appointed the reluctant Chłopicki 'dictator'. Paradoxically, Chłopicki hated all disorder and was eager to achieve a reconciliation with the tsar-king, but Nicholas refused to negotiate or to make any concessions that might have appeased Polish opinion. On 17 December he offered an amnesty but demanded unconditional capitulation. Unable to deliver what Nicholas wanted and unwilling to crush the rising, Chłopicki resigned on 18 January 1831. Little could now prevent an irrevocable break with Nicholas. On 25 January, after two months of indecision, the Sejm deposed Nicholas by public acclamation. By this act the Sejm broke with legality and defied the treaty of Vienna which had sanctioned the Kingdom's union with Russia. Polish claims that Alexander's and Nicholas' violations of the constitution justified the deposition were essentially flawed.

There now ensued an internal struggle over the nature, methods and aims of the insurrection. To prevent the ultra-patriots and the radicals of the Patriotic Society from seizing power, moderate conservatives like Czartoryski felt that they had no option but to assume the leadership of the insurrection. The five-man National Government elected on 30 January by the Sejm included Lelewel but was presided over by Czartoryski, who acquired special responsibilities for foreign policy. Furthermore, on 8 February, the Sejm declared that Poland would remain a hereditary constitutional monarchy and that only the existing Sejm had the authority to elect a new king. While the radicals wanted a 'people's war' against Russia, the moderate leadership hoped that a successful military campaign would force Nicholas and the Great Powers to revise the clauses of the Vienna treaties relating to Poland. Secretly, Czartoryski was even willing to retain a loose dynastic link with Russia. He was anxious to reassure the governments of Europe, especially Austria and Prussia, that the Polish revolution was national, that its aim was the Kingdom's independence, and that it was in no way socially subversive. Yet the force of events extended Polish war aims. The spread of the insurrection to the western *gubernii* of Russia compelled the Sejm, in another act of defiance against the treaty of Vienna, to pass a bill in May 1831 incorporating that vast area into the Polish state. Nicholas in the meantime had resolved that he would reduce the Kingdom's autonomy, while to surrender to the full territorial demands of the Poles would be tantamount to relegating Russia from the ranks of the Great Powers. The Poles were now left with no alternative but to fight and win a war with Russia.

The well-trained Polish army, which reached 80,000 effectives, gave a good account of itself. On 25 February Chłopicki halted the Russian advance on Warsaw at Grochów, the largest land battle fought in Europe between Waterloo and the Crimean War. A string of subsequent Polish successes in the spring alarmed St Petersburg, but the defeat of the indecisive General Skrzynecki at Ostrołęka on 26 May turned the scales of the war against the Poles. Commanded by the experienced campaigner Paskevich, the Russian army was able to cross the Vistula near the Prussian border and approached Warsaw from the west. The prospect of defeat led to vicious street unrest in Warsaw in mid-August and to recriminations within the National Government. Czartoryski's suggestion that the Poles

20   The battle of Grochów, fought on 25 February 1831. Painted in 1887, and improved in 1928, by Wojciech Kossak (1856–1942), the scene depicts the 4th regiment of the line of the Polish army in action. General Chłopicki, the overall Polish commander, can be seen on horseback in civilian dress. Observing the battle on the Russian side was Grand Duke Constantine, who had commanded the Polish army in 1815–30 with brutal discipline. He expressed perverse but understandable delight at seeing 'his' soldiers perform so well.

should seek Austrian protection infuriated Lelewel and the radicals who now pressed for the creation of an egalitarian republic. The government resigned and full power was finally conferred on one man, General Jan Krukowiecki, who restored order. But by then it was all too late. Conscious of the ignominious behaviour of the Targowica Confederacy in 1792, the Polish civilian and military leadership refused to capitulate to the tsar and went into exile.

The glaring differences in resources between Russia and the landlocked Congress Kingdom were bound to tell eventually on the war's outcome, yet there were specific failings on the Polish side. The Poles lacked political unity during the early stages of the insurrection. Some of their leaders were doubtful about their chances of success, while the 200–man Sejm retained effective control of the war effort and deprived the National Government of real power. On balance, the Polish high command showed less initiative than Marshal Paskevich. The rising also lacked wide social support. No imaginative attempt was made to win over the peasant masses; even a modest government bill to enable peasants on crown lands to purchase their own freeholds was rejected by the Sejm in April. And for all its respect for the social order, the Polish leadership failed to win any effective international support. The enthusiasm for the Polish cause among the public of Britain, Germany, and especially France was widespread. Casimir Delavigne's impassioned song 'La Varsovienne' was sung in Paris in March 1831 to the stirring music by d'Auber, and rapidly acquired in translation a prominent place in the repertoire of Polish patriotic songs. Across much of Germany resounded songs (the so-called *Polenlieder*) in praise of the valiant Poles. Yet nothing could sway the governments into action. The cabinets of Berlin and Vienna remained neutral but essentially hostile, while the British and the French were preoccupied with acute domestic problems and were at loggerheads over the Belgian Question.

The cost of defeat for the Poles was disastrous; not only did the mirage of a large independent Poland dissolve into thin air but most of the limited gains of 1815 were also lost. Nicholas I formally respected the Vienna treaties by retaining the Kingdom as a separate administrative and legal unit, but he abolished the constitution, the Sejm and the Polish army. The university of Warsaw was closed

down. Excluded from a general amnesty were the original conspirators, all members of the Sejm and of the National Government, and
all exiles. Paskevich, now created 'prince of Warsaw', remained an
all-powerful viceroy with a permanent army of occupation. In
1833 martial law was introduced, and a vast citadel-prison was
built to overawe the restive city.

The end of the Kingdom's statehood encouraged Prussia and
Austria to rescind some of their concessions to the Polish nationality. In 1833–4 the three partitioning powers mutually guaranteed
their respective Polish possessions and committed themselves to the
suppression of all revolutionary activity. The 'Holy Alliance' was
back in business. Even the papacy, committed to the preservation of
the international order, condemned the insurrection. In the western
gubernii the local insurgents had to endure hard labour, servitude
in the tsarist army, and the loss of their property. The closure of the
university of Wilno (except for the medical and theological facul-
ties) and of the entire network of Polish schools was a tragic blow
to Polish culture, yet only the beginning of the region's further
russification.

With the collapse of the insurrection in 1831, about 10,000
Polish exiles, including much of the Kingdom's political, military
and cultural elite, headed west, mostly to France. They promoted
among their hosts an idealized vision of Poland as a heroic victim
of tsarist tyranny and did much to promote russophobia among
western liberals and radicals. In the West the exiles were also free to
assess the causes of their failure and to discuss and prepare various
plans for their country's future salvation. Indeed, the next decade
and a half witnessed among the 'Great Emigration' an extraordinary flowering of Romantic literary creativity and of political
and social thought which was to exert a deep impact on Polish
national consciousness. Of the exiled bards the greatest was Mickiewicz. In his *Books of the Polish nation and Polish pilgrimage*
(1832) he called on the exiles ('the soul of the Polish nation') to
prepare for 'a universal war for the freedom of peoples', and gave
expression to his messianic vision of Poland as the 'Christ of
Nations' whose resurrection would bring about the religious regeneration of mankind. In his lectures at the Collège de France
between 1840 and 1844 Mickiewicz was to develop his subversive

attacks on the existing European order, drawing on himself inevitably the opprobrium of the French authorities. The poet Juliusz Słowacki considered nations as spiritual categories that should be led by revolutionary spiritual elites. While endorsing the ideal of national self-determination, the conservative Zygmunt Krasiński was disturbed by the notions of popular sovereignty advocated by Mickiewicz and Słowacki, and in his *Undivine comedy* (1835) presented an apocalyptic vision of the destruction of the old social order by 'the hungry and the poor'. Mickiewicz's revolutionary eschatology was also attacked by Cyprian Norwid, the last of the great philosophizing poets of the Romantic period, who was to warn against raising patriotism into an 'unjustified religion'.

What emotionally united all the poets and all the exiles was the music of Frédéric Chopin: from the powerful 'Revolutionary' *étude* (op. 10 no. 12 in C minor), in which the composer was believed to express his anguish on hearing of Warsaw's fall in September 1831, to his preludes, mazurkas and *krakowiaks* which conveyed sentiments of yearning for the distant homeland. More than the written word, it is Chopin's music that remains the purest and the most universally accessible expression of Polish Romantic feeling. It is extraordinary how this frail and sickly man, who never lifted a sword or gun in the national cause, is revered to the present day as a sacred national icon.

The political and ideological disputes that had raged in Warsaw during the insurrection acquired even greater intensity in exile in a climate of mutual recrimination. Within the wide spectrum of émigré political groupings, the most prestigious was that led from Paris by Prince Czartoryski, whose support for a modern constitutional monarchy based on a propertied and educated electorate attracted moderate conservatives and liberals. As a statesman of international renown, Czartoryski cultivated unofficial links with the governments of Britain and France and established across Europe an extensive network of agents. At first he concentrated on defending Poland's limited rights as defined by the treaties of 1815, a legalistic position tactically justified to win international support but condemned by many of his less restrained fellow exiles. Two conditions, Czartoryski sensibly argued, had to be met for a Polish national uprising to succeed: it had to coincide with a major European war between Russia and the Western Powers, and it had to enjoy wide peasant support, which could only be gained if the nobility voluntarily endowed the peasants with their own landholdings. The vital lessons of 1831 had clearly been learnt, not that they brought independence any nearer. In 1840 Czartoryski adopted a more independent policy by using his agents to weaken Russian influence in the Balkans and to promote the cause of nationality in general. He also persuaded the papacy to modify its originally negative stance towards Polish nationalism.

Despite his relentless defence of the Polish cause, the majority of the exiles turned their backs on the aristocratic Czartoryski and sought more radical if equally fruitless solutions. While Czartoryski considered the traditions of the *szlachta* as the essential ingredient of Polish national values, Lelewel found theoretical inspiration for his collectivist brand of democracy in his romanticized pseudo-historic accounts of primitive Slavonic communes in pre-Christian Poland. With his associates from the Patriotic Society Lelewel put his hopes in the early overthrow of the continental autocracies by the *carbonari*; he joined 'Young Europe', the international revolutionary republican brotherhood led by Giuseppe Mazzini. The efforts of Lelewel's emissaries to rekindle the flames of insurrection in Russian Poland not only failed but also provoked the tsarist authorities to weaken even further Polish and Catholic influence in the western *gubernii*. In 1839 the Greek Catholic Church with its 2 million adherents was formally absorbed by the Russian Orthodox Church. In 1840 the Lithuanian legal code, the last functioning institutional link with the old Polish-Lithuanian Commonwealth, was replaced by Russian law, and in the south-western (Ukrainian) *gubernii* Governor-General Bibikov zealously implemented the policy of reducing the legal status of the petty *szlachta* to that of 'one-dwelling peasants'.

As the conspiratorial work of Lelewel's Young Poland fizzled out in the late 1830s, it was replaced as the main left-wing rival to Czartoryski by the more realistic and larger Polish Democratic Society, founded in Paris in 1832. The Democratic Society called for the removal of all social privileges, and for the inclusion of all social groups within a modern democratic nation of equal citizens.

After bitter internal wrangles most of the democrats acknowledged that the participation of the *szlachta*, with its tradition of political and personal liberty, was essential for the recovery of independence; at the same time they insisted that the peasants had to acquire full property rights to their holdings without the payment of any indemnity. After 1840 the Polish Democratic Society was run from Versailles by a five-man directorate; its most outstanding strategist was Wiktor Heltman. The Democratic Society's critical but ultimately conciliatory approach to the nobility and its acceptance of private property as the basis of society was not shared by one of its splinter groups, the Commune of the Polish People formed in Portsmouth by exiled non-commissioned officers and soldiers. Drawing eclectically on all schools of French socialist and democratic thought, and inspired by Lelewel's theories of primitive Slav communalism, the Commune called for the overthrow of the nobility, the introduction of collective landownership, and the rejection of western industrialization. Isolated from the majority of the exiles and weakened by internal feuds, the populists were soon to learn how poorly the cause of agrarian socialism was to fare in Poland.

It was clear by the 1840s that all active émigré groups in various degrees accepted the involvement of the peasantry in the national struggle as a precondition of a successful insurrection. It was an urgent matter since it was feared that the partitioning governments would improve the peasants' lot and thereby rob the peasants of the material incentive to join the national cause. At the same time it needs to be borne in mind that the Polish radicals and democrats saw in the Lithuanian-, Belorussian- and Ukrainian-speaking serfs of the western *gubernii* future equal citizens of a democratic Polish nation embracing all the lands that had constituted the Polish-Lithuanian Commonwealth in 1772. In that sense they identified Polish territorial claims in the east with the universal cause of liberty. Whether this generous vision had any mileage within the complex and increasingly confrontational ethnic, religious and social realities of that region remained to be seen.

For those educated Poles who did not have to choose exile, and who eschewed political agitation or revolutionary conspiracy, there remained some scope for legal economic and cultural activity

21 'Organic work' in action: the Cegielski factory in Poznań (Posen). Established by the industrialist Hipolit Cegielski (1813–68) in 1855, the factory produced agricultural equipment and machines, and contributed to the modernization of agriculture on Polish-owned farms in Poznania. Gegielski also helped to create a Polish-language press and promoted Polish cultural life under Prussian rule. In 1849 he served as deputy to the Prussian parliament. The photograph dates from 1883.

within the limits set by the governments of the partitioning states. It was in Poznania that political and material conditions were most favourable in the 1840s for all such work of social improvement, which became known in Polish as 'organic work' (*praca organiczna*). Prussian rule mellowed under the liberal-minded Frederick William IV, and it was possible for the philanthropist Karol Marcinkowski to launch a variety of practical initiatives in the fields of education, commerce and the crafts. A conceptual framework for this activity was provided by the eminent Hegelian philosopher August Cieszkowski, who endorsed modern scientific and bourgeois civilization. Modern agricultural methods also raised the productivity of noble-owned estates and peasant farms in Poznania. The increased cultivation of the potato, in western and then central Poland, added a much welcomed nutritional boost to the peasants' staple diet of brown bread and vegetables, especially the ubiquitous cabbage. Industry and commerce continued to make impressive inroads in the Congress Kingdom in the 1830s and 1840s, especially in textiles and railway building; the Warsaw–Vienna railway, financed by private investors, was completed in 1848. Many of the Kingdom's substantial landowners accepted the necessity of modernizing the retarded rural economy; the case was growing for commuting peasant labour dues into money rents, and even for introducing a land reform on the Prussian model. It is noteworthy that it was in Russian-occupied Wilno in the early and mid-1840s that Stanisław Moniuszko, the creator of the Polish national opera, wrote and produced some of his earliest works. In Galicia, however, backward social conditions and the absence of committed activists militated against 'organic work'.

Against this background of gradual economic improvement, wealth creation and political realism, the scheming exiles and revolutionaries seemed at times to be a peripheral element in the daily lives and concerns of their fellow countrymen. For all their zeal the different Polish movements for national and social liberation had clearly failed by 1840 to overthrow the foreign yoke: there was no great European war nor was there a great rising of the peoples of Europe. Yet this did not deter further attempts to challenge the political and social order in Poland; Czartoryski continued with his propaganda and the exiled Polish Democratic

Society set about restoring an underground network across Poland in the early 1840s. While the programme of the Democratic Society was potentially relevant in the more advanced Poznania, the ground in Russian and Austrian Poland was less fertile for modern democratic ideas. Yet it was there that a new generation of impatient radicals set to work. Henryk Kamieński and his nephew Edward Dembowski, two 'penitent' noblemen, espoused the cause of a peasant revolution and of a 'people's war' as the only solution to Poland's national and social predicament. Dressed as a peasant, Dembowski wandered through the villages of Galicia preaching his revolutionary gospel, only to realise that his listeners were more interested in property rights than in rural socialism. He duly felt obliged to modify his message, but his call for action found a response among the leadership of the Democratic Society which was also encouraged by the existence in 1844 of a populist conspiracy led by Piotr Ściegienny, a revolutionary parish priest in Lublin province.

The continuing rumbles of discontent in the villages of Galicia and of the Kingdom were interpreted by the democrats as evidence of an imminent revolutionary outburst that had to be channelled in the national cause. There was no time to waste. The directory of the Democratic Society in Versailles co-ordinated plans for a national insurrection throughout Poland for 1846. The forces of the partitioning states were to be destroyed piecemeal by a mass peasant army at the head of which was to stand the 32-year-old émigré Ludwik Mierosławski, in whom the democrats recognized a rare but so far unproved strategic genius. Even Czartoryski, unable to halt the revolutionary movement yet desperate to prevent an internecine class war, urged the nobility to participate. But the agitation of the democrats and populists among the peasantry was nothing less than playing with fire; their failure to appreciate the deep social and cultural divisions in large areas of the Polish countryside was soon to be borne out in a horrifying and tragic fashion.

Mierosławski and his associates were betrayed to the Prussian police before any action could begin in Poznania; the Russians too quickly foiled the conspiracy in the Kingdom. Conditions were more favourable in the Republic of Kraków, where the free and propertied peasants rallied in support of the democratic revolutionary government established in February 1846, which Prince Czartoryski recognized out of patriotic solidarity. In the western half of Galicia, however, the gulf between the patriotic and democratic ideology of the insurgents and the class antagonism of the semi-serfs ended in catastrophe. The Polish-speaking Catholic peasants turned against the rebels and their liberal gentry sympathizers in an orgy of killing and destruction. Dembowski, who joined the Kraków revolution, was killed by the Austrians while leading an unarmed religious procession from the city on 27 February in a desperate bid to win over the Galician peasants. Having manipulated the peasants' fury in suppressing the insurrection, the Austrian government then forced them back to their villages, and to their feudal duties. The Republic of Kraków, the last island of Polish freedom, was annexed by Austria, with Russian and Prussian consent and despite British and French protests. The mirage of national and social solidarity burst in the aftermath of the Galician jacquerie. While the authorities mopped up what was left of the revolutionary network, many landowners came to the conclusion that they would have to seek government protection of their economic and social interests. At the same time Tsar Nicholas moved briskly in 1846 and 1848 to reduce the danger of a peasant explosion in his Polish lands and to lessen the influence of the Polish nobility there; in the Kingdom he granted security of tenure to the peasants, and in the western *gubernii* he placed firm limits on the seigneurial exploitation of the serfs.

Just as the events of 1846 exposed the gross unreality of a 'people's war', so too did the ideal of the brotherhood of nations founder on the rocks of conflicting nationalisms during the revolutions that gripped much of continental Europe in 1848 and 1849. Russian Poland remained sullenly quiet in 1848–9 as Nicholas I tightened his repressive controls. Elsewhere, however, in exile and at home many Polish patriots were galvanized into action by the revolutionary wave that seemed to herald the collapse of absolutism in Prussia and Austria, and of the international order that sanctioned the subjugation of their country. Mickiewicz threw himself body and soul behind the cause of revolutionary internationalism in Italy and France; Mierosławski was released from prison in Berlin and set to work to organize a Polish army and administration in Poznania, where the poet Słowacki also arrived to lend encouragement. Alluring prospects of an alliance between the new Liberal government of Prussia and the Poles, supported by the French Republic, against Russia proved short-lived. In the end Berlin was not willing to go beyond the division of Poznania into two ethnic areas and when this was rejected by the Poles the Prussian army restored full control in April and May 1848. The initial support, in March, of the German Pre-Parliament in Frankfurt for Polish independence evaporated in July in acrimonious arguments over Germany's future eastern border; only a handful of radicals remained true to German solidarity with Polish national aspirations. In Paris, on 15 May, thousands of workers, to the cry of 'Vive la Pologne!', invaded the National Assembly. Lamartine spoke movingly in Poland's favour, but the French Republic dared not risk waging a major war for Poland's liberation.

Memories of the tragedy of 1846 were all too recent in Galicia and the response of the local Poles to the Viennese revolution in March 1848 was initially cautious and limited to a petition for autonomy for the province. In a separate attempt to win over the peasants to the national cause, the Polish national committees in Kraków (reinforced here by members of the Democratic Society) and in Lwów invited the landed nobility voluntarily to abolish labour dues on Easter Sunday. They were outmanoeuvred by the Austrian governor Stadion, who pre-empted the Polish leaders by first announcing the end of the corvée in the Emperor's name on Easter Saturday, and then bombarding Kraków into submission on 26 April. Continuing revolutionary ferment in Vienna in May 1848 and the spread of nationalist uprisings in Italy and Hungary encouraged the Poles to rally again. This time a 20,000-strong national guard was created; there was even talk of Galicia becoming a kind of Piedmont, an independent Polish centre from which would proceed the liberation of the rest of Poland.

By now, however, Polish aspirations clashed in the east of Galicia with those of the young Ukrainian national movement, focused around the Uniate Church, which demanded imperial protection against the Poles and the division of Galicia along ethnic lines. In the summer and autumn of 1848 the imperial authorities showed considerable powers of recuperation: they exploited all inter-ethnic conflicts, and found that many peasants, now emancipated and free from the corvée, showed limited support for national movements led by the gentry and the intelligentsia. Province after province fell to the imperial forces, which eventually in November restored full control over Galicia. About four thousand Polish fighters managed to escape across the Carpathian mountains to join the Hungarians, who still defied the Habsburgs. The Polish generals Józef Bem and Henryk Dembiński, veterans of the 1831 war against Russia, were given high commands; Bem was eventually appointed overall commander of the Hungarian army. At this juncture the Habsburgs turned to St Petersburg for help. Implacably hostile to the national awakening in central Europe and to any developments that might raise the hopes of his ungrateful Polish subjects, Tsar Nicholas willingly obliged and in May 1849 dispatched a Russian expeditionary force under Field-Marshal Paskevich, the conqueror of Warsaw in 1831. Within three months the Hungarians were crushed and thousands of exiles, including the Poles, had to flee into Ottoman territory.

The Polish contribution to the revolutions and wars of liberation in Italy, western Germany and Hungary in 1848–9 did more than justice to the Polish patriots' internationalist slogan of 'For Your Freedom and Ours', but the national rivalries in Poland and elsewhere also revealed that the Romantic belief in the brotherhood of Europe's nations was mostly wishful thinking. In the long run the events of 1848–9 did contribute to the strengthening of Polish national consciousness. The brief revolutionary period witnessed the blossoming of unfettered journalism and public debate in both Prussian and Austrian Poland. The willingness of the emancipated peasants of Poznania to rally to the national cause was profoundly telling, and helped in due course to shape the sturdy Polish nationalism of that region. And even in Silesia the social upheavals of 1848–9 reawakened among the Polish-speaking peasantry an attachment to their mother tongue. By the same token, the end of serfdom in Galicia was to begin the lengthy process of integrating the Polish-speaking peasants there into a wider Polish community. In the eastern part of that province Ukrainian national feeling was to prevail.

On the other hand, the contrasting experiences in the separate parts of Poland in 1848–9 only accentuated the already pronounced regional differences between them. The partition frontiers appeared as firmly drawn as ever. Inevitably, the influence of the émigrés plummeted; many educated Poles in Poland now resented the claims of the exiles to guide the nation's destiny. In the years that followed, the advocates of non-revolutionary methods gained the upper hand in the Prussian and Austrian parts. Conservative Polish deputies attended the Prussian parliament, established in 1851, while the appointment in 1850 of a Polish viceroy in Galicia, Count Agenor Gołuchowski, encouraged the loyalism of the Galician aristocracy to the Habsburgs.

The outbreak in 1854 of the Crimean War, in which Britain, France and Turkey challenged Russian ambitions in the Balkans, appeared at first to be Providence's answer to the lengthy prayers of the dejected Polish exiles, who promptly raised a variety of armed formations to fight against Russia. Mickiewicz, the embodiment of Polish Romantic defiance, himself arrived in Constantinople to help the military effort, only to be struck down by cholera. However, by agreeing to sue for peace in 1855, the new tsar Alexander II successfully deflected the British and French threat to widen the conflict to embrace the Polish Question, which was excluded from the agenda of the Paris peace conference of 1856.

At the same time the era of reforms that Alexander II launched after the debacle of the Crimean War could not ignore Russia's Polish lands. An amnesty for political prisoners, the suspension of military recruiting, the opening of a medical academy in Warsaw, and the appointment of the conciliatory Prince Gorchakov as viceroy in the Congress Kingdom all heralded a much-welcomed political thaw, which also coincided with a period of vigorous economic growth. Police controls were eased and restrictions on public activity lifted. In 1858 Count Andrzej Zamoyski, the largest landowner in the Kingdom, was permitted to launch an Agricultural Society which attracted the old established landed nobility as well as landowners of recent bourgeois, including Jewish, origin. While initially concerned with the urgent issue of agrarian reform, the Agricultural Society became in effect the national forum for moderate opinion in the Kingdom, a kind of substitute Sejm. The cause of peaceful modern progress was also promoted by Leopold Kronenberg, Warsaw's most influential banker and industrialist, and a Jewish convert to Calvinism, who associated himself closely with Zamoyski.

Among Warsaw's intelligentsia voices could also be heard calling for the introduction of accountable local government and for wider social reform, including Jewish emancipation and the abolition of peasant labour dues. More alarming for the tsarist authorities was the growing receptivity of the younger generation to radical ideas and to Polish Romantic literature, which became more accessible in the new freer climate. The anticipation of change was encouraged by the authorized debate on peasant emancipation in Russia, and by the achievement of Italian and Romanian unification between 1859 and 1861. From his exile the indefatigable yet reckless Mierosławski resumed his urgent call for an early national insurrection which would pre-empt the tsar by offering a generous land settlement to the peasants in the Kingdom and especially to the serfs of the western *gubernii*.

The Russian authorities, faced with the growing ferment in the Kingdom in 1859–60, found themselves in an awkward situation characteristic of authoritarian imperial regimes that embark on liberal reform; repression would only inflame Polish patriotic feelings while concessions would only encourage the Poles to ask for more. Demonstrations became increasingly frequent in Warsaw. In October 1860 stink bombs were let off in the Great Theatre at a performance attended by Tsar Alexander, Emperor Franz Josef of Austria and the prince regent of Prussia. The singing of patriotic songs in churches and in the streets heightened popular feelings. In early 1861 events took an alarming turn. In response to the tsar's February decree emancipating the serfs of the Russian Empire, the Agricultural Society in Warsaw formally called on 26 February for the granting of full property rights to the Kingdom's peasant leaseholders. A series of demonstrations was violently dispersed and in one instance Russian troops fired on the crowd, killing five people. The tsar, with one eye on improving relations with Napoleon III, offered to introduce limited cultural and administrative concessions in the Kingdom, but also resolved to crush all unrest and to curtail all independent political initiatives.

On 27 March Marquis Aleksander Wielopolski was appointed head of a revived department of religious and educational affairs in Warsaw. Wielopolski was a conservative patriot who had participated in the anti-Russian uprising of 1831 but who, under the impact of the horrors of the Galician jacquerie of 1846, had accepted the necessity of collaboration with Russia. Now in 1861 he saw himself as a man of Providence who believed he could restore to the Kingdom a measure of its lost autonomy while at the same time keeping at bay all the restless and subversive elements in Polish society. Unfortunately, his strategy also entailed the dissolution on 6 April of the Agricultural Society and of the City Delegation, two institutions which enjoyed considerable moral authority in the city. The crowds that gathered in Castle Square on 8 April to protest against the authorities' actions displayed patriotic and religious emotions of an unparalleled intensity; many of those present continued to pray on their knees as Russian troops fired into the crowd killing over one hundred people. Public opinion was enraged, collaboration with the tsarist authorities was discredited, and a state of national mourning was declared; the women of Warsaw, of all social ranks, wore black for the next two years. Many of the city's Jews, encouraged by the chief rabbi Beer Meisels, also joined the protest movement. In towns across the Kingdom and even in the western *gubernii*, vast congregations attended patriotic religious services. Significantly enough, much of the countryside remained aloof from the outburst of patriotic grief, preferring to agitate against labour dues, which Alexander finally replaced with cash payments in October.

The stick-and-carrot policy was not abandoned. The promised local authority elections, in which only 25,000 persons qualified to vote, took place in the autumn of 1861. But the new viceroy Lambert introduced martial law and banned all public gatherings, some of which had been highly symbolic and provocative, such as the celebration of the anniversary of Poland's union with Lithuania or the quasi-royal funeral of the popular archbishop of Warsaw Fijałkowski. On 11 November, the anniversary of Kościuszko's death, crowds again poured into Warsaw's churches. This time Russian soldiers entered the churches and proceeded to arrest thousands of worshippers. In a dramatic gesture against this profa-

22   The closure of the churches, painted by Artur Grottger (1837–67) in
1861. All places of worship were closed in Warsaw as a protest against
Russian soldiers arresting worshipers on 11 November 1861. Patriotism
and religion made a powerful combination in Russian Poland in the run-up
to the insurrection of 1863. Like many Polish artists of his generation,
Grottger focused on patriotic themes, making the insurrection his major
subject in a series of symbolic paintings. He had studied at the Vienna
Academy before returning to Kraków.

nation, the ecclesiastical authorities of all faiths ordered the closure of all the city's Catholic and Protestant churches and of all its synagogues. Wielopolski resigned and left for St Petersburg.

All this played into the hands of conspiratorial radical groups, now styled the 'Reds', who embarked on preparations for an uprising. Links were established with radical officers in the tsarist army while Mierosławski's followers, trained in Italy with Garibaldi's blessing, slipped into the Kingdom. Zamoyski, Kronenberg and other moderate 'White' leaders remained bitterly hostile to such adventurism, and concentrated on mobilizing Polish and foreign opinion in favour of the peaceful extension of Polish national rights. In mid-1862 events seemed to favour their cause. The government's relations with the Catholic Church were eased by the appointment of a new archbishop of Warsaw, while Wielopolski's dignified and sensible arguments finally persuaded Alexander II to restore to the Kingdom much of its lost self-rule. The tsar's liberal-minded brother Constantine was appointed viceroy, and all non-military matters in the Kingdom were placed in the hands of a civilian government led by Wielopolski, who immediately proceeded with some badly needed social and educational reforms. The compulsory commutation of labour dues into rents was a step forward, although it did not satisfy peasant demands for land and did not bridge the gulf between the nobility and the peasantry. The Jewish population finally obtained equal legal rights. The university of Warsaw and a network of Polish schools were restored.

There was, however, no extension of political liberties, and Wielopolski's unpopularity did little to enhance the objective attractiveness of the reform package. If anything, the youthful Reds, led by Jarosław Dąbrowski, stepped up their revolutionary preparations: the rudimentary structures of an underground state were put into place under the direction of a Central National Committee, a secret paramilitary force was raised, and plots were hatched to assassinate the viceroy and Wielopolski. Many young Catholic clerics found themselves drawn to radical beliefs akin to modern liberation theology. The position of the Whites, unwilling to alienate public opinion by co-operating with Wielopolski yet not wishing to give the Reds any advantages in the patriotic stakes, was becoming increasingly difficult. In September 1862, in an attempt to seize the patriotic high ground and to marginalize the Reds, Zamoyski proposed to Grand Duke Constantine that the western *gubernii* should be reunited with the Kingdom and that the 1815 constitution should be restored in its entirety, with the Sejm and a separate army. The tsar exiled Zamoyski for his audacity, but thereby weakened the influence of those Poles who wished to avoid an uprising. The middle ground in Polish politics was fast disintegrating.

The conspirators, led by the 22-year-old Stefan Bobrowski and the 28-year-old Zygmunt Padlewski, were planning to strike in the spring of 1863. However, their hand was forced when Wielopolski ordered, on 14 January 1863, the round-up and conscription into the tsarist army of 12,000 urban youths known to the police for their radicalism. With one surgical cut Wielopolski hoped to destroy the Reds in the middle of the winter when conditions were least favourable for an insurrection. To the consternation of many of their fellow conspirators in the provinces, the Red leadership decided to act. On 22 January 1863 the Central National Committee proclaimed itself the 'Provisional National Government', and declared war on Russia for the liberation of all of Russia's Polish lands within the limits of 1772. The insurgents initially had at their disposal merely 6,000 poorly armed men, mostly urban workers, artisans and impoverished nobles, against a Russian army of 100,000 in the Kingdom and a further equal number in the western *gubernii*. Most men of property looked aghast at the sheer irresponsibility of the young Reds.

The self-styled National Government hoped to lessen the disparity between the forces by winning over the mass of the peasantry to the struggle. To this end it issued a decree granting the peasants full property rights to all their holdings, and promising rewards in the form of land to all landless peasants who joined the insurrection. In mid-February Mierosławski, aspiring to become the Polish Garibaldi, was back in Poland as 'dictator'. The initial peasant response to the uprising was generally favourable but muted. The insurrection turned into a guerrilla war in which no more than 30,000 insurgents at any one time pitted themselves with little more than shotguns and scythes against the largest army in Europe. Yet despite their enormous military superiority and their early victories over Mierosławski's units, the Russians were unable to stamp out the insurgents whose hit-and-run tactics proved highly effective in the forests of Poland and Lithuania. Wide expressions of public sympathy in the West, and official British and French diplomatic protests to St Petersburg, only encouraged the insurgents in their illusions that foreign intervention would save their cause; as a result, support for the rising spread within Poland to groups hitherto opposed to the armed struggle. The Whites could not stomach Mierosławski and some were unhappy about the anonymous character of the National Government, but they were persuaded to join the insurrection when command was assumed by the moderates Marian Langiewicz and later Karol Majewski. The insurrection engulfed much of Lithuania and western Belorussia but not the Ukraine, while numerous volunteers crossed the border from Poznania and Galicia.

In April 1863 the tsar's offer of an amnesty was rejected and the rising entered a more bitter phase. Alexander II dismissed Wielopolski, and replaced Grand Duke Constantine as viceroy with Field Marshal Berg, whose harsh methods emulated those of Mikhail Muraviev, the governor-general of Vilna, whose pitiless repression in the east earned him lasting notoriety in Polish patriotic tradition as 'the hangman'. The Reds took the reins of the National Government and responded with their brand of terror, deploying a security corps of so-called 'stiletto-men' against Russian officials and their Polish collaborators. Desperate to prolong the struggle until the spring of 1864, in the hope that France might yet intervene, the insurgents elected a new leader in October 1863: Romuald Traugutt, an experienced professional officer from the tsarist army who had resigned his commission in 1862 and who had proved his mettle as a guerrilla commander in the woods and marshes of Polesie. Traugutt's political sympathies lay with the Whites, but he infused the underground state with a renewed determination to survive; the insurrectionary army was reorganized and a unified military and civilian command created.

But the tide of events was turning against the insurgents. They were unable to establish effective control over any sizeable region of Russian Poland and were thus unable to implement systematically their land reform. The tensions between the Whites and the

Reds weakened Traugutt's authority. The vocal support for the Polish cause of the Russian radicals Herzen and Bakunin, and of the Russian revolutionary organization 'Land and Will' produced limited practical benefits. Indeed, most of Russian public opinion, including many liberals and Slavophiles, rallied against the Poles in a powerful outburst of indignant patriotism. And once again the international situation, so vital a factor in the Poles' calculations and hopes, proved unfavourable. Austria and Prussia, in league at the time over the Danish problem, both adopted a hostile attitude to the Polish insurrection; Bismarck even offered to help the Russians against the rebels. Cut off from the rest of Europe, the Polish insurgents soon learnt that all the expressions of support and sympathy from Paris, London and elsewhere were a cruel deception. There was to be no European Congress to discuss the Polish issue, let alone any military intervention on their behalf.

In early March 1864 the tsarist authorities made a bold stroke to outmanoeuvre the National Government in the struggle for the hearts and minds of the peasants. The liberal Russian reformer N. N. Miliutin had finally persuaded the tsar that to offer the peasants the same property rights as those promised by the revolutionary government would do more than anything else to restore Russian control in the Kingdom. Indeed, following Tsar Alexander's generous decree of 2 March on land reform, support for the insurrection in the Polish countryside began to slacken as the peasants turned to securing their new rights. Traugutt and his associates were arrested in April and executed on 5 August 1864, by which time the remaining flames of insurrection had been largely snuffed out. The last insurgent unit, led by the radical priest Stanisław Brzóska, held out in Podlasie until 1865.

For those thousands of insurgents who were spared the gallows, there awaited the long march to penal servitude in Siberia. Landowners who had sympathized with or supported the uprising faced fines or the confiscation of their property. Yet another Polish generation paid the price for a heroic but ultimately doomed attempt to challenge the Partitions. However, it was a remarkable feat that the uprising managed to last for eighteen months against such overwhelming military odds. The insurgents proved to be an elusive and tenacious foe. From its hideouts in Warsaw the

National Government was able to function under the very noses of the tsarist police, and in the countryside its secret agencies played hide-and-seek with the Russian army. In many areas landowners and peasants paid a 'national tax' and offered supplies to the insurgents who, although often surrounded and defeated, would quickly reform and resurface with fresh volunteers. The secret underground state that operated over much of Russian Poland in 1863–4 was an extraordinary phenomenon in the history of nationalism in nineteenth-century Europe. In the words of Viceroy Berg, it had been 'a truly devilish conspiracy'. But it could not hold out indefinitely against an army of nearly 400,000 men (half of the entire Russian land forces) which flooded the tsar's Polish lands, and especially with the demoralizing absence of any foreign intervention. Increasingly harsh reprisals and finally the tsar's gesture to the peasants also took their toll. Yet through its endorsement of the peasant cause, the insurrection had prompted the tsarist authorities to offer to the Kingdom's peasantry a far more generous deal than that contemplated by Wielopolski or indeed offered by the tsar to the peasants in Russia proper.

It now remained to be seen whether the peasants of Russian Poland would become the grateful and loyal subjects of their imperial master in St Petersburg, or whether, with their immediate economic demands satisfied, they would find a common national identity with their fellow countrymen. The international order that emerged after 1864 also represented a watershed in the history of the Polish struggles for independence. With the rise of Bismarckian Germany as the major power on the continent of Europe, and the consequent eclipse of France, all Polish illusions of western help died. The era of Romantic insurrections had come to an end. Nevertheless, the memory of the heroism and sacrifice of 1863–4 and the sense that a great injustice had been done were to leave a bitter and potent legacy.

5

An era of transformation,
1864–1914

The crushing of the insurrection of 1863–4 dealt what seemed to
be a final and fatal body blow to the cause of Polish independence.
A new wave of exiles, as defiant but not as illustrious as their
predecessors of 1831, sought sanctuary in the West. Militant
radicals amongst them joined the cause of international socialism,
and many went to fight, and perish, on the barricades of the Paris
Commune. The moderates set about devising no less unrealistic
plans to preserve the national cause. Some of their ideas and
activities were to germinate in the long run into vigorous socialist
and nationalist movements within Poland, but at the moment, with
every year that passed, the Polish Question as an international issue
faded more and more into the distant background. The Russo-
Turkish war of 1877–8 and the resulting Eastern Crisis raised a few
desultory hopes, only to dash them. Indeed, the 1870s and 1880s
witnessed a reinvigorated campaign by both the Russian and
Prussian authorities to weaken still further the Polish character of
their respective shares of old Poland. It was ironically in Austria,
which had been least well disposed to Polish national aspirations in
the early decades of the century, that Polish fortunes were to
improve.

The distinct administrative status of the Congress Kingdom was
much reduced, and Russian was imposed as the language of
administration and of the courts. In 1874 that ill-fated creation of
the Congress of Vienna was even formally renamed 'the Vistula
Land' (Privislansky Kray), and the office of viceroy was abolished.

Censorship and strict police controls became the order of the day, and steps were taken to weaken the influence of the nobility among the Kingdom's peasantry. In the western *gubernii* the purchase of land by individuals of Polish or Catholic origin and the public use of the Polish language were forbidden. The Poles' sense of political impotence was further reinforced when two important liberal reforms, introduced in the 1860s in the rest of the Russian Empire by Tsar Alexander II, were not extended to any of the ex-Polish lands. These were the *zemstva*, elected district councils with extensive responsibilities for health, education and the economic infrastructure; and secondly, the jury system in the law courts. On the credit side, however, Polish conscripts into the tsarist army were at least able to benefit from Miliutin's humane army reforms which ended the system of twenty-year military servitude.

The active involvement of the Roman Catholic clergy in the recent uprising brought upon the Church increased restrictions, in both the Kingdom and the western *gubernii*. Most monasteries were closed, and surviving ones were forbidden to admit new members. A fifth of all Roman Catholic parishes in Lithuania and Belorussia were dissolved. Protesting bishops were deported, with the result that by 1870 all but one of the Kingdom's dioceses were unoccupied. The surviving Greek Catholic diocese of Chełm in the south-east of the Kingdom was compelled to return to Orthodoxy in 1875; troops were used to whip the reluctant villagers into submission. An agreement between St Petersburg and the papacy in 1882 brought only limited respite to the Church in Russian Poland.

The Kingdom's educational system was not spared either. In the mid-1860s Russian became the obligatory language of instruction in all secondary schools, followed by all elementary schools in 1885. In 1869 a Russian-language university was opened in Warsaw to replace the closed 'Main School'. The humiliation experienced in 1878 by the young Maria Skłodowska (later Curie), and her fellow pupils, when instructed by a government school inspector to recite the Lord's Prayer in Russian and then to enumerate from memory all members of the imperial family, was a characteristic feature of those years.

The distinct status of Prussia's ex-Polish provinces was also eroded. Poznania and Danzig Pomerania (West Prussia), which had

not been included in the German Confederation of 1815, were now
fully integrated within the new Germany after 1871. German was
finally established as the exclusive language of local administration,
the courts and, by 1887, of all schools, with the notable exception
of religious instruction. Nothing was now left of earlier Polish
hopes for the creation of a Polish university in Poznań. Bismarck
was not a modern-style German nationalist, and initially considered Polish-speaking peasants capable of loyal service to the Prussian state. But he was adamant that Polish aspirations to statehood
were fundamentally incompatible with Prussian and German state
interests, and that Polish nationalism, represented primarily by the
nobility and the clergy, was on a par with Catholicism as a
centrifugal force hostile to the new Reich. Bismarck's attempt in the
1870s to subordinate the Roman Catholic Church to the German
state and to limit its influence in society, the so-called *Kulturkampf*,
acquired in the east a distinctly anti-Polish character. In the
Poznań-Gniezno archdiocese most remaining monasteries and convents were dissolved, and between 1873 and 1877 30 per cent of
the parishes were deprived of their priests by police arrests. The
ultramontane Archbishop Ledóchowski was imprisoned for two
years and was then obliged to leave for Rome. Yet the unintended
outcome of the *Kulturkampf* in the east was the strengthening of
the links between religion and nationality, most unexpectedly in
Upper Silesia. In response to growing nationalist demands within
the Reich to strengthen even more the German character of the
Prussian east, Bismarck created in 1886 a special fund to buy out
Polish-owned estates with the aim of distributing the land among
German settlers. Except for a short conciliatory period towards the
Poles under Chancellor Caprivi between 1890 and 1894, when the
government needed the support of the Polish deputies in the Reich-
stag, the resulting struggle over land added yet another dimension
to the persistent nationality conflict in the east.

The policies of the Austrian government towards its Polish
subjects in the latter part of the nineteenth century provided a
sharp contrast to developments in Russia and Prussia. Major
defeats at the hands of France and Prussia, in 1859 and 1866
respectively, weakened the Austrian Empire and obliged Vienna
to make constitutional concessions. The creation of a partly repre-

sentative Council of State and of regional parliaments in the early 1860s led in 1867 to the more thorough transformation of the empire into the Austro-Hungarian Dual Monarchy. Inhibited by still vivid memories of the jacquerie of 1846 and apprehensive about the Ukrainian national revival, the predominantly conservative Polish leadership in Galicia contented itself with a limited degree of autonomy within the Austrian half of the Dual Monarchy.

In return for loyalty to Austria, control of Galicia's internal affairs was gradually transferred to the local Polish elite. Until 1918 the posts of viceroy and of the minister for Galicia in the Viennese cabinet were both held by Poles. A narrow class-based franchise ensured a landed and middle-class domination of the provincial Sejm in Lwów, and of the Galician representation to the central Austrian parliament. Between 1877 and 1889 there were no peasant representatives in the provincial Diet, and only a handful of Ukrainians. A number of Polish aristocrats held high office in Vienna: Count Alfred Potocki and Count Kazimierz Badeni served as Austria's prime ministers in 1870–1 and 1895–7, respectively; Count Agenor Gołuchowski (the elder) was interior minister and minister of state from 1859 to 1860, while his son served as foreign minister between 1895 and 1906. Polish national culture was allowed to flourish; after 1870 the Polish language was restored in the administration, the courts, the schools and in the two universities of Kraków and Lwów. The hitherto passive Catholic hierarchy in Galicia acquired a more pronounced national character and greater freedom of action: in 1879 the patriotic Albin Dunajewski was nominated archbishop of Kraków, and in 1890 was elevated to the cardinalate. Kraków emerged as the centre of the Polish world of art, to be dominated for three decades by Jan Matejko, whose vast historical canvases portrayed a glorified and dramatic vision of Poland's past. Compared to what had existed before, and to what was happening in Russian and Prussian Poland, these were substantial political and cultural benefits; yet they did not quickly bring commensurate economic and social progress to what remained for decades a backward province of the Austrian Empire.

The new realities within Poland and across Europe as a whole compelled many educated Poles to reassess critically their nation's predicament and its prospects for the future. The first and most vigorous intellectual and historical condemnation of the futility of political Romanticism and of the tradition of armed insurrections came in 1869 from a group of erstwhile freedom fighters, now prominent intellectuals in Kraków: the historian Jan Szujski and the literary historian Stanisław Tarnowski. In Szujski's memorable phrase, *liberum conspiro* (the freedom to conspire) was an anarchic and destructive principle on a par with the old *liberum veto*. To this was added, in the late 1870s, a scathing critique of Poland's past by the influential historian Michał Bobrzyński. Known in Poland as the 'Stańczyks', with reference to Stańczyk, a sixteenth-century court jester, they endeavoured to influence Polish public opinion in the spirit of political realism, hard work and social conservatism. The essential unity of Polish culture had to be promoted, ran their message, but politically the Poles had little alternative but to accept 'tri-loyalism', or co-existence with their three respective governments. It was a position easier to adopt under the Habsburgs' tolerant rule in Galicia than under the strict tsarist regime in Warsaw; nevertheless, to many conservative men of property across Poland tri-loyalism offered a prudent way of coming to terms with difficult political realities.

The futile heroism of the insurrectionary tradition was also condemned in the 1870s by the Positivists of Warsaw. Drawing heavily on the values of western rationalism and empirical philosophy, and on the tradition of 'organic work', they called on the Poles to focus on strengthening the economic, social and cultural sinews of the nation. Modern European civilization had to be the way of the future, not impractical dreams. The leading Positivists, such as the journalist and publicist Aleksander Świętochowski, the novelists Bolesław Prus (the Polish equivalent of Dickens) and Eliza Orzeszkowa, or the poet Adam Asnyk, offered in their work a realistic and anti-obscurantist approach to social problems which did much to promote the cause of progress in their country. One of the main achievements of the Positivists was a clandestine 'flying university', founded in 1886, offering rigorous academic courses in Polish. By the 1880s, however, it was becoming clear that industrialization and urbanization, especially in Russian

Poland, were creating social divisions and tensions rather than the social harmony and national unity of which they dreamt.

The latter objectives were most successfully promoted in Poznania where Polish landowners, artisans, peasants and priests found common ground in the defence of their faith, their land and their nationality against German nationalist pressure. Economic co-operatives and self-help educational societies, many led by priests, flourished. Over a thousand Polish libraries, mostly of a religious and moralistic character, operated in Poznania and Silesia. The Polish-owned Peasant Bank, founded in 1872, had 125,000 members by 1910. In 1888 the Poles of Prussia even founded a Land Bank to counteract Berlin's policy of buying out Polish landowners. The strong sense of nationality of the Poznanian peasants was not only a reaction to the *Kulturkampf* but also a reflection of the advanced level of civilization in Prussia's Polish lands. The emergence in Prussian Poland of a modern, highly productive system of agriculture owed much to the early Prussian land reform which had favoured the creation of economically viable large and medium-sized farms. It was also encouraged by the demand for food in Germany's expanding industrial cities, by the German government's protectionist tariffs on agricultural products, and by the construction of a dense railway network throughout Prussia.

The pace of economic development and social change during the last four decades of the nineteenth century was markedly different in each of the regions of partitioned Poland. In the former Congress Kingdom the tsarist land reform of 1864 had created an uneven patchwork of reduced landed estates and numerous small and fragmented peasant holdings. Agricultural productivity here was much lower than in Poznania. Indeed, the entire rural sector was badly hit by the agricultural slump of the 1880s. In contrast to the wealthier aristocracy, many landowners among the lesser gentry did not survive the crisis and drifted into the urban professions and into the growing ranks of the intelligentsia, which retained many of the gentry's cultural values and genteel habits. Among the peasants, too, the more robust coped, but many had to sell their uneconomic holdings (most were under 15 hectares in size) and seek new jobs or join the armies of seasonal labourers that criss-crossed this part of Europe at harvest time. On the other hand, there was a striking

23 Weaving hall of Karl Wilhelm Scheibler's cotton mill in Łódź, the 'Manchester of Poland'. The importance of Łódź as a textile centre dates from the 1820s. The abolition of the customs barrier between Russia and the Kingdom of Poland in 1850 and the arrival of the railway in 1866 stimulated the city's economic expansion. By the 1870s, the German-born Scheibler (1820–81) was the leading mill-owner in Łódź, and his textile business the largest in the Russian Empire. The dynamic, acquisitive and socially divided world of Łódź, with its Polish, German and Jewish inhabitants, was recreated in the novel *Ziemia obiecana* ('The promised land') (1898) by Władysław Reymont. Two film versions of the novel have been made, one in 1927 and one in 1974, by Andrzej Wajda.

growth of industry, of towns and of railway construction, even if modest by English or German standards. The population of Warsaw, now an important metallurgical centre, doubled between 1864 and 1890 to nearly half a million and reached over 760,000 in 1910; that of Łódź, which attracted much German capital and which directed much of its vast textile production to Russia and the Far East, increased spectacularly from 28,000 in 1860 to 410,000 in 1910. Coal-mining expanded in the Dąbrowa basin near the Silesian border. The proportion of the urban population of the Kingdom grew from just over a fifth of the total in 1872 to about a third in 1909, by which time the value of industrial production exceeded the agricultural. In economic terms, the former Kingdom had become the most advanced region of the Russian Empire.

Much less developed was Galicia with its dense patchwork of small and frequently subdivided peasant holdings, its abject rural poverty and its socially conservative elite. Until 1890 the province remained in debt to the central government in Vienna and was burdened by indemnity payments to landowners following the peasant emancipation of 1848. It trailed far behind industrialized Teschen Silesia as well as other western regions of Austria. At the beginning of the twentieth century, out of a population of 7.3 million, Galicia had no more than 60,000 industrial workers. Its only significant industrial activity was the extraction of oil (over 5 per cent of world production in 1909) around Borysław and Drohobycz in the south-east. Economic expansion did accelerate after 1890, and the cities of Lwów and Kraków reached a respectable size by 1910, with 207,000 and 174,000 inhabitants respectively.

The last decades of the nineteenth century witnessed substantial demographic growth across Poland, with the resulting mass exodus of poor peasants to the industrial areas of Westphalia and subsequently overseas, mainly to the United States and Brazil; about 2.5 million peasants are estimated to have left the ethnic Polish lands between 1870 and 1914. The Polish character of large parts of Chicago in the first half of the twentieth century owed much to this early wave of job-seeking emigrants. In the absence of adequate cultural and educational institutions, especially in Russian Poland, many talented Poles of gentry or middle-class background also left

24   Marie Curie-Skłodowska: a Nobel Prize winner, photographed in
1913 in Birmingham. After training herself in chemical analysis in the
laboratories of the Museum of Industry and Agriculture in Warsaw, she left
to study in Paris, where she graduated in physics and mathematics. In 1895
she married the physicist Pierre Curie. In 1898 she discovered two highly
radioactive new elements, polonium and radium. She was twice awarded
the Nobel Prize: in 1903 (together with her husband and Henri Becquerel)
for physics, and in 1911, alone, for chemistry. She always maintained close
contact with her native country, and was instrumental in the establishment
of the Radium Institute in Warsaw in 1932.

to make careers abroad. Joseph Conrad (Korzeniowski), Ignacy Paderewski and Maria Curie-Skłodowska provide three most eminent examples. To these one could also add the names of two future presidents of Poland: Gabriel Narutowicz, an expert on hydroelectricity, and the chemist Ignacy Mościcki, both of whom acquired their professional reputations in Switzerland. By the same token, numerous Polish engineers made their fortunes in the Russian interior and Siberia where their Polish origins were not a liability. Nor did his national background prevent Wacław Niżyński (better known as Vaslav Nijinsky) from making a glittering career as a star of Russian ballet.

The western *gubernii* of the Russian Empire retained a predominantly rural character, although the coming of the railways did stimulate economic activity. Nevertheless, rural over-population took its toll here too; nearly a quarter of the ethnic Lithuanian population emigrated, mostly to the United States, between 1864 and 1914. Belorussia, with its poor soil and extensive forests, remained most backward; among the isolated and self-sufficient marshland communities in Polesie primitive conditions continued well into the twentieth century. In the Ukraine west of the river Dnieper, substantial Polish landed fortunes managed to survive; their owners, such as the Potockis or the Branickis, had the scope and resources to modernize their estates and to develop ancillary food industries, especially the highly profitable refining of beet-sugar. Until 1917 Kiev was home to a large and thriving Polish intelligentsia.

Economically, the separate zones of what had once been the Polish-Lithuanian Commonwealth were moving in different directions and according to different rhythms. The growing dependence of Poznanian agriculture on the German market and of the Kingdom's industrial sector on the Russian market integrated those regions with the German and Russian economies. The railway systems constructed across Poland in the nineteenth century reflected this vividly. Warsaw's long circuitous railway links with Poznań, Kraków and Lwów were hardly those that would have been built had Warsaw been the capital of a united Poland. Only with Wilno was a direct line established in 1862 as part of the Warsaw–St Petersburg railway. The railway networks continued to

25   A scene of peasant life in Polesie. The photograph was taken in 1938, but it reflects a way of life that had changed little since the late nineteenth century. Much of Polesie, perhaps the most backward part of the lands of the former Polish-Lithuanian Commonwealth, consisted of marshland fed by the river Pripet and its tributaries. The region's rural inhabitants were mostly Orthodox and spoke Belorussian. They would most probably refer to themselves as 'tutejsi' – 'we who live here'. Illiteracy here still amounted to well over 70 per cent in 1914.

grow, but even as late as 1914 only three mainline and three secondary rail routes crossed from Prussia into Russian Poland. A cursory glance at a map of the Polish state railways today clearly highlights the dense network in the areas that had belonged to the German Reich before 1918.

Against this background of economic and social change it is difficult to be precise about the degree and extent of the Polish-speaking peasantry's national sentiments. A complex set of regional factors was at play here. While military service, especially in the Austrian army, had some influence in inculcating loyalty to the three empires among young male Poles, official Prussian and Russian hostility towards Catholicism and the Polish language, not to mention a misguided tsarist campaign against the wearing of national dress, had the opposite effect. The migration of thousands of peasants into the towns also affected cultural and social mores. The peasants brought with them traditions of rural religiosity and in turn were exposed to the patriotism of the urban artisans and to the ideas of the early socialists. The end of serfdom and the growing awareness through education and literacy of a wider world beyond the village community were undoubtedly key factors in shaping the peasants' consciousness. Yet there were unusual contrasts in this respect. In Prussian Poland primary education was compulsory and illiteracy was virtually eliminated by 1900, but all schools used German as the language of instruction; nevertheless, evidence of an emerging Polish identity could be observed even among the Kashubians of Danzig Pomerania who started electing Polish deputies to the Reichstag. In Russian Poland, government-sponsored primary education was in Russian, but the provision of schooling at all levels remained woefully inadequate; at the end of the nineteenth century illiteracy levels there still hovered about the 65 per cent mark. The teaching of the Polish language, in both Prussian and Russian Poland, became the activity primarily of voluntary and autodidactic educational societies sponsored by private philanthropists and by socialist and nationalist parties. By the early 1900s such secret teaching embraced about a third of the Kingdom's population. In aristocratic and well-to-do families, and among the intelligentsia, the written language was taught at home by the ladies of the house or by tutors. At all levels of society effective counter-measures were deployed against the onslaught of cultural germanization and russification.

Only Galicia enjoyed a formal system of primary education in Polish, even though as late as 1900 it was available to only about 30 per cent of the province's children; in the case of Ukrainian youngsters the proportion was even lower. A major government-sponsored expansion of village schooling under viceroy Bobrzyński between 1908 and 1913 did lower illiteracy levels to below 50 per cent. Galicia's extensive national and political freedoms (universal male franchise was introduced in Austria in 1907), its Polish-language schools and newspapers, and opportunities of participating in public life all helped to nurture a sense of a Polish identity among the rural population. The memoirs of Jan Słomka (1842–1927), the first written by a Polish peasant, who described the evolution from serfdom to constitutional government in Galicia, provide a vivid illustration of this process.

Just as feelings of national consciousness were spreading among wider sections of the Polish-speaking population, so similar developments could be observed among other ethnic groups inhabiting what had been the eastern half of the former Commonwealth. In due course, the new national movements in the east, led by the native clergy and the emerging local intelligentsias of peasant descent, acquired a political character; they rejected the concept of the old multicultural Commonwealth and challenged the continuing Polish social and cultural supremacy in the east. The earliest strides in this direction had been made by the Ukrainians of eastern Galicia where, in conditions of relative freedom under Austrian rule, their cultural and learned societies gave evidence of impressive vitality. Conservative clerical leaders among the Galician Ukrainians initially favoured closer bonds of affinity with Russia, but in the 1880s they were successfully challenged by a younger radical group, inspired by the writer Ivan Franko, which espoused the cause of an all-Ukrainian national identity, clearly distinct from Russians and Poles alike. Many Polish and Ukrainian communities existed peacefully side by side under Habsburg rule, but the Polish domination of Galicia's public life and the prevalence of Polish-speaking landlords in eastern Galicia accentuated inter-ethnic and class resentments and eventually contributed to bitter mutual antagonism. A Ukrainian literary and cultural movement also emerged in the Russian Empire in the 1840s; its chief ideologist was Mykola Kostomarov and its leading bard Taras Shevchenko. A single Ukrainian literary language, based on the dialects of the Poltava and Kiev regions, was eventually adopted by Ukrainian writers and publicists on both sides of the Austro-Russian border.

The tsarist government was not only uncompromisingly hostile towards all Polish-inspired secessionism, but it also adopted a negative attitude to the awakening of other local national cultures in the western borderlands of the Russian Empire. The Ukrainian language, for instance, was banned from Russian schools in 1863, and from printing and publishing in 1876. Discriminatory restrictions were also applied to the Lithuanian language which until 1904 could only be printed in the Cyrillic alphabet. However, the Russian authorities could not effectively prevent the illegal distribution from East Prussia of Lithuanian-language publications printed in the Latin alphabet and vigorously expressing a new linguistically based Lithuanian national identity. The most important journal was *Auszra* (Dawn), edited by Jonas Basanavičius and Jonas Šliupas. In 1863–4 most ethnic Lithuanians had sided with the Poles against tsarist despotism, but the paths of the two nationalities began to diverge soon after that. Indeed, the new Lithuanian national revival, despite its indebtedness to Polish Romanticism and the support of several eminent bi-cultural bishops and writers, acquired strong anti-Polish characteristics, born out of a resentment towards the cultural polonization of most of the *szlachta* and of the educated classes in the former Grand Duchy of Lithuania. The modest beginnings of a Belorussian literary revival, based largely on Polish models and even encouraged by local Polish patriots as a means of resisting Russian influence, could also be observed in this period. The pattern of inter-ethnic relationships in the western *gubernii* was complicated by social, linguistic and religious factors. While the Roman Catholic faith tended to reflect Polish cultural orientation in Belorussia and in the Ukraine, it was the linguistic divide, and not religion, that came to distinguish modern Lithuanians from Poles or polonized Lithuanians.

The world of the Jewry of the former Polish-Lithuanian Commonwealth was also changing. In the Congress Kingdom the process that had begun with the emancipation decree of 1862 continued; many able, better-off and enterprising Jews left the confines of their traditional religious and cultural communities to play a full part in the Gentile world. Indeed, in large urban centres cases of assimilation into the upper bourgeoisie and the intelligentsia were not uncommon, the most prominent examples being the banking and industrial families of the Kronenbergs, the Blochs and the Poznańskis. Assimilation could also be observed in Galicia, especially in Kraków and Lwów, where Jews were granted equal civil rights after 1867. On the other hand, large numbers of poorer Galician Jews sought a better life by migrating to Vienna. In Poznania most Jews gravitated towards German culture, and indeed left for Germany proper. In the western *gubernii*, where about 40 per cent of the urban population was Jewish, secularized Jews were increasingly drawn to Russian culture, despite the

26 Feast of the Trumpets – Jewish New Year. Painted by Aleksander Gierymski (1850–1901) in 1884. Orthodox Jews singing and praying on the banks of the Vistula in Warsaw. Gierymski, a realist painter sensitive to the effect of strong light, painted many memorable scenes of Jewish life. In the background a steam train crosses the Kierbedź railway bridge. It was Gierymski's elder brother, Maksymilian (1846–74), who painted *The insurgents' patrol* shown on the cover of the book.

continuation there of a wide range of tsarist restrictions on Jewish
life.

The expansion of industry and trade, and the rising proportion
of Jews in the towns of the Kingdom also accentuated the economic
rivalry between Gentile and Jewish shopkeepers, pedlars and all
sorts of middlemen, and added a further dimension to popular anti-
Jewish sentiments. These were also fuelled by the arrival there in
the 1880s of thousands of russianized Jews (the so-called 'Litvaks')
fleeing poverty and pogroms in western Russia, and by the emergence of an exclusive ethnically based Polish nationalism. The
hopes that Gentile and Jew would act together in the cause of civil
rights and of national liberation, so strong in the Kingdom from
1861 to 1864, burnt much less brightly as the century wore on,
although they did continue in the Polish socialist movement and
among the progressive intelligentsia. Jewish emigration, especially
to the New World, grew apace; over a million Jews left the lands of
the former Commonwealth between 1870 and 1914. The extraordinary diversity of the Jewish world was further accentuated in
the late 1890s by the rise of two rival secular political movements:
Zionism, with its vision of Jewish statehood, and the socialist
Bund, which set out to embrace the large Jewish working population of the Russian Empire.

As elsewhere in east-central Europe, new ideological and political movements were emerging in Polish society: socialism,
modern nationalism and agrarian populism. A new generation of
radicals took up the mantle of the exiles of 1864 and challenged the
Polish elites who had sought some form of accommodation with
the prevailing political realities. Although these movements were
eventually to acquire a mass and pan-Polish dimension, they also
possessed their own specific regional characteristics, reflecting the
different conditions under Russian, German and Austrian rule.

Modern Polish socialism, which appeared in the 1870s, drew not
only on the inspiration of Marx and Engels but also on the native
Romantic insurrectionary tradition and the revolutionary potential
of Russia's militant populists (the Narodniks). From the start there
were tensions between the movement's national and internationalist objectives. The early socialist Bolesław Limanowski, who was
based in Geneva, favoured the former; Ludwik Waryński, who in

1882 founded the first Marxist group on Polish soil, stressed the primacy of the latter. Waryński's organization was quickly broken up by the tsarist police and the focus of Polish socialist activity moved abroad. In 1892 in Paris the Polish Socialist Party (the PPS) was formed, soon to be led by the conspiratorial Józef Piłsudski.

Just as the earlier generations of radicals hoped to mobilize the peasants in the struggle for independence, so now Piłsudski saw in the growing industrial working class of Russian Poland a revolutionary instrument with which to overthrow tsarist rule. Central to this was the presupposition that socialism could only be achieved in an independent and reunited Poland, which would be open on a voluntary basis to all its historic national groups. This met with the bitter opposition of those doctrinaire Marxists, like Rosa Luxemburg, who rejected the cause of Polish independence as fundamentally incompatible with the supranational nature of socialism, and running in the face of capitalist development which had bound the Kingdom economically to Russia. In 1893 Luxemburg and her associates formed the rival Social Democratic Party of the Kingdom of Poland (the SDKP); in 1900 it was given a new lease of life, largely through the efforts of Feliks Dzierżyński (Dzerzhinsky), as the Social Democratic Party of the Kingdom of Poland and Lithuania (the SDKPiL). In terms of size the PPS was to have a marked advantage over the SDKPiL, with 50,000 members compared to 30,000 in 1906; but it was clear that Polish socialism was bitterly divided. It is ironic that Piłsudski and Dzierżyński, who both experienced tsarist repression in their youth and whose personal careers were to lead in totally different directions, both came from gentry families in Lithuania. The two socialist parties were to remain unreconciled over the 'national question'; and even within the PPS tensions between the party's social and national objectives would surface repeatedly. And although Rosa Luxemburg was a secularized Polish Jewess from Zamość, the establishment in 1898 in Russia of a distinct Jewish socialist party, the Bund, was a further reflection of the problematic relationship between socialism and nationality in eastern Europe.

Whether in its German or its Polish variety, socialism failed to strike deep roots in Prussian Poland. In Poznania the number of industrial workers was small, and the association of Polishness

with Catholicism was too strong. In Upper Silesia the large industrial labour force (numbering about 360,000 in 1900) tended to
vote for the German Catholic Centre Party until the 1890s. The
advanced system of social security introduced in the 1880s by
Bismarck also lessened material deprivation and class tensions in
the German east. Socialism made a little more headway in Galicia,
where it tapped into the local radical traditions. The socialist party
was able to function legally in Austria and adopted a gradualist
non-revolutionary programme of extending workers' political and
social rights. But socialism in Austria had to contend with the
monarchy's complex nationality problems which brought about the
movement's fragmentation into autonomous linguistic-ethnic components. The most outstanding among the Polish socialists in
Galicia was Ignacy Daszyński, a talented orator and future parlia-
mentarian; among the Ukrainian socialists it was Ivan Franko and
Mykhailo Pavlyk.

However significant the rise of socialism in Poland, there existed
in Polish society even more powerful nationalist undercurrents
which could be tapped and profitably manipulated by a modern
nationalist party. The potential attraction of nationalist sentiments
was reflected, for instance, by the enormous popularity of Henryk
Sienkiewicz's historical *Trilogy*, published between 1883 and 1888.
Set in the seventeenth century during Poland's difficult wars against
rebellious Cossacks and invading Swedes and Turks, Sienkiewicz's
swashbuckling epic provided a powerful Romanticized vision of
Poland's past which was to leave its mark on the historical
consciousness of subsequent Polish generations. Strong anti-
German sentiments were also given vent in Bolesław Prus'
Placówka (The outpost) of 1885 which dealt with the rivalry of
Polish and German peasants over land, and in Sienkiewicz's
medieval tale of conflict with the rapacious Teutonic Knights
(*Krzyżacy*, 1890).

The origins of the modern Polish nationalist movement can be
traced to the clandestine Polish League founded in Geneva by the
émigré Zygmunt Miłkowski, a veteran of the 1863–4 insurrection,
and to the secret youth organization 'Zet' created by Zygmunt
Balicki in Kraków, both in 1887. Miłkowski's nationalism,
however, contained too many liberal elements to be acceptable to

Warsaw's hard young nationalist activists such as Roman Dmowski. The movement was renamed in 1893 the National League and then, in 1897, the National Democratic Party (nicknamed in Polish the 'Endecja'). Dmowski and his associates attacked the political passivity of the Positivists, the tri-loyalism of the conservatives, as well as all manifestations of the 'sentimental patriotism' and 'false doctrinaire humanitarianism' of the Romantic era. New strategies were needed if the Poles were to survive under foreign rule in the age of imperialism and *Realpolitik*. Without abandoning the dream of independence, the National Democrats focused on pragmatic but effectively organized political action, and developed a nationalist ideology that owed much to the new ideas of Social Darwinism. A naturalist by education, Dmowski was attracted to the idea, best expressed in his book *Thoughts of a modern Pole* (1902), that a struggle for survival existed among states and national groups, and that conflict had a vital functional role in strengthening the identity and resilience of a nation. The ethical values of the individual, Balicki argued in turn in his *National egoism and ethics* (1903), had to be subordinated to the collective national interest.

By moderating their early social radicalism, which had initially alarmed many wealthy Poles, the National Democrats made impressive strides in the Kingdom, winning considerable middle-class and artisan support. Their skilful propaganda campaigns and educational activities in the countryside also brought them many peasant adherents, just as their gymnastic societies and youth organizations attracted many youngsters. By emphasizing their opposition to socialism, the National Democrats were able to attract many members of the Catholic clergy, although in the Kingdom the party's relationship with the Church was not always harmonious. The anti-German stance of the ND party also enabled it to extend its influence in Poznania and among the industrial workers of Upper Silesia where the local ND leader Wojciech Korfanty attained prominence. The ND attitude to the non-Polish nationalities in the east, especially to the Ukrainians in Galicia, was uncompromising: they had to submit to cultural and linguistic polonization or had to prove their own claim to nationhood in an uneven political and economic battle with the Poles. Hardly surprisingly, anti-Semitism became a key element in the ND ideology. The Jews were depicted not just as a prominently visible alien religious-cultural entity, but also as an economic and elemental threat, all the more menacing through their influence on Polish intellectual life, to the creation of a strong integrated and ethnically based Polish nation. It was all a categorical repudiation of the early Romantic vision of a pluralist Poland bringing freedom to all its national and ethnic groups, and as such horrified Polish conservatives and left-wing democrats alike. Nevertheless, the National Democrats were to succeed in inculcating xenophobic attitudes among numerous Poles who were at this time acquiring a semblance of political awareness and a sense of their national identity.

The modern Polish populist or peasant movement made its gradual appearance in Galicia in the mid-1870s. Much of the early leadership was provided by Stanisław Stojałowski, a priest with a considerable flair for demagogy who tried to instil among the peasants of Galicia the virtues of self-reliance, economic co-operation and civic patriotism. The sight of Stojałowski entering Kraków in 1883 at the head of a 12,000-strong peasant rally to commemorate the bicentenary of Sobieski's victory over the Turks outside Vienna must have amazed anyone still remembering the jacquerie of 1846. But Stojałowski's methods soon met with the strong disapproval of state and church authorities alike, and his influence waned. More lasting proved the efforts of Bolesław Wysłouch, an exile from Russian Poland, who as a student in St Petersburg had been associated with Russian populists and later with Polish socialists in Warsaw, and who had since settled in Lwów. In his journals, in the late 1880s, Wysłouch attacked the conservatism of the Stańczyks and outlined the vision of a prosperous, fully politicized and nationally conscious peasantry as the basis for a future democratic Polish state that would embrace all ethnic Polish lands and which would recognize the national rights of the Ukrainians and of other peoples in the east. With his indefatigable wife Maria and his talented follower Jan Stapiński, Wysłouch launched his political peasant party in Rzeszów in 1895. Although its anticlericalism brought it into conflict with the Catholic Church, the new party successfully entered Galician political life, and gradually widened its ambitions; in 1903 it adopted the title of the Polish Peasant Party (the PSL).

The response of the Catholic Church to the new social conditions and to the accompanying ideological ferment varied in the different regions of the country. As already indicated, the *Kulturkampf* had strengthened the link between Polishness and Catholicism in Prussian Poland. In Galicia the Church's privileged position in public life and its long hostility to independent political action among the peasantry militated at first against the emergence of a priest–peasant solidarity of the Poznanian type. Although the clergy here were heavily involved in the rural temperance movement, it was only during the first decade of the twentieth century that the Church hierarchy modified its negative attitude to the populist movement.

Despite a welcome general thaw in tsarist policy towards the Kingdom after the accession of Tsar Nicholas II in 1894, the scope for open social and educational work by the Church in Russian Poland was hampered by the authorities until 1905. Considerable help to the rural and urban poor was provided by worker-nuns, who wore ordinary clothes, lived privately or at home, and thereby concealed their membership of officially banned religious orders. The Church's involvement in social work was encouraged by Pope Leo XIII's encyclical 'Rerum Novarum' (1891) which recognized the rights of workers to form trade unions and to receive fair pay. It was a belated but significant response by the Vatican to the problems of modern industrial society and to the threat of godless socialism. Out of this arose in the Polish lands a Church-sponsored Christian political-social movement which promoted social harmony; it struck roots especially in Prussian Poland and, not surprisingly, was to find much common ground with the programme of Dmowski's National Democrats.

The outbreak of the Russo-Japanese war in February 1904 and the Russian Revolution of 1905 brought out in sharp relief the political and social divisions in the Kingdom; like an X-ray, the Revolution illuminated starkly the new realities that had arisen in Russia's Polish lands since 1864. All political groupings expected some benefits for Poland from Russia's discomfort in the Far East. Conservative elements among the Kingdom's wealthy classes formed a Party of Realistic Politics, and hoped that their public loyalty to the tsar would be rewarded with religious, linguistic and legal concessions. Dmowski's NDs hoped for a fair degree of autonomy. The PPS, on the other hand, as the inheritor of the Romantic insurrectionary tradition, started preparations for an uprising. To seek assistance against Russia Piłsudski even travelled to Japan, only to discover that Dmowski had preceded him there and had helped to dissuade the Japanese from sponsoring a Polish revolt against Russia. Nevertheless, Piłsudski did return with some funds and arms to equip PPS fighting squads. Tension continued to grow in the Kingdom. The war disrupted trade, brought a fall in industrial production, and increased unemployment. The situation was exacerbated by a poor harvest and widespread opposition to the mobilization for the Russian army. Demonstrations became more frequent, and PPS squads started regular shoot-outs with the police. News of 'Bloody Sunday' on 22 January 1905, when tsarist troops fired into a procession of unarmed workers outside the Winter Palace in St Petersburg, electrified opinion throughout the Kingdom, which was soon paralysed by a month-long general strike of industrial workers. Students and pupils boycotted Russian schools and demanded the restoration of Polish in educational institutions. The peasants, increasingly aware of their nationality and responsive to political militancy, also agitated for the wider use of the Polish language in public administration.

In April 1905 the tsarist government introduced religious toleration and rescinded some of the restrictions on the use of local languages. Worker protests, inspired by the socialist parties, continued regardless. Even agricultural labourers stopped work and demanded higher pay. In June an armed workers' uprising gripped Łódź, resulting in the loss of hundreds of lives. An all-Russian railway strike in October led to a general strike throughout the empire, plunging Russia further into revolutionary chaos. Disorder spread in the Kingdom, and the scale of terrorist attacks on tsarist officials and policemen approached that of 1863. The gulf between the militant PPS and the pragmatic NDs widened as a result, and then degenerated into mutual hatred. The NDs condemned the unequal struggle against the tsarist regime as grossly irresponsible, and formed their own worker organizations and fighting squads to oppose the socialists. The revolution in Russian Poland was turning into a civil war. The conservative Realists and the Catholic hierarchy, led by the archbishop of Warsaw Wincenty Popiel, increasingly felt obliged to look to the tsarist government for the preservation of the threatened social order. Tsar Nicholas II's October Manifesto, promising political liberalization and the introduction of a Russian parliament (the Duma) gave heart to the NDs and to the Realists in their hope that the restoration of a Polish administration would calm tempers in the Kingdom and weaken the forces of socialism; it was a calculation very reminiscent of Wielopolski in the early 1860s. But the Russian authorities were not prepared to make any substantial political concessions to the Poles; a delegation of ND and Realist leaders returned empty-handed from St Petersburg. On 11 November martial law was introduced in the Kingdom. Political polarization in Russia continued as the future of the revolution hung in the balance. On the heels of the workers' uprising in Moscow in December, the PPS made another armed bid to overthrow the tsarist regime in the Kingdom, and to transform the revolution into a national uprising. But events were slowly turning in favour of the authorities.

The Russian army, which in the main remained loyal to the tsar, proceeded to crush the remaining pockets of resistance within the Russian Empire. Moderate elements in the Kingdom, as in Russia proper, remained willing to participate in the new constitutional order promised by the tsar. Fissures emerged within the PPS: between the young left-wingers ready to seek benefits for Poland within a wider revolutionary settlement in Russia, and the 'elders' under Piłsudski, with his paramilitaries, who continued to press for an independent socialist Poland. In November 1906 the PPS formally split into the 'Revolutionary Fraction' under Piłsudski, and the 'Left', which then gravitated to the SDKPiL, hostile as ever to independence. Piłsudski reorganized his fighters, who continued their terrorist attacks throughout 1907, until the futility of the internecine killings between the PPS and the NDs made both sides see sense.

None of the political parties operating in the Kingdom gained their full objectives during the revolutionary turmoil. Tsarism had survived, the Kingdom's status was not altered, and martial law remained. The animosities and hatreds exacerbated by the revolution left their poison in Polish society. On the other hand, 1905 did bring about important benefits to the Poles under Russian rule. Workers' pay and conditions improved, trade unions were legalized, and a vigorous co-operative movement was able to mushroom. The lifting of many restrictions on political, social and cultural life, and on the public use of the Polish language was welcomed by the Poles, especially in the western *gubernii* where they were again allowed to buy land. A 'Polish Circle' of fifty-five deputies, dominated by the NDs and led personally by Dmowski, was to sit in the Duma. Dmowski had every intention of using his team in parliamentary horse-trading to win further benefits for the Poles, playing a role not dissimilar to Redmond's constitutional Irish Home Rule party in Westminster. There is also no doubt that the dramatic events of 1904–7 heightened the political awareness of wider sections of the urban and rural population, and gave encouragement to the radicals. On the other hand, for many men of property and for many Catholic clergymen the attraction of the National Democrats, as a force against socialism and all revolutionary methods, grew.

The failure of the bishop of Wilno to create a broad Catholic front embracing Poles, Lithuanians and Belorussians demonstrated that new national loyalties were also at work among the population of historic Lithuania. Lithuanian political agitation in 1904–5 had won concessions for the use of the Lithuanian language in primary schools and in village administration. There were unmistakable stirrings among the Belorussians, the least advanced of the nationalities in the east, who were allowed to publish their first newspaper. Among Ukrainian radical activists in the Russian Empire there was even less interest in a Polish connection, and most preferred to co-operate with their larger Russian counterparts, especially the pro-peasant Socialist Revolutionaries and the Russian Social Democrats.

The ripple effects of the 1905 revolution in the Kingdom reached Galicia with some force, encouraging the left-wing parties to attack the conservative-dominated constitutional order. Demands for democratizing the Austrian electoral system were successful: in 1907 universal male suffrage was introduced for elections to the central

27   A hunting party in the Grodno *guberniya*, 1908. Local Polish gentry gather at Wężowszczyzna, the home of Stanisław Żórawski, east of Grodno (today Hrodna in Belarus). Despite tsarist repression during the nineteenth century, about 60 per cent of land in historic Lithuania was still in Polish hands in 1914. The world of the Polish aristocracy and gentry in this area finally came to an end with the Soviet invasion in 1939.

Austrian parliament in Vienna. But there were strings attached. The NDs, who had established themselves as a major party in Galicia in 1905, secured the continuation of Polish influence in east Galicia by the creation there of two-member constituencies. Further attempts to abolish the class-based system of electoral colleges in elections to the Galician Sejm in Lwów were bogged down until 1914 in complex political horse-trading, made all the more acrimonious by the rise in Polish and Ukrainian nationalist passions. In 1908 the viceroy, Count Andrzej Potocki, was assassinated by a Ukrainian student, while in 1913 his moderate successor, the history professor Michał Bobrzyński, was forced to resign by an ND-led campaign for promoting reconciliation between the two communities. In 1913 the NDs succeeded in splitting the peasant movement, winning over its right wing (PSL-Piast) led by Wincenty Witos. The left-wing peasant group now veered towards Piłsudski's pro-independence socialists. It was yet another contributory factor to the continuing polarization of Polish politics in a period that witnessed increasing international tension over the Balkans and ominous talk of a general European war.

How the Poles should react to the growing likelihood of a conflict between Austria-Hungary, supported by Germany, and Russia inevitably came to prey on Polish political thinking. Several conflicting strategies emerged, based on different geopolitical calculations and ideological preferences, and shaped by contrasting experiences of life in Austrian and Russian Poland. Many of Galicia's conservatives and democrats, acutely conscious that only in Austria did the Poles enjoy full political and cultural freedoms, favoured the so-called 'Austro-Polish Solution'; in the event of war, the former Congress Kingdom would be attached to Galicia, to form the third component of a triune Austro-Hungarian-Polish state. However, the increasingly enlivened political and intellectual climate in Galicia also encouraged more adventurous concepts. The Young Poland (Młoda Polska) movement in literature and the arts, of which the most outstanding and original representative in Kraków was Stanisław Wyspiański, issued a neo-Romantic challenge to the complacency and conservatism of Galicia's traditional elite. The impact of Wyspiański's dramas, with their blend of mystical visions and national myths, was electrifying. In his historical play *November night* (1904), set in Warsaw in 1830, Wyspiański utilized the Greek legend of Demeter and Persephone to produce a powerful poetic expression of faith in Poland's rebirth. The acquisition in 1905 by the Galician authorities of the former royal castle of Wawel (the 'Polish Acropolis'), hitherto used as an Austrian army barracks, and its subsequent restoration to its former glory, was not without symbolic significance.

It was therefore hardly surprising that it was in Galicia, where he had moved in 1908, that Piłsudski found many students and youngsters responsive to his charismatic appeal and ready to join his paramilitary riflemen formations which he was able to organize with the tacit approval of the Austrian military authorities. Piłsud-

28 Stanisław Wyspiański (1869–1907). Self-portrait, 1902. Playwright, poet, painter, designer of furniture and textiles, and an innovator in the graphic arts, Wyspiański was the most outstanding and versatile artist of the neo-Romantic Young Poland movement in literature and the arts. Creator of modern Polish drama, his plays drew on tragic episodes in Polish history and on ancient Greek myths. Wyspiański's artistic life was closely associated with the city of Kraków.

ski's flirtation with Marxism was coming to an end; he was now studying Napoleon and Clausewitz, and preparing for the moment when he could assume the mantle of Poland's military liberator. The riflemen's role was enhanced when they were recognized as the military wing of a broad pro-independence association, formed in 1912. This included representatives of most of Galicia's left-wing parties and PPS-controlled groups in the Kingdom. In the event of

war, Piłsudski's 10,000 riflemen were to fight alongside the Austrians, but above all they were to promote an uprising in Russian
Poland and, ultimately, to provide the nucleus of a future Polish
army. In such a climate the influence of the internationalist left was
weakening across Poland.

Diametrically opposed to Piłsudski stood Dmowski, who argued
in 1908 that German imperialism, and not tsarist Russia, posed the
fundamental threat to the survival of the Polish nation. He considered it unlikely that an independent Polish state would emerge out
of a major European war; the most realistic solution, in the short
run, was the reunification of all Polish lands as an autonomous unit
under the tsar. Dmowski's appeal for Russo-Polish reconciliation,
and his endorsement of neo-Slavism (with its emphasis on the
equality of all Slavs) echoed some of the ideas of Adam Czartoryski
a century earlier. And like Czartoryski, Dmowski discovered that it
was not easy to win over to his 'realistic' programme either Russian
officialdom or indeed many of his own fellow countrymen. The
Russian government under the premiership of Stolypin and his
successors was at that very moment pursuing nationalist policies
against many of the minorities of the western borderlands, including Jews, Finns and Poles. If anything, the behaviour of the
Russian authorities was a slap in Dmowski's face: in 1907 the size
of the Polish representation in the Duma was cut by two-thirds,
and appeals for Polish autonomy were rejected. In 1911 local
elected councils (*zemstva*) were finally introduced in the western
gubernii, but on the basis of a restricted franchise that favoured
ethnic Russians; Russian officials were also given disproportionate
voting rights in the municipal councils introduced in the Kingdom
in 1913. And 1912 proved to be a particularly bad year for Russo-
Polish relations: the region of Chełm was detached from the
Kingdom and incorporated administratively and legally into the
empire as a new Russian *guberniya*; the Russian state purchased
the Warsaw–Vienna railway and dismissed many of its Polish
employees. The recently completed Orthodox cathedral of St Alexander Nevsky, in the very centre of Warsaw, already provided a
monumental symbol of Russia's domination of the 'Vistula Land'.

In such circumstances, Dmowski's geopolitical calculations
seemed to make little sense. Many of his disenchanted younger and

more radical followers seceded from the NDs and gravitated towards Piłsudski. To counter this serious haemorrhage from his movement, Dmowski turned increasingly, from 1911 onwards, to anti-Semitic propaganda. His call for an economic boycott of Jewish shops met a favourable response among large sections of the Kingdom's lower middle classes, although it alienated enough voters for him to lose his seat (representing Warsaw) in the 1912 Duma election. Yet for all their reverses the NDs remained the largest political movement in the Kingdom, with tentacles reaching far beyond, and with a claim to a monopoly on Polish patriotism.

Dmowski's anti-Germanism found an exceptionally fertile soil in Prussian Poland, where the German–Polish struggle over land and language resumed with extra vigour after 1902. The former was graphically illustrated by the case of the peasant Michał Drzymała, who defied a 1904 law restricting the right of the Poles to build on newly purchased land, by living in a circus caravan which he had wheeled onto his plot of land. Drzymała lost his case, but not without a legal battle that went on for many years and ended in the Prussian supreme court. Berlin's policy of promoting German settlement in the east was not always as successful as expected, with many Germans in the east even preferring to move to seek better-paid industrial jobs in western Germany. The Poles managed to hold on tenaciously to the land they had, but in the long run their prospects seemed grim: among the estate-owners and the upper bourgeoisie of Poznania and Danzig Pomerania (West Prussia) the German element was already dominant, while a government bill introduced in 1908 authorized for the first time the compulsory purchase of Polish-owned estates.

Other forms of administrative pressure were also deployed. First came the replacement of Polish with German as the language of religious instruction in primary schools. The large-scale resistance of pupils and parents, which lasted from 1901 to 1906, was eventually broken by the use of the cane, fines and even imprisonment. Numerous towns and villages received new German names, and in 1908 restrictions were placed on the use of Polish at public gatherings. Extra numbers of German civil servants and teachers were directed to Poznania, giving that province the highest ratio of state officials to the size of the population within the Reich. It was all a boon for the NDs whose influence increased in most Polish cultural and social organizations of Prussian Poland. The NDs came to dominate the Polish Circle of parliamentary deputies in the German Reichstag, and in 1912 voted against further credits for the German naval programme. The ability of the NDs to establish an active and co-ordinated political presence in all parts of Poland and in the parliaments of the three occupying empires was a remarkable achievement.

Nothing could disguise the fact that as 1914 approached the lands of the former Commonwealth were deeply divided by conflicting political preferences, ideological values and ethnic loyalties, as well as profound economic, social and legal disparities brought about by the simple fact of partition and the integration of the ex-Polish lands within three very different empires. No region of what could be considered 'Poland' was exclusively homogeneous in terms of nationality, religion or speech: there were numerous Germans in the west and north-west, large highly diversified Jewish communities in the centre and the east, and of course substantial non-Polish populations in the east. Different historical experiences accentuated local identities and created different regional flavours of Polishness. With its largest concentration of Polish-speakers, and with its traditions of conspiracy and insurrection centred on Warsaw, the primacy of Russian Poland was unquestioned. It was here that Polish Romanticism and Positivism first appeared as well as Polish socialism and modern nationalism as mass movements. Yet despite its largely archaic social order, Galicia's role as the centre of free political and cultural expression could not be under-estimated. Here conspirators and exiles from Russian Poland could find refuge; here Poles of both sexes from all parts of the partitioned country could study in Polish universities; here great national anniversaries, such as the 500th anniversary of the Polish victory over the Teutonic Knights at the battle of Grunwald (1410), could be publicly celebrated. Here too the Poles gained the widest experience of parliamentary government (of a specific Austrian variety) and developed a native class of professional civil servants and educationalists which would play a crucial role in independent Poland after 1918. In their turn, the Poles of Prussia were economically hardened and socially disciplined through their exposure to and confrontation with Prussian rule.

The trappings of modern civilization, in the shape of electric trams, luxury hotels, telephones (first introduced in Warsaw and Łódź in 1883), or Parisian fashion, could be observed in all major cities of partitioned Poland. The cinema too was making inroads in the provinces. On the other hand, in the central and eastern regions there were overcrowded urban slums in which Gentile and Jewish families eked out a miserable daily existence. There was poverty and disease in the countryside. The ratio of one doctor per 800 people in the larger towns and one per 30,000 in the rural districts is just one indicator of the deep contrasts in the former Kingdom. In fact, an unmistakable civilizational faultline could be traced between the more advanced territories of the German Reich and those within the Austrian and Russian Empires. In terms of levels of literacy, agricultural and industrial productivity, urban infrastructures, and the general standard of living, Prussian Poland outclassed the other regions. At the same time it was in Prussian Poland that clerical and National Democrat influences were strongest; ironically, it was also in Poznania that the percentage of the Jewish population was the lowest of all regions of historic Poland.

The different standards and quality of public administration in the three parts of Poland also helped to shape different cultures of civic behaviour. In Russian Poland the wholesale evasion of government rules and regulations, as an expression of contempt for the tsarist regime, was proverbial; it was a habit that was to weigh heavily on life in restored Poland after 1918. In one anecdote among many, a Jewish merchant living near the meeting point of the three empires complained that German customs officials never took bribes, that the Russians always did, and that with the Austrians it was never quite certain. Different lifestyles also generated popular inter-regional prejudices; jokes abounded about 'Galician misers', about 'dopey Poznanians', or about Warsaw's notorious 'tricksters'. The mutual distrust between the neighbouring industrial communities of Upper Silesia (in Prussia) and the Dąbrowa basin (in Russian Poland) continues to be reflected to the present day in the intense hostility between the football clubs of the two regions.

Yet for all the regional and social differences, there were also strong cohesive cultural forces at work. Despite the absence of a Polish state, Polish national consciousness had spread widely since 1864 among the Polish-speaking sections of the urban and rural population. The growing emphasis on an ethnic-linguistic national identity meant, however, that Polish influence was on the retreat in the east, that it was consolidating in the centre, and that it was making some gains in the west. On the eve of the First World War about 15.5 million Polish-speakers occupied a relatively compact area of settlement in the basin of the Vistula and Warta rivers, and along the upper Oder. A further 1.3 million lived in eastern Galicia, constituting a third of that area's population, and perhaps 2 million Poles lived scattered along the length and breadth of Russia's western *gubernii*, with a substantial concentration in the Wilno area.

The Poles' distinct sense of nationality was fostered by extensive cultural bonds which transcended the state frontiers and reached wider sections of society. A single literary language and a common literary tradition, dating back to the sixteenth century, linked all educated Poles, irrespective of where they lived. Poems, novels, plays and works of scholarship criss-crossed the borders. In one way or another literacy was growing among the masses. A vivid example of the existence of a single Polish reading public was the simultaneous serialization in 1911 of Sienkiewicz's best-selling adventure story *W pustyni i w puszczy* (In desert and wilderness) in Polish-language newspapers of Warsaw, Wilno, Poznań and Lwów. The lives of great poets and writers were celebrated with festivities in the major cities of Austrian and Russian Poland: in 1898, on the centenary of his birth, statues of the great Romantic bard Adam Mickiewicz were erected in Warsaw, Kraków and Lwów. The Polish universities and other institutions of higher learning in Kraków and Lwów attracted and brought together students from all parts of Poland. Journalists, physicians, scientists and musicians attended professional gatherings spanning all regions of the country. The impressive development of historical scholarship and scientific research; the existence of a diverse press and of a lively theatre scene; the emergence of a native cinematography; the musical accomplishments of Karol Szymanowski and of Ignacy

29 The Teatr Miejski (Municipal Theatre) in Lwów (L'viv) in Galicia. Built in 1897–1900, it was one of the most modern theatres in contemporary Europe, and was one of the great centres of Polish drama in the early twentieth century, although it never equalled Kraków in this respect. Among the better-known actors and actresses who made their debut or appeared on its stage were Ludwik Solski and Helena Modrzejewska (known as Modjeska in the English-speaking world).

Paderewski; the literary achievements of Henryk Sienkiewicz (Nobel Prize in 1905), of Stefan Żeromski, or of Władysław Reymont (Nobel Prize in 1924), not to mention the bohemian artistic milieu of Kraków, all provide compelling evidence of a creative cultural vibrancy during the two decades or so before 1914.

And despite the Roman Catholic Church's potentially divisive leanings towards the National Democrats, traditional Catholicism played an important integrating role in Polish society, still predominantly rural and in the main conventionally pious. Without belittling the existence of well-established but relatively small

30 Our Lady of Ostra Brama (Aušros Vartų Madona) in Wilno (Vilnius),
photographed in 1927. The icon was painted by an unknown local artist
around 1620–30, and was probably based on a sixteenth-century Flemish
print. The cult of the Ostra Brama Madonna started in the second half of
the eighteenth century, and has since spread throughout Poland, Lithuania
and Belorussia. The Madonna is venerated by Roman and Greek
Catholics, and Orthodox alike.

Polish-speaking Protestant, Moslem or Armenian communities in
some areas of the country, it was Roman Catholicism which high-
lighted most Poles' difference from the predominantly Protestant
Prussians and Orthodox Russians, not to mention the unassimi-
lated bulk of the Yiddish-speaking Jewish population. Polish
hymns and carols, religious festivals, and the intensely moving

atmosphere of the Christmas Eve supper held in most Polish homes all promoted powerful emotional bonds. These were reinforced at a popular level by the annual participation of hundreds of thousands of people from all parts of Poland in pilgrimages to the shrine of the Black Madonna in Częstochowa, to that of Our Lady of Ostra Brama (Aušros Vartų Madona) in Wilno, and to many other lesser centres of Marian devotion.

In the realm of culture Poland certainly existed, although very few ordinary Poles realistically expected the early arrival of reunification and independence. As the clouds of war gathered over Europe in July 1914, few contemporaries could have foreseen the extensive human losses, the large-scale material destruction, and the unexpected political vicissitudes that this disparate nation would soon experience.

6

Independence regained and lost,
1914–1945

The outbreak of the First World War created an unprecedented situation in the Polish lands. For the first time since the destruction of the old Polish-Lithuanian Commonwealth the three partitioning powers (or their successor states) were now at war with each other: on the one side Germany and Austria-Hungary (the Central Powers), and on the other Russia in alliance with France and Great Britain (the Entente). Some patriots in the previous century had considered that an independent Poland could only emerge out of a great European war. Yet there was nothing inevitable about Polish independence. Although both sides in the war were to make general appeals to their Polish populations, for neither of them was Polish independence initially a war aim. However, by the end of 1918 the core of an independent Polish state had come into being, made possible by the unexpected collapse of the three eastern empires, and by the readiness of the Poles to exploit this advantageous situation.

The outbreak of the war found the Poles bitterly divided. The anti-Russian Piłsudski was the first to act, anxious to establish a distinct Polish military presence in the war with Austrian permission. The incursion of his riflemen into the former Kingdom in August 1914 ended in a fiasco; the local population was unmoved by the appeal to rise against the Russians. As a result Piłsudski had to submit his legions to stricter Austrian control. The legions' subsequent exploits against the Russians on the Galician front were to sow the seeds of a legend which was to elevate Piłsudski to the status of Poland's man of Providence. But at the turn of 1914–15 Piłsudski's cause seemed unpromising. Not only were the National Democrats hostile to Piłsudski's anti-Russian campaign but they also welcomed the manifesto of the Russian commander-in-chief Grand Duke Nicholas Nicholaevich of 14 August 1914 which called, albeit in vague and semi-religious language, for a reunified autonomous Poland under the tsar. Indeed, the prevailing mood of the population in the Kingdom was at first pro-Russian. The Russians even created a volunteer Polish force of their own to counteract Piłsudski's legions.

The first year of the war brought no significant political gains for the Poles, but much suffering and destruction. Conscripted in their hundreds of thousands into the three fighting armies, the Poles found themselves killing each other for the tsar and for the two kaisers. The eastern front ran across historic Polish lands, whose economic resources were ruthlessly exploited by the warring sides. The occupation of the whole of the former Kingdom by the Central Powers in August 1915 altered the situation dramatically. The century-old Russian occupation of Warsaw ended, while Dmowski and the leadership of the ND and of the Realist parties left for Petrograd; there they continued their thankless task of lobbying the tsarist government to declare itself more resolutely on the issue of Poland. Frustrated by the lack of progress, Dmowski left Russia in November 1915 to campaign in Britain and France. In the meantime the Germans embarked on wooing the Poles of the Kingdom with significant concessions: the use of the Polish language was permitted in local government, in the courts, and especially in education, and a Polish university and polytechnical institute were reopened. The idea of a Habsburg kingdom of Poland was briefly floated in Vienna, but the Austrians finally gave way to Berlin's proposal for a small puppet Polish state under German control which could provide the German war machine with Polish cannon-fodder. On 5 November 1916 the German and Austrian emperors issued a decree proclaiming the creation of a Polish constitutional monarchy. This kingdom still had no fixed borders and no monarch, while its Provisional Council of State was granted merely consultative powers. Nevertheless a breakthrough had been made. Piłsudski agreed to head the new kingdom's military department, but insisted that the formation of a regular Polish army had to be conditional on the creation of a genuine Polish state. This the Germans were not prepared to accept at this stage.

Although ousted from their Polish lands, the Russians were encouraged by the western allies to respond to the German initiative. On 1 January 1917 Nicholas II announced as a war aim the restoration of a free and reunited Poland in union with Russia. The bartering for Poland's future took a further step when the February Revolution toppled the Romanov dynasty. Both the Petrograd Soviet and the Russian Provisional Government, encouraged by the Polish liberal Aleksander Lednicki, declared their support for an independent Poland, but left the issue of borders to a future Russian Constituent Assembly. The Provisional Government not only permitted the Poles in Russia to organize their own military formations but also agreed to the creation of a Polish army in France to fight on the side of the Entente. Now that their Russian ally had publicly endorsed Polish independence, both France and Britain no longer felt restrained in their attitude to the Polish Question and recognized Dmowski's Polish National Committee (established in Paris in August 1917) as an 'official Polish organization'.

While the prospect now appeared of Poland becoming, at least on paper, a member of the Entente, the realities in the country were still determined by the Central Powers. The refusal of Piłsudski and most of his legions to take an oath of 'military brotherhood' with the armies of the Central Powers ruined Berlin's plan to raise a 'polnische Wehrmacht', and obliged the Germans to raise their bids in the Polish stakes. Piłsudski was imprisoned for his defiance, but on 12 September 1917 the Central Powers bestowed on their Polish Kingdom the equivalent of 'home rule': a three-man Regency Council was created with powers to appoint a government with full control of educational and judicial affairs, as well as a partially elected legislative body. There was still no king. On the Regency Council sat three highly respectable figures: the archbishop of Warsaw Aleksander Kakowski, Prince Zdzisław Lubomirski and Count Józef Ostrowski. But no sooner had the Regency Council been established when the political and military landscape in eastern Europe went through another convulsion brought about by

31   The Polish National Committee in Paris, 1918. Roman Dmowski is
seated in the centre front. On the left is Count Maurycy Zamoyski, the
largest landowner in Poland, and on the right is Erazm Piltz, a conservative
politician and publicist who had lived in St Petersburg. The Committee
acted as the official Polish delegation at the peace conference at Versailles,
where it pressed for the weakening of German power in the east. Although
Dmowski was one of Poland's leading political figures, he held high office
only once, as foreign minister in 1923.

the Bolsheviks' seizure of power in Petrograd and their readiness to
sign a separate peace with the Central Powers. As the former
Russian Empire disintegrated, German priorities and tactics in the
east changed, to the marked disadvantage of their puppet Polish
Kingdom. Berlin recognized Ukrainian and Lithuanian statehood,
while the Austrians also agreed to create out of eastern Galicia a
separate imperial Ukrainian crownland within the Dual Monarchy.
The treaty of Brest-Litovsk with Bolshevik Russia, signed on 3
March 1918, confirmed the total victory of the Central Powers in
the east. In view of Berlin's aims to extend the eastern frontier of
the Reich into formerly Russian Poland, it was clear that what

remained of the Polish Kingdom would end up as little more than a dependency of a German-dominated *Mitteleuropa*.

Poland's fate did not rest, however, entirely in German hands. The energetic campaigns led by Dmowski and Paderewski on both sides of the Atlantic in the cause of Polish independence were having a marked impact on governments and public opinion alike. The inclusion of the demand for the restoration of an independent Poland with access to the sea in Woodrow Wilson's Fourteen Points of January 1918 was highly significant. The treaty of Brest-Litovsk, which took Russia out of the war, and the failure of the great German offensive in the West in March to May 1918 removed whatever reservations the Entente Powers had with regard to Poland. On 3 June 1918 the restoration of an independent Poland was officially endorsed as a war aim by the Entente. Not that the Poles were passively awaiting developments: an anti-German Polish army in Russia was 30,000 men strong, while the Polish army in France under General Józef Haller attracted thousands of volunteers, many from Polish communities in America, and fought alongside the western allies in France.

With the evident exhaustion of Germany and Austria-Hungary, and with the growing prospect of independence, the struggle for political power in Poland resumed with intensity between the pro-independence left and the National Democrats. The NDs, however, only brought ridicule on themselves by an inept attempt to seize power from the Regency Council which was in any case trying to wriggle out from German tutelage. The situation was further complicated by the disintegration of Austria-Hungary at the end of October. Local Poles took control of parts of Teschen Silesia and of western Galicia. In Lublin a pro-independence left-wing People's Republic, led by the socialist Daszyński and supported by Piłsudski's allies, was proclaimed on 6–7 November as a rival to the Regency Council in Warsaw. Workers' councils appeared in the Dąbrowa basin and other industrial centres. The outbreak of revolution in Germany, the creation of a socialist government in Berlin on 9 November, and the all-important decision of the German garrison to evacuate Warsaw removed the remaining obstacles to independence. In December the Poles of Poznania took up arms and wrested the control of their province from the Germans.

The three empires that had ruled Poland in 1914 were no more; the unbelievable had happened. But a single Poland still had to be created out of the disparate regions and out of the conflicting political and social forces that were now in the open. Piłsudski's return from German captivity on 10 November provided the catalyst for the dramatic events of the following days. His role proved providential. His legendary exploits as a fighter for national freedom, his left-wing background yet his readiness to rise above party factionalism, and his sixteen-month spell in German captivity had earned him wide support among a population desperate to escape wartime privations yet euphoric about the imminence of independence. On 11 November the German troops in Warsaw allowed themselves to be disarmed. On the same day (celebrated since as Poland's Independence Day) the Regency Council appointed Piłsudski commander-in-chief of its armed forces. Three days later, before dissolving itself, it conferred on Piłsudski the authority of head of state with almost dictatorial powers. On 18 November the People's Republic in Lublin recognized Piłsudski's authority, while the new head of state nominated the socialist Jędrzej Moraczewski to lead a left-wing government. Piłsudski's position was very strong: it had been sanctioned by the conservative Regents and enjoyed the undisputed support of the pro-independence socialist and peasant parties. To win even wider popular support for the reborn state, Moraczewski's government introduced a wide package of social reforms and welfare measures, and an eight-hour working day; it also promised compulsory land reform. Yet all was not harmony. The NDs resented Piłsudski's authority, and the predominantly ND-run administration in Poznania still refused to recognize the left-wing government in Warsaw. The SDKPiL and its allies, who merged in December 1918 to form the Communist Workers' Party of Poland, refused to recognize Polish independence altogether, and put their faith in local workers' councils and the imminence of a Bolshevik-led universal revolution.

Industry was paralysed and over four-fifths of industrial workers were unemployed, communications were severely ruptured, agricultural production had fallen dramatically, and poverty and malnutrition stalked the land. About 400,000 Poles had perished while serving in the three imperial armies. The new state, which now consisted of the former Congress Kingdom and western Galicia, also faced the burning and intractable issue of frontiers. Fighting raged for control of Lwów (L'viv) with the West Ukrainian Republic which had established itself in eastern Galicia. The situation in the borderlands between Poland and Russia was ominously fluid as the Red Army advanced west in the wake of the German forces retreating from Russia (in accordance with the November 1918 Armistice provisions), and as local national movements laid conflicting claims to the region. The precise delimitation of the boundary between Poland and Germany had to await the decision of the Versailles peace conference.

The Entente Powers still recognized the Paris-based and ND-led Polish National Committee, and not the government in Warsaw, as Poland's official representation. It was clearly apparent to Piłsudski that national unity, so vital if Poland was to exert any effective influence at the peace conference, could only be achieved by a compromise with the NDs, and consolidated by early democratic parliamentary elections. In an inspired move to ease internal tension, Piłsudski replaced Moraczewski with the eminent pianist Paderewski, who was highly respected by the NDs, as head of a non-party government of experts. The elections of January 1919, based on universal suffrage and proportional representation, produced a fragmented but relatively evenly balanced Sejm (parliament). Just over a third of the seats went to the NDs, who emerged as the single largest grouping, while about 30 per cent each went to the centre (including the peasant PSL-Piast led by Wincenty Witos) and to the Left (including the left-wing peasant parties and the socialists). The communists' appeal for a boycott of the elections was largely ignored.

On 20 February the new Sejm adopted the so-called 'small' constitution modelled on that of the French Third Republic: ministers were to be responsible to the Sejm which also elected a head of state with very limited powers. Piłsudski retained the latter post which was now shorn of effective constitutional authority; his position as commander-in-chief, however, gave him considerable influence. Indeed, the creation of a large national army within months of independence was a remarkable early achievement. In late February the restored Polish Republic was finally recognized by France, Britain and Italy. It now faced the daunting task of securing its frontiers.

Poland's western borders and its access to the sea proved to be the most contentious territorial issue at the Versailles peace conference. Dmowski's extensive claims were challenged by Lloyd George and had to be modified. The treaty of Versailles (28 June 1919) transferred outright to Poland Poznania and most of Pomerania along the lower Vistula (West Prussia), providing Poland thereby with direct if narrow access to the Baltic Sea. Some compromises had to be made: Danzig (Gdańsk), Poland's natural and historic port but with an overwhelmingly German population, became a Free City under the League of Nations and within the Polish customs area; plebiscites were to decide the future of Upper Silesia and the southern part of East Prussia.

In the south-east the Poles destroyed the West Ukrainian Republic and occupied eastern Galicia. But since the Ukrainian cause enjoyed some Entente support at the peace conferences, the province's future was by no means a closed issue. Of even greater magnitude and complexity was the question of the future western frontier of Russia, still in the throes of a civil war. The Entente, especially France, hoped in 1919 for a White victory which would restore France's earlier anti-German alliance with Russia. The NDs too, in line with Dmowski's earlier geopolitical thinking, believed in the possibility of an accommodation with a non-Bolshevik Russia. In his turn Piłsudski refused to support the Whites, whose traditional nationalism appeared more anti-Polish than the internationalism of the Bolsheviks.

There existed two conflicting visions of Poland's role in the eastern lands of the former Polish–Lithuanian Commonwealth with their complex mosaic of intermingling nationalities and religions. Overall, Polish or polonized Roman Catholics, landowners, various professionals, as well as *déclassé* petty nobles and peasants, were in a minority here, but were important economically and socially. The narrowly nationalistic NDs called for the outright annexation of Lithuania, most of Belorussia and western Ukraine, areas which they considered could be effectively absorbed within a unitary Polish state. Piłsudski and his associates, on the other hand,

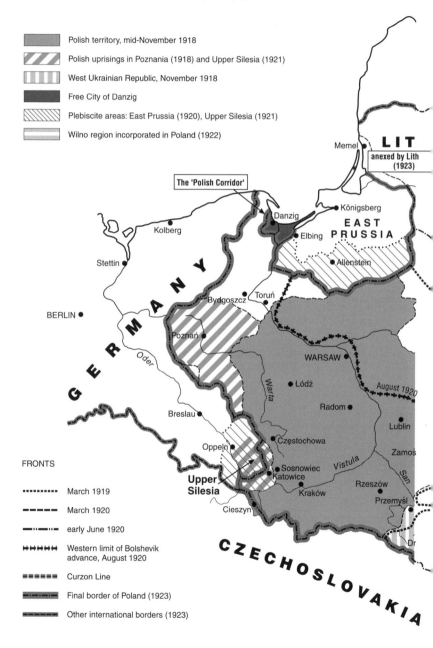

Map 8   Rebirth of the Polish state, 1918–23.

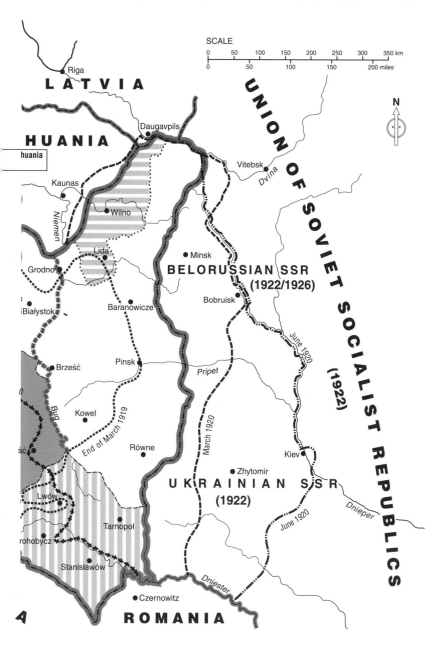

felt that there existed a rare historic opportunity to achieve wider regional security under Polish leadership against a resurgent Russia by creating an extensive east European federation, encompassing ethnic Poland, the Baltic states, Belorussia and the Ukraine. But the so-called 'Jagiellonian Idea', with reference to the vast Polish-Lithuanian realm of the late Middle Ages, could only be achieved by war. Despite ND opposition and the misgivings even of his left-wing allies, but in the light of Bolshevik intentions to transport their revolution to the West, Piłsudski won approval for his plan. Consequently, while retaining the contested east Galicia, Poland recognized the independence of the Ukraine, and formed a military alliance with the Ukrainian government of Symon Petliura which was battling against the Red Army.

The Poles and their Ukrainian ally launched their offensive on 25 April 1920; on 7 May they entered Kiev. But the euphoria proved short-lived. The Poles had underestimated Bolshevik strength and overestimated popular support in the Ukraine for Petliura. Bolshevik forces under Tukhachevsky counter-attacked in the north while the cavalry army of Budenny struck in the south. Numerous former tsarist officers, enraged by the Polish attack, rallied to the cause of 'National Bolshevism'. The Poles had to retreat. It was now Lenin's turn to implement his grand vision; over the corpse of 'bourgeois Poland' the Red Army was to bring the proletarian revolution into the heart of Europe. In the van of the Red Army travelled a committee of Polish communists, including Felix Dzerzhinsky, all set to bolshevize their country.

In the face of a possible disaster, the Polish government sought Entente mediation in the war and reluctantly accepted the so-called Curzon Line (named after the British foreign secretary) as a provisional demarcation line in the east, corresponding roughly with the eastern limit of the former Congress Kingdom. The Bolsheviks ignored the proposal and continued their advance towards the Vistula. Across western Europe and in Germany workers and trade unions protested against Polish 'aggression'. The workers and peasants of Poland did not, however, rise to welcome the Red Army. If anything, the threat of godless Bolshevism generated an outburst of patriotism. On 24 July an all-party Government of National Defence was formed in Warsaw under the premiership of

Renja → Slucka 29/7. 1919

x Boguslaw Zaleski

32   Polish cavalry in Slutsk in Belorussia, August 1919.

33   A Polish armoured train, *The General Sosnkowski*, during the Polish–
Bolshevik war, 1920. The long struggle for Poland's frontiers between
1918 and 1922 witnessed the rapid growth of the Polish Army, from 6,000
men in November 1918 to 600,000 in autumn 1919, reaching 900,000 in
July 1920. Unlike the trench war on the Western Front during the First
World War, the war between reborn Poland and Bolshevik Russia from
1919 to 1921 was one of considerable mobility over a vast area of eastern
Europe, and involved large numbers of cavalry and even armoured trains.

the peasant leader Witos and with the veteran socialist Daszyński
as deputy. Its radical programme of land reform helped to neutra-
lize Bolshevik propaganda. Thousands of volunteers, including
students and schoolboys, rallied to the colours as the Bolsheviks
approached Warsaw. It was not the French military mission under
General Weygand, whose unhelpful advice was ignored, which
turned the tide of the war, but Piłsudski's bold counter-attack on
16–18 August from the south against the over-extended Bolshevik
lines east of Warsaw. And in the last great cavalry battle of modern
warfare, involving 20,000 horsemen on each side, Budenny's army
was destroyed near Zamość. The Bolshevik rout was confirmed by
a subsequent Polish victory on the Niemen river in September.

Not since Sobieski's triumph outside Vienna in 1683 had Polish
arms met with such success; but the so-called 'Miracle on the
Vistula' was a close-run thing. What the impact of a Soviet victory

in 1920 would have been on the much-troubled societies of Germany and western Europe can only be speculation. The Poles like to think that in 1920 they saved Western Civilization from the Bolshevik hordes. In one sense they certainly repaid some of their debt for the Entente's victory over Germany which had made Polish independence initially possible in 1918. The Polish–Soviet war ended with the peace of Riga of 18 March 1921. It established a frontier well to the east of the now infamous 'Curzon Line', but Piłsudski's federal scheme, for which so much blood had been shed, lay in ruins. By the same token, Bolshevik ambitions of a European revolution had been checked. In Moscow the idea of Socialism in One Country was born, while Lenin's New Economic Policy represented a partial compromise with capitalism.

While fighting for its very survival against the Bolsheviks in the summer of 1920, the fledgling Polish state was unable to press its territorial claims effectively in southern East Prussia, where the Polish-speaking Mazurians, whose national identity was still indeterminate, voted overwhelmingly to remain in Germany rather than risk inclusion in a Bolshevik Poland. At the same time the Czechs obtained the Entente's recognition of their occupation of the disputed industrial region of Teschen (Cieszyn), a move that was to damage Polish–Czech relations during the rest of the inter-war period. The violent Polish–German dispute over Upper Silesia, one of the main industrial areas of central Europe, was not resolved until October 1921 when, following a plebiscite, the League of Nations divided the region: Poland obtained only 29 per cent of the territory but 46 per cent of the population and most of the mines and industrial plants.

The city of Wilno (Vilnius), which the new Lithuanian state claimed as its historic capital but whose population was predominantly Polish and Jewish, was seized in October 1920, with Piłsudski's unofficial authorization, by allegedly mutinous local Polish units. But Piłsudski's proposal for a bi-cantonal Lithuania (including Wilno) in a federal association with Poland was rejected both by the Lithuanians and by the Wilno regional assembly which voted in January 1922 for simple incorporation into Poland. The old multilingual Grand Duchy of Lithuania could not be recreated in an age of ethnic nationalism. Unreconciled to the loss of Wilno, the Lithuanians established a provisional capital in Kaunas, and insisted until 1938 that a formal state of war existed with Poland. Polish attempts in the 1920s to create a Baltic security zone were to suffer as a consequence.

It was only in March 1923 that the Conference of Ambassadors in Paris, acting as the executive organ of the Allied Powers, finally recognized Poland's eastern frontiers. The struggle for the frontiers had lasted for over four years, almost as long as it took to achieve a final settlement in the lands of the former Ottoman Empire. Poland's inter-war borders were no more unfair than many of those redrawn elsewhere in central and eastern Europe. Most Poles now found themselves within a Polish nation-state; nevertheless, national minorities constituted nearly a third of Poland's population of 27 million in 1921. While the western border corresponded roughly with the ethnic-linguistic division (and with Poland's pre-partition frontier), that was mostly not the case in the east, where strategic considerations were paramount. What was more worrying was that Poland had emerged as a sizeable independent state only because of the temporary weakness of Germany and Russia. Only with Latvia and Romania was Poland to maintain good neighbourly relations throughout the inter-war period. Security against Germany was provided, for the time being, by a French alliance of February 1921, but no major power was committed to defending Poland in the east. Poland's sovereignty was also restricted by international treaty obligations with regard to the legal rights of its national minorities.

A new constitution, adopted in March 1921, symbolized the consolidation of the Polish Second Republic, but also introduced what was to prove an unwieldy system of parliamentary government. Fearing Piłsudski's return to power, the NDs prevented the creation of a strong presidency. In their turn, the left-wing parties secured the introduction of proportional representation in parliamentary elections to prevent the domination of the NDs, who were the largest party. But since the Polish parliamentary scene was composed of at least eighteen parties, it was a recipe for unstable coalition government. A wide range of civil rights and political and religious freedoms was guaranteed as well as the sanctity of private property; it was clear that the land reform, so eagerly adopted in

1920 and so important in a country in which a third of all peasant holdings were under two hectares in size, was going to be a limited affair. On the other hand, the advanced social welfare provisions of 1918 were retained.

A kind of normality began to return after the political and military upheavals of the war years. The outburst of patriotic feelings in 1920 and the start of post-war reconstruction did much to dampen the earlier social tensions. The authority of the new state was also increasingly felt in most areas of national life as the previously disparate regions of the country were gradually reintegrated administratively and economically. A vigorously expanded national system of education and a national army provided two important foci for the cultivation of a supra-regional national identity. Yet the new state lacked a well-established tradition of constitutional government, while within its new borders there still functioned four different legal systems. The inheritance of three different railway systems also hampered communications. The strong regional differences, in terms of contrasting levels of economic and social development and popular literacy, remained, and were further accentuated by the existence of national minorities.

The largest minority, concentrated in the south-east and numbering over 4 million, were the Ukrainians, many of whom retained strong aspirations for their own statehood. The idea of autonomy for eastern Galicia had been mooted since 1919, but the fact that nothing was to come of it had damaging results for inter-ethnic relations. Indeed, in the early 1920s Ukrainian nationalists waged an underground war against the Polish state. Among the 1.5 million Belorussians there was social unrest. As for the Germans, many thousands had left Poland by 1921, but there remained a scattered yet economically and socially important German minority of nearly 1 million; those in the ex-German regions resented their separation from the Reich. In 1921 Poland's highly diverse Jewish population numbered about 2.2 million, of whom well over four-fifths used Yiddish as their mother tongue. While Polish national aspirations were alien to most Jews, many members of the Jewish intelligentsia were willing to co-operate with the Polish state. Assimilated Jews could be found among the ranks of Polish

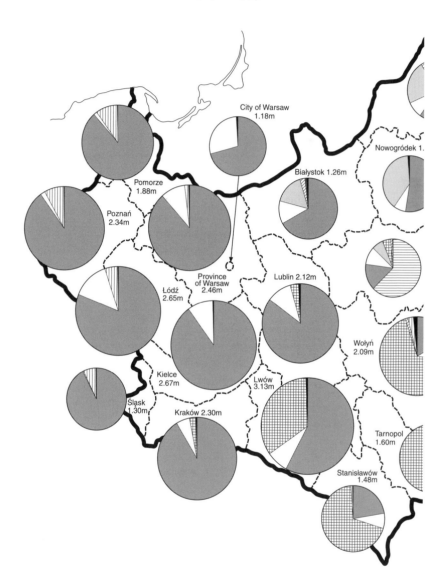

Map 9   Inter-war Poland: a land of many nationalities and faiths.
         Source: *Petit annuaire statistique de la Pologne 1939* (Warsaw, 1939).

Nationalities according to language (Polish 1931 census):
Each pie-chart on the map represents a province (*województwo*) with its population in millions. The City of Warsaw enjoyed the status of a separate province. Divisions of the pie-charts represent percentages.

Key

	Polish
	Ukrainian
	Yiddish
	Belorussian
	'Local'
	German
	Russian
	Lithuanian
	Others

Wilno 1.28m

.06m

Polesie
1.13m

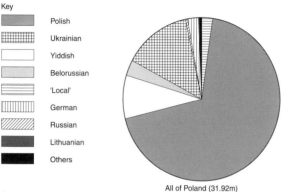

All of Poland (31.92m)

Notes

1. Ukrainian includes Ruthenian (*ruski*) which was a separate category in the census.

2. Yiddish includes Hebrew which was declared by 7.8% of the Jews, although few of them would have used it in daily life.

3. 'Local' was declared as their mother tongue by 707,000 Belorussian-speakers in Polesie.

Religious affiliations 1931

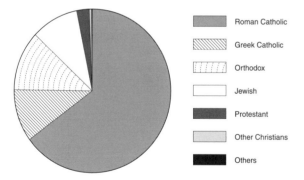

	Roman Catholic
	Greek Catholic
	Orthodox
	Jewish
	Protestant
	Other Christians
	Others

patriots, for instance the eminent historian Szymon Askenazy who from 1920 to 1923 represented Poland at the League of Nations. On the other hand the anti-Semitism propounded by the NDs did much to poison Jewish–Gentile relations, and only increased among many young Jews the attraction of communism and Zionism. The Jewish contribution to Polish life, however, whether in medicine, law or literature, was to be enormous in the inter-war period. The poet Julian Tuwim and the writer Bruno Schulz provide just two examples of a remarkable Polish–Jewish cultural osmosis.

With the achievement of independence, Polish writers, poets and artists were freed from the obligation to fight for the national cause. Some remained involved in politics, as apologists for Piłsudski and the legend of his legions, or as commentators on the lives of ordinary working people, but others embarked on the search for new forms of expression. Among the most creative were the lyrical poets of the 'Skamander' group who tackled exotic, sexual and surreal themes; amongst them stood out the painter, playwright and novelist Stanisław Ignacy Witkiewicz, known simply as Witkacy.

With the end of the national emergency of 1920–1 the NDs renewed their struggle for political domination. They toppled Witos' centre-left government in June 1921, and consolidated the forces of the right in the so-called Christian Union of National Unity, but failed to secure a majority in the parliamentary elections of November 1922. The defeat of the ND candidate in the presidential election a month later and the victory of Professor Gabriel Narutowicz, made possible by the support of the parties of the left and the centre and of the National Minorities Bloc, drove the NDs to fury. On 16 December an ND fanatic assassinated the president-elect. Only narrowly did Poland avoid an outbreak of the kind of wider violence that was raging at the time in Germany, Italy and Spain. The murder of Poland's first president brought no immediate gains to the shamed NDs, who felt obliged to draw back and meekly accept the appointment of a strong government under General Władysław Sikorski and the election as president of the veteran socialist Stanisław Wojciechowski.

The National Democrats had to acknowledge that to achieve 'a government of the Polish majority' they would have to make concessions. In May 1923 they reached a compromise agreement with Witos' centrist peasant party Piast, the second largest grouping in the Sejm, and assumed office in a coalition government led by Witos. In return for the ND offer of support for a moderate land reform, PSL-Piast moved to the right and endorsed the NDs' programme to restrict the rights of the national minorities, and to reduce Piłsudski's influence by subordinating the army to a Ministry of War. Piłsudski thereupon resigned as chief of the General Staff. But the centre-right's success was blighted by the impact of the economic depression that had started in March. Inflation wreaked general havoc. In practical terms, a peasant who had borrowed funds from the state in 1919 to buy twelve horses was able to repay his debt in August 1923 for the equivalent of one kilogram of meat. Social distress grew as well as the number of strikes, from which Piłsudski's hawks and both the constitutional and revolutionary left hoped to benefit. In an atmosphere of mounting tension, accompanied by terrorist outrages, Witos' government decided to act against the left; in October it placed striking railwaymen under military discipline. A general strike on 5 November, initiated by the socialists, led to bloody confrontations with the army and the police. Witos' government lost its parliamentary majority when Piast split over the proposed land reform, and resigned in December.

The prospect of political and economic disaster brought the main parties to their senses. The moderate non-party government that took office in December under the stern Władysław Grabski was empowered by the Sejm to restore financial stability and to come to grips with the escalating inflation; between June and December 1923 the value of the Polish mark had fallen from 71,000 to 4.3 million to the US dollar. Grabski's policy of financial retrenchment, coupled with the rigorous collection of taxes, put brakes on inflation and restored confidence. In April 1924 a new currency, the Polish złoty, was introduced. But the effectiveness of Grabski's reforms was blunted by a disastrous harvest in 1924 and the damaging tariff war started in early 1925 by Germany, with which Poland conducted half of its trade.

Indeed, associated with the German economic offensive against Poland was Gustav Stresemann's avowed intention of recovering some of the territories lost to Poland at Versailles. For General von Seeckt, the commander of the German army since 1919, the destruction of hated Poland was the ultimate objective. Already alarmed by the willingness of Weimar Germany and the USSR to co-operate at Rapallo in 1922, the Poles now observed with nervous concern the weakening of French influence after the Ruhr crisis and the international rehabilitation of Germany with a permanent seat on the Council of the League of Nations. The inviolability of Germany's western border, guaranteed at Locarno in October 1925 by the west European powers, was not extended to Germany's eastern frontier. Neither an arbitration treaty with Germany nor a much diluted Franco-Polish mutual assistance pact could conceal the reversal suffered by Poland.

At home, Grabski's government succeeded in other important areas of national life. In 1925 construction began of a new port and city in Gdynia which, unlike Danzig, was situated on sovereign Polish territory, and of a railway between Gdynia and Upper Silesia to facilitate the export of Polish coal. In February 1925 state–church relations were regularized with the signing of a Concordat which granted considerable privileges to the Roman Catholic Church in return for a government say in episcopal appointments, and for the recognition by the Vatican of Poland's new state boundaries. A moderate land reform, passed in December 1925, provided for the annual transfer of 200,000 hectares, on a voluntary basis and over a ten-year period, from large landed estates into peasant ownership. The government also came to grips with Soviet-inspired agitation along the long eastern frontier by creating a special border force and by encouraging the settlement of military colonists, although the latter were often deeply resented by ·the local non-Polish populations. Indeed, official policy towards the national minorities was hardening. A law of 1924 promoting bilingual schools led to a drastic reduction of single-language Ukrainian schools in eastern Galicia; another law in the same year banned the use of the Ukrainian language in governmental agencies.

In November 1925 the renewed economic crisis overwhelmed Grabski's administration. Alarmed by the prospect of yet another political crisis and by the mutinous rumblings among Piłsudski's

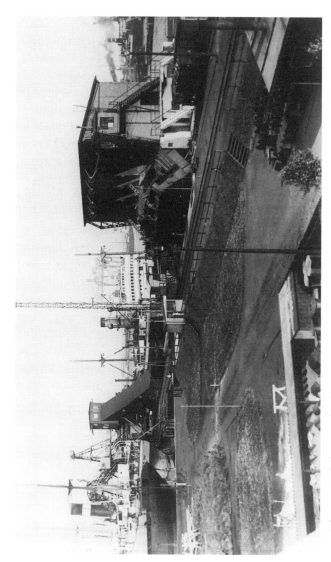

34   The new Polish port of Gdynia in the 1930s. From a fishing village of a thousand souls in 1921, Gdynia expanded to a city of 120,000 people in 1939. In the mid 1930s it overtook Danzig (Gdańsk) as the main port for Poland. In 1938 nearly four-fifths of Poland's total trade (in tonnage) and over three-fifths (in terms of value) went by sea. The so-called 'Polish Corridor' to the Baltic Sea was of vital economic importance for the inter-war Polish state.

followers in the army, the main parties patched up their differences in a grand coalition government under the even-tempered Aleksander Skrzyński, a distinguished diplomat and recent foreign minister with no formal party affiliation. But the days of Poland's young parliamentary system of government were numbered. A sense of disillusionment with the political order was growing, exacerbated by financial scandals and by a lack of consensus for dealing with the continued economic difficulties. Matters came to a head after Skrzyński's resignation on 5 May 1926 and the failure of the president to recreate Grabski's non-partisan administration. As a result the peasant leader Witos returned to office on 10 May at the head of a centre-right cabinet. But memories of Witos' disastrous administration of 1923 were still very fresh. Piłsudski now took it upon himself to save the country from what he saw as a contemptible breed of corrupt and bickering politicians. From his country retreat in Sulejówek outside Warsaw he marched on the capital on 12 May at the head of rebel army units. At a dramatic meeting on the Poniatowski bridge over the Vistula, President Wojciechowski rejected Piłsudski's unconstitutional demands for a change of government. After three days of fighting between Piłsudski's men and government troops, both the president and Witos agreed to resign. A railwaymen's strike, inspired by the socialists, prevented pro-government reinforcements from reaching Warsaw. Piłsudski's coup was welcomed by all the non-communist left, by Poland's industrialists, and by wide sections of the population, including many Jewish organizations. Only in ND-dominated Poznania were there mass protests. There were specific Polish causes and features of Piłsudski's 1926 coup, but it does provide another instance of the fragility of parliamentary institutions in much of continental Europe after the First World War.

Piłsudski had no wish to assume a public role as a dictator, preferring to deploy lesser figures to carry out his ultimate objective of introducing strong presidential government in Poland. The overawed and humiliated Sejm legalized the coup. Piłsudski's choice, the former socialist and eminent chemist Ignacy Mościcki, was elected president by the National Assembly. Kazimierz Bartel, another professor of no party affiliation, was to serve intermittently as prime minister until 1930. Until his death in 1935 Piłsudski

35   The 1926 coup. Marshal Piłsudski (fourth from left) crosses the
Poniatowski bridge into Warsaw on 12 May 1926, in the company of loyal
officers, to confront President Wojciechowski. 'For me,' declared the
Marshal, 'the legal road is closed.' He had hoped that a military
demonstration would suffice to topple Witos' centre-right government.
The fighting that ensued cost 379 lives.

retained control of the army as minister of war and as the General
Inspector of the Armed Forces.

Piłsudski's coup was carried out in the name of Sanacja, a term
used in the sense of restoring 'health' to the body politic, and which
gave the name to the political regime that continued until 1939.
With its emphasis on discipline, anti-corruption and loyalty to the
state, the Sanacja hoped to appeal to a wide cross-section of the
population, including the national minorities. Formally Poland
retained a multi-party parliamentary system, but the constitution
was modified in August 1926 by the augmentation of the president's powers to dissolve parliament and to rule by decree, and also
to determine the state budget. With no political party at his
disposal, the marshal exerted his authority indirectly through his
faithful followers within the parties of the centre and the left, and
those promoted in the armed forces and the civilian administration.

Not wishing to be beholden to the left, and determined to weaken the right, Piłsudski skilfully engineered a rapprochement with the conservative elements in Polish society: aristocratic landowners, industrialists and even the once hostile Catholic Church.

Piłsudski's regime was further strengthened by the marked improvement of the Polish economy between 1926 and 1929. The pace of cultural life also quickened, whether measured by the expansion of the press and periodicals, or by the number of radios, which increased from 120,000 in 1927 to 246,000 in 1930. Elementary education expanded with extra vigour, and social security provisions were further extended. Considering Poland's very modest economic base of 1921 these were noticeable improvements. Yet while the demand for agricultural products brought substantial gains to the peasantry, the 1925 land reform was inadequate to resolve the acute problem of rural over-population, especially in the south of the country. Alleviation continued to come in the form of large-scale emigration to the Americas, and especially to France, which alone received 320,000 Polish immigrants between 1925 and 1930; most headed for the coal-mines in the region of Lille, where their descendants still represent France's largest Polish community. The existence of only 30,000 passenger cars in 1930, representing one-ninth of Germany's car ownership on a per thousand of population basis, provides a telling index of Poland's relative poverty. The cost of maintaining Poland's armed forces, which consumed 35 per cent of total state expenditure in 1929, continued to be an unavoidable burden on a country in a precarious geopolitical position.

Conditions were now ripe for Piłsudski to consolidate his regime. Despite his aversion to party politics, the marshal realized that he needed a formal pro-government political grouping in the Sejm. The resulting Non-Party Bloc of Co-operation with the Government (BBWR), formed in early 1928, embraced individuals of diverse ideological standpoints; its two guiding principles were service to the state and loyalty to the marshal. Although the 1928 election saw the effective eclipse of the National Democrats and of Piast, the BBWR won only a quarter of the parliamentary seats, not enough to push a revision of the constitution through the Sejm. A long war of attrition now began against the opposition in the Sejm.

Jadwiga Smosarska
w filmie „Ziemia Obiecana
Wytw. „SFINKS".

36   One of the great stars of the inter-war Polish cinema: Jadwiga Smosarska (1900–1971) in a still from the 1927 film ('The promised land') *Ziemia obiecana* (see plate 23). Between 1919 and 1937 she appeared in twenty-five films, and also frequently played on stage. She was typical of many of her generation in that the war forced her into exile, in her case in the United States. She revisited Poland on several occasions after 1958 before returning for good in 1970.

To browbeat the Sejm into submission, the marshal deployed a variety of intimidatory tactics, including placing in office hard-line 'colonels' from among his close ex-legionary followers. The public declaration in July 1929 by Walery Sławek, the most ambitious of the colonels, that 'it is better to break the bones of one deputy than to bring machine guns into the streets', well reflected the incipient threat of violence. Determined to restore full parliamentary democracy, the parties of the centre and the left formed an alliance in September 1929; their cause was facilitated by the impact of the Great Depression, which by mid-1930 had brought a painful end to the recent years of relative prosperity. With the virtual paralysis of parliamentary government, the centre-left embarked on a campaign of mass public demonstrations, starting in Kraków on 29 June

1930. But it underestimated the marshal's readiness for a final confrontation.

On 25 August 1930 Piłsudski personally assumed the premiership, announced new elections for November, and on the night of 9–10 September had the opposition leaders, including Witos, arrested and incarcerated in the fortress of Brześć. Thousands of opposition activists were detained. The inability of the centre-left to establish a common front with the National Democrats, the communists and the national minorities prevented the creation of a broad movement of resistance to the regime. The elections of November 1930 finally yielded an absolute parliamentary majority of 55.6 per cent of the seats to the BBWR. The centre-left alliance altogether managed to muster only 21.9 per cent, while the NDs tailed far away with 14 per cent. The victory of the Sanacja was such that Piłsudski could afford to pass the premiership back to Sławek and to leave the country on a three-month rest cruise to Madeira.

In the meantime the Great Depression was making ever deeper cuts in the Polish economy. By 1932 industrial production had fallen to 54 per cent of the 1929 level, and in 1933 nearly a third of the industrial workforce was unemployed. The steep fall in agricultural prices brought severe hardship to the peasants. The regime's initial response to the crisis was a deflationary economic policy aimed at maintaining the value of the złoty, and the tightening of political control over the judiciary, local government and academic institutions. The arrested opposition leaders were tried in Brześć between 1931 and 1933 and either jailed or, as in the case of Witos, obliged to leave the country. A 'camp of isolation' was established at Bereza Kartuska in 1934 for the most militant critics of the regime: communists, right-wing extremists and Ukrainian nationalists.

The Sanacja under Piłsudski was a secular authoritarian system of government of a non-fascist type. The government did try to mobilize mass support for the regime, but large areas of national life remained outside its direct control: opposition political parties, many trade unions, a host of social, cultural and sporting organizations from the co-operative movement to the scouts, much of the economy and the press (although subject to limited censorship), as well as the country's many religious denominations with their charitable societies. Many of the old *szlachta* values of individualism and personal liberty remained deeply ingrained in many areas of Polish culture. The creation of a strong modern state did, however, open a multitude of careers to the intelligentsia: in the civil service, in education, or in the armed forces. Responses to the new political realities among the intellectual and artistic elite varied. Some writers, like Julian Kaden-Bandrowski, the father of the Polish political novel, endorsed the Sanacja; others, such as Witold Gombrowicz or Julian Tuwim (especially in his scathing poem 'The ball in the Opera' written in 1936), responded with acid satire. The greatest asset of the Sanacja was of course Marshal Piłsudski himself, with his brusque manner, simple lifestyle, and heavy-handed paternalism. Until his death from cancer in May 1935 he concentrated on military and foreign affairs and left the day-to-day business of government to his colonels.

Essentially Poland was still a pluralist society. Nevertheless, the scale of the Great Depression obliged the authorities to consider increasing state intervention in the economy. Some of the opposition parties, even those with a democratic pedigree, now veered towards more radical collectivist solutions to Poland's problems. In 1931 the main peasant parties united to form a single Polish Peasant Party (PSL) of 100,000 members, which adopted as its programme the expropriation, without compensation, of private landed estates. In its turn, in 1934 the PPS called for the nationalization of the major branches of the economy, and even endorsed the principle of 'the dictatorship of the proletariat' as a temporary necessity. Needless to say, the communist KPP gained new followers. The Christian Democrats, weakened by desertions to the government camp, turned towards ideas of Catholic corporatism. The National Democrats, relying increasingly on the Gentile lesser bourgeoisie, moved even further to the right; in 1932 the elderly but still active Dmowski launched the so-called Camp of Greater Poland with 250,000 members, only to see it banned by the government the following year. The appeal of fascism and of anti-Semitism was most pronounced among young radical NDs, who in 1934 formed the 'National-Radical Camp' (ONR), from which emerged the distinctly totalitarian ONR-Falanga under Bolesław

Piasecki. The grim warnings coming from Witkacy, the leading 'catastrophist' writer, about eastern totalitarianism and about the creation by contemporary civilization of a 'socially perfect, mechanized man' seemed particularly apposite in the new anti-democratic and anti-liberal climate sweeping the continent in the 1930s.

On the other hand, the Roman Catholic episcopate, led since 1926 by the calm but resolute Cardinal August Hlond, distanced itself from its earlier pro-ND tendencies. Despite the Church's good relations with the state, Hlond publicly criticized the authoritarianism creeping into government policy in the 1930s. Indeed, this period witnessed the revitalization of Polish Catholicism and the rise of the Church's moral prestige across a broad spectrum of the Polish population. The parochial system was reformed and expanded; seminaries were improved. The growth of lay Catholic organizations, such as Catholic Action and the so-called 'rosary brotherhoods', involved many millions of faithful, mostly in the rural areas; membership of Christian trade unions exceeded membership of those of the socialists. The introduction of religious instruction in schools, the creation of a Catholic university in Lublin, the appointment of inspired university chaplains, and the Church's concern for the easing of social tensions helped to weaken the anticlericalism that had been widespread among the left-wing and liberal intelligentsia before 1918, and promoted the emergence of a new open-minded Catholic intelligentsia. All this provided the roots of the Church's resilience during the ordeals that were to face it and the nation after 1939.

In the meantime, Poland's continuous search for security presented new problems, new opportunities and new traps. In July 1932 Poland signed a non-aggression treaty with the USSR which strengthened Poland's hand in responding to Hitler's rise to power. Indeed, the ideological enmity between Nazi Germany and the USSR militated against the 'spirit of Rapallo' and encouraged Piłsudski, through his new foreign minister Colonel Józef Beck, to develop a policy of 'balance' with regard to Poland's two dangerous neighbours. Increasingly apprehensive about the reliability of the French alliance and sceptical about French plans for an eastern security pact, Piłsudski decided on a direct resolution of all Polish–German problems. In his turn, Hitler was eager to separate the

Poles from the French. The ensuing Polish–German non-aggression treaty of January 1934 ended the tariff war, but equally raised French fears about Polish intentions. Piłsudski was under no illusion about Poland's vulnerability; confidentially he predicted in 1934 that Poland had gained perhaps four years of breathing space in its relations with Germany.

In view of Piłsudski's rapidly declining health and the growing political radicalism in the country, the Sanacja moved to give a new legal framework to the post-1926 system of government. A new constitution, introduced in April 1935, emphasized the primacy of the state and endowed the president, who would now be elected by a small electoral college, with enormous powers. By the same token the powers of the Sejm were reduced, while a subsequent electoral law abolishing proportional representation nearly halved the number of deputies, and gave the authorities a major say in the selection of parliamentary candidates. The election of the Senate ceased to be by universal and direct voting.

Marshal Piłsudski did not live long enough to assume the new-style presidency, which had been the original idea. Despite the highly controversial nature of his regime, Piłsudski's death on 12 May 1935 was deeply felt by the majority of the population which recognized his enormous contribution to the struggle for independence. But his death deprived the ruling elite of its main focus of unity. President Mościcki, hitherto an obliging executor of Piłsudski's wishes, refused to surrender his office to Sławek, envisaged as Piłsudski's successor; rejecting the advice of the colonels, Mościcki appointed General Edward Rydz-Śmigły as head of the armed forces. The elections of 1935, boycotted by over half of the electorate, further accelerated the divisions within the Sanacja. Two distinct groupings emerged: one centred around President Mościcki and the distinguished economist Eugeniusz Kwiatkowski which laid emphasis on efficiency and professionalism in government, the other of a more military and authoritarian flavour around Rydz-Śmigły. A compromise between the two in May 1936 resulted in the creation of a surprisingly stable caretaker administration under the malleable General (and ex-physician) Felicjan Sławoj-Składkowski which survived until the outbreak of war in 1939. Although lacking the necessary political talents, Rydz did not abandon his ambition of stepping into Piłsudski's shoes. In November 1936 he was promoted to the rank of marshal, and in 1937 his followers formed a new highly centralized political party, the Camp of National Unity (Ozon), with a strong nationalist and anti-Semitic programme. This attempt to appeal to the right backfired on Rydz, who had to moderate his tone; too many of Piłsudski's followers, including the Mościcki group, were horrified by this betrayal of the dead marshal's essentially non-extremist ideals.

The failure of the Sanacja to win wider popular support was vividly portrayed by the continued political agitation and social turmoil in the country which was only slowly emerging out of the Depression. During 1936 and 1937 the police responded violently to large-scale outbreaks of strikes by industrial workers and peasants. On the other hand, the opposition parties were too divided to organize an effective common front against the Sanacja. The National Democrats, still the largest party in the country, refused to have any dealings with socialists and freemasons, and spent most of their energies on anti-Semitic outrages and internecine leadership struggles for the succession to Dmowski (who was to die in January 1939). As a result only a small, if eminent, group of centrist politicians, including Sikorski, Witos and Paderewski, was involved at the inception of the 'Morges Front', named after Paderewski's Swiss residence. The socialist and peasant parties refused to collaborate in a 'Democratic Front'. The prospect of a 'Popular Front', launched by the Comintern in Moscow in 1935 to unite all European left-wing and democratic parties against fascism, fared little better in Poland; in 1937 Stalin put to death most members of the Polish Communist Party (KPP) residing in the USSR, and in 1938 dissolved the entire organization on charges of Trotskyism.

The Great Depression, and the political and nationalist radicalism it encouraged, accentuated the problems of Poland's national minorities. The Greek Catholic (Uniate) Church under the outstanding leadership of Metropolitan Sheptyts'kyi, the extensive Ukrainian co-operative movement, and moderate Ukrainian political parties strove through legal means to protect Ukrainian cultural and economic interests. The horrors of Stalin's collectivization in the Soviet Ukraine had also dissolved any attraction the

USSR might have exerted on Poland's Ukrainians. However, despite some conciliatory gestures made by the Polish government in the mid-1930s, instances of official anti-Ukrainian discrimination only hardened the bitterness of the increasingly assertive Ukrainians. Nationalist paramilitary groups turned to terrorism to undermine Polish rule. The social and material position of Poland's Jews also deteriorated in the 1930s. Polish nationalist groups encouraged peasants to boycott Jewish shops and organized anti-Jewish demonstrations at the universities. Some professions imposed restrictions on Jewish membership, while the government even endorsed unrealistic plans for Jewish emigration. The Zionist movement also promoted Jewish emigration to Palestine, although, of the 400,000 Jews who left Poland between 1921 and 1937, only about a third headed there. Nevertheless, by 1937 Polish Jews constituted 40 per cent of the mandate's Jewish population. The growth of Nazi influence among Poland's German minority further compounded nationalist tensions in the country.

The most constructive undertaking of the Sanacja in this period was the new interventionist economic policy inaugurated in 1936 by Kwiatkowski, deputy prime minister and minister of finances since 1935. The most important element in his four-year state investment plan was the establishment of the Central Industrial Region (COP) in the most over-populated and strategically secure area between the Vistula and the San rivers. The construction of hydroelectric power stations, of aircraft, rubber and motor vehicle factories, of chemical plants, and of a new industrial centre at Stalowa Wola was to make possible the modernization of the armed forces, due to be completed by 1942. Further investment plans envisaged the modernization, by 1954, of Poland's communications, agriculture and education. Already in 1938 Poland's industrial production and real industrial wages well exceeded those of 1928.

By 1939 an entire generation had been brought up for whom national independence was the norm. After the long period of partitions, the different parts of the country had been quite successfully reintegrated, and the process of unifying the legal system was far advanced. The railway network had been expanded; several shipping lines and a national airline 'Lot' had been created. Higher

37   Peasants harvesting near Nowy Sącz in southern Poland, 1936. It was in the south of the country that the greatest fragmentation of holdings existed; in 1921 four-fifths of all holdings there were less than 5 hectares (12.5 acres) in size. In the whole of Poland in 1939 there were only 2,000 tractors, compared to 30,000 in France. Note the scythe with a pitchfork attachment.

and secondary education was still limited but of a good standard; popular illiteracy, still mostly evident in the eastern provinces, had been reduced from 33 to 15 per cent; mortality rates had been cut by half; the infrastructures and appearance of most towns had been improved; and by 1939 wireless ownership had reached 1 million. Overall, however, living standards were still modest, and in the countryside hidden unemployment affected an estimated 5 million people. The nationalities issue also remained as intractable as ever; Polish officialdom continued to perceive the nationalist aspirations of the minorities as a threat to the integrity of the Polish state.

However impressive the early fruits of Polish economic *étatisme*, Poland had neither the means nor the resources, nor the totalitarian controls, ever to achieve economic or military parity with either of its two big neighbours. In 1937 Polish steel production was 1.5

million tons, that of Germany 19.8 million, and of the USSR 17.8 million. And time was running out. While Warsaw considered the USSR temporarily weakened by Stalin's purges of the Red Army, Poland's international position became increasingly vulnerable as a result of Hitler's blatant policy of overthrowing the Versailles system, and the irresolute response to the dictators by Britain and France in their anxiety to avoid war. France's failure to challenge Hitler's remilitarization of the Rhineland in March 1936 undermined Foreign Minister Beck's confidence in the French alliance. However, Beck's sceptical attitude to collective security, and his attempt to strengthen Poland's position without unduly irritating Berlin, gave the misleading impression that Poland was acting in collusion with the predatory dictators. When Hitler annexed Austria in March 1938, Beck, with a veiled threat of war, forced Lithuania to establish diplomatic relations with Warsaw. Even more shameful was the manner and timing of Poland's annexation of Teschen (Cieszyn) in October 1938 from a prostrate Czechoslovakia which had been sacrificed at Munich by Britain and France in the greatest act of appeasement.

Germany's sights focused next on Poland itself. Initially Hitler's preferred intention was to turn Poland into a vassal state which would act both as a springboard for the conquest of *Lebensraum* in the USSR, and as an eastern screen should Germany first have to fight France. Poland's anti-communist record and anti-Russian traditions, the anti-Semitism of its right-wing parties, and even from a 'racial' point of view the strong Baltic and Germanic elements in its population qualified Poland in Hitler's eyes as a possible and useful ally. To establish Germany's domination over Poland, Berlin requested the return of Danzig, already controlled by local Nazis, and the creation of an extra-territorial highway and railway across Polish Pomerania (the so-called Polish Corridor); the Poles were also invited to join the Anticomintern Pact.

Hitler's occupation of Prague on 15 March 1939 and the destruction of the rump of Czechoslovakia proved to be a turning-point for Poland and for the Western Powers. Hitler's attempt to intimidate the Poles into subservience had the opposite effect, while the collapse of appeasement prompted Britain and France to show more resolve in checking Nazi expansion. On 26 March the Polish government politely but unequivocally declined the Führer's 'magnanimous' offer. Chamberlain's public declaration of support for Poland on 31 March was followed by a formal British guarantee on 6 April, which only stiffened Polish resolve to resist Hitler's demands. Hitler responded furiously by repudiating both the Anglo-German naval agreement of 1935 and the Polish–German non-aggression treaty of 1934. The *Wehrmacht* was now instructed to plan an attack on Poland. On 19 May France signed a military agreement with Warsaw and committed its forces to a full-scale offensive against Germany on the fifteenth day of a German attack on Poland.

The deterioration of international relations in 1938 and 1939 and the economic recovery had calmed political tensions within Poland and encouraged national solidarity. The election of November 1938, held under the restricted arrangements introduced by the 1935 constitution, and coinciding with the twentieth anniversary of independence, proved a success for the government, which gained more than 80 per cent of the parliamentary seats. The government rejected all suggestions for the creation of a coalition government of national defence on the 1920 model. Nevertheless, its decision to defend the country's sovereignty had the overwhelming backing of Polish public opinion.

Just as Poland had refused to be drawn into the German embrace, so it also remained highly suspicious of British and French efforts to include the USSR in an eastern 'peace front'. For the Polish government the Soviet conditions for such co-operation were unacceptable for they were equally tantamount to the loss of sovereignty. Moscow demanded the stationing of Soviet troops in eastern Poland, the dissolution of the Polish–Romanian alliance, and the limitation of the British guarantee to Poland's western frontier. In his turn, Stalin was deeply mistrustful of western motives, especially after Munich, and was keen to buy time. Placing imperial interests over ideology, Stalin opted for a deal with Hitler, who offered him more than the West. The secret clauses of the Nazi–Soviet non-aggression pact of 23 August 1939, revealed only in 1946 but denied by the USSR until 1989, provided for the joint division of eastern-central Europe and the partition of Poland.

Hitler now schemed hard to drive a wedge between Warsaw and

the Western Powers in order to complete his victim's isolation. However, the failure of Franco-British talks in Moscow and the signing of the Nazi–Soviet pact removed the last obstacle to the conclusion, on 25 August, of a formal treaty of alliance between Britain and Poland. Hitler was momentarily unnerved, while the West persuaded the Poles to delay their mobilization in the hope of last-minute talks. Hitler did not really expect the West to fight for Poland; and in any case, in this game of double bluff, he was willing to take the risk. Early in the morning of 1 September Germany unleashed the bulk of its forces against Poland. Two days later Britain and France declared war on Germany.

Poland would fight. Honour and national interest made the alliance with Britain and France, whose effective help had been promised and was expected, preferable to becoming a German satellite. The September campaign was an uneven struggle. The bitter resistance of the partly mobilized Polish armed forces could not alter the enormous superiority of the Nazi war machine in terms of men, modern equipment, mobility and firepower. While the Germans applied the new doctrine of *Blitzkrieg* with awesome effect, the Poles tried to defend their long and over-exposed frontiers. Yet the campaign was no simple walk-over. The small Polish air force bravely harried the *Luftwaffe*, while from 9 to 12 September the Polish counter-attack on the river Bzura, west of Warsaw, mauled five German divisions. The Germans suffered a total of 50,000 casualties and lost 500 aircraft and over a thousand armoured vehicles. Polish military casualties numbered over 200,000, not to mention the civilian victims of indiscriminate German bombing, or the mass executions of Polish officials and civilians. The promised French general offensive in the west, which might have turned the course of the campaign, never materialized. Plans to create a redoubt in the south-east, along the Romanian border, were finally dashed by the entry of Soviet troops on 17 September, which sealed the Poles' fate. Warsaw did not surrender until 27 September, while General Kleeberg's Polesie Army held out against both Soviet and German forces until 5 October, the day on which Hitler presided over a victory parade in the Polish capital. A Nazi–Soviet agreement of 28 September divided Poland fairly equally along the rivers Narwa, Bug and San (the original plan had

38   Poland's state-of-the-art bomber, the PZL P.37 Łoś ('Elk'). With a
maximum speed of 277 m.p.h., a range of 932 miles and a bomb load of
4,850 pounds, it compared favourably with the best medium bombers in
service anywhere in the world. But the Poles had too few modern aircraft
to face the Nazi and Soviet onslaughts in 1939. Only 180 of these
machines were produced between 1936 and 1939.

envisaged the line of the Vistula), although the Germans acquired
the more populous and more developed regions.

   The Polish state, in Molotov's words 'that hideous creation of the
Versailles treaty', had yet again been wiped off the map. But for the
Poles the war was by no means over. Tens of thousands of soldiers
and airmen managed to escape via Hungary and headed for France;
most of the Polish navy had earlier left the Baltic for British ports.
The Polish government and high command refused to capitulate
and sought refuge in Romania where, to their surprise, they found
themselves interned. On 1 October, under French pressure, Presi-
dent Mościcki appointed Władysław Raczkiewicz, a moderate
Sanacja politician, as his successor, while General Władyslaw
Sikorski became prime minister of a broad coalition government-
in-exile, residing in Paris and recognized by Britain and France.
Constitutional legality was thus preserved. As commander-in-chief,
Sikorski began the business of reconstructing a Polish army in

France, and established contact with the resistance groups that were sprouting in occupied Poland. A quasi-parliamentary body, a National Council, with representatives from all the main political parties, was also formed; significantly enough, it included a Jewish Bundist member, but none from the other national minorities.

Both occupying powers focused their terror on the educated and ruling elite of the country, and, in the Nazi case, also on the Jews. The eastern half of Poland, except for the region of Wilno (Vilnius) which was handed over by the Soviets to the Lithuanians, was formally annexed by the USSR after bogus local plebiscites. Mass arrests took place of key figures in the Polish military, political and economic establishment, of civil servants and trade union leaders. All private and public enterprises were taken over; the press was shut down; and all Polish political, cultural and social organizations were dissolved. At first the Soviets made strenuous efforts to win over the local non-Polish populations by promoting the Belorussian and Ukrainian languages, and by distributing confiscated landed estates among the peasants. Once effective control had been established, the Soviets launched an attack on all religions, dissolved all local autonomous organizations, including the highly developed Ukrainian co-operative movement, and arrested all local Ukrainian and Zionist leaders. In April 1940 Soviet-style collectivization was imposed. The entire population was now terrorized into obedience.

In 1940 and 1941 upwards of 1 million people from all social classes and all ethnic groups, but mostly Poles, were deported from the Soviet-occupied territories to Siberia and Soviet Central Asia. Entire families, deemed in any way 'unreliable' by the Soviets, suffered this ordeal; scores of thousands were to perish in the inhospitable conditions of their places of exile or from forced labour in the Gulag. By mid-1941 many small towns of pre-war eastern Poland had lost much of their Polish character. The NKVD meted out special attention to captured Polish officers (regulars and reservists), civil servants, policemen and border guards. On orders signed on 5 March 1940 by Stalin and the Politburo, over 21,000 such prisoners were shot in April 1940; of these 4,000 perished in Katyn near Smolensk. For half a century, until Gorbachev's admission in April 1990, Soviet governments were to deny their responsibility for these atrocities. Yet while merciless to those he considered enemies of Soviet power, Stalin sought to recruit Poles, especially left-wing intellectuals, willing to co-operate with the USSR. This policy gained momentum after the unexpected defeat of France in June 1940 which left the USSR alone facing a Nazi-dominated European continent. In any confrontation with Germany, the Poles could be useful. In the autumn of 1940 the 85th anniversary of Mickiewicz's death was publicly celebrated in Lwów (L'viv), and in early 1941 the Comintern revived its Polish section.

Soviet terror was soon outstripped by its Nazi counterpart. The Nazi occupation lasted longer, it affected the majority of the Polish population (indeed, between 1941 and 1944 Nazi control extended to the entire area of pre-war Poland), and it took a heavier toll of life. A vast tract of western Poland, including Poznań and Łódź (renamed Litzmannstadt), was incorporated directly into the Third Reich, and its population classified according to crude and inconsistent 'racial' criteria. To affirm the German character of Upper Silesia and especially of Pomerania, two-fifths of their population were registered wholesale as 'German' (and therefore subject to military service) as opposed to 2 per cent carefully screened in the Wartheland. Those classified as 'Poles' were reduced to the status of a helot underclass, deprived of all property and of access to all but the most basic schooling, and subject to compulsory labour or deportation. In the Wartheland virtually all Polish Catholic churches, monasteries and charitable institutions were closed; in Upper Silesia and Pomerania German was enforced as the language of religious life. Patriotic Polish priests were either expelled, arrested or shot. The central part of Poland, administered separately by the Germans as the so-called General Government (to which east Galicia was added in 1941), was subject to a regime of terror, semi-starvation and ruthless economic exploitation. It became a dumping ground for all unwanted Poles and Jews from the lands annexed by the Reich. Most Catholic parishes were allowed to function in the General Government but under many restrictions. Polish Protestants were especially victimized by the Nazis. A policy of 'spiritual sterilization' brought with it an attack on Polish high culture: museums, libraries, universities, most secondary schools, and theatres were closed down, and the public playing of Chopin's music was forbidden. Only some primary schooling and limited technical training was permitted, while cheap entertainment was provided in the cinemas and through a so-called 'reptile' gutter press.

The incarceration in concentration camps in September 1939 of the staff of Kraków University was a foretaste of the fate awaiting the entire Polish educated class under Nazi rule. Indeed, a large proportion of the Polish intelligentsia and professional classes, including of course most of the Jews amongst them, perished through mass executions or in concentration camps: from 15 per cent of all teachers and 18 per cent of the Catholic clergy to 45 per cent of all doctors, 50 per cent of all qualified engineers, and 57 per cent of all lawyers. The rest of the Poles were treated as a slave workforce, 'ein Arbeitvolk'; from 1939 to 1944 about 2.8 million Poles were sent to Germany as compulsory labourers. About 200,000 Polish children with 'racially appropriate features' were removed from orphanages and from their parents in order to be brought up as 'Aryan' Germans in Nazi homes. And for every German killed in occupied Poland a hundred hostages were executed. Public hangings and shootings became commonplace in towns and villages. The Nazi 'Generalplan Ost' of April 1942 envisaged that the remaining Poles would eventually be scattered over the eastern wastes of conquered Russia as so much unwanted, racially inferior trash. All of Poland was to become a region of German settlement.

However vicious and costly in lives the Nazi treatment of Polish Gentiles was, the fate of the 'subhuman' Jews and Gypsies of Poland was to be catastrophically worse. Subject to mass killings and brutal maltreatment from the very beginning of the war, the Jews were herded into 400 sealed ghettos, where disease and hunger ravaged their inhabitants; the largest was the Warsaw ghetto with 450,000 people. After the German invasion of the USSR in 1941 the Nazis were able to get their clutches on the Jews of eastern pre-war Poland. At the notorious Wannsee conference in January 1942, the Jews of occupied Europe were condemned to total extermination. To implement this unprecedented act of genocide a whole system of death camps was developed in occupied Poland, the largest centres being Auschwitz-Birkenau

Map 10   Poland during the Second World War, 1939–1944.

(Oświęcim-Brzezinka), Majdanek and Treblinka. Here the inhabitants of the ghettos and Jews from all over occupied Europe were transported by the trainload. The uprising in the Warsaw ghetto in April and May 1943 was a hopeless but powerfully symbolic act of Jewish defiance against their oppressors. By the end of 1944 the Nazis had put to death about 90 per cent of pre-war Poland's Jewish population of 3 million, and had virtually wiped out a community which had been on Polish soil for centuries.

The reaction of Polish Gentiles to the fate of their Jewish fellow citizens during the Holocaust varied. On the dark side there were extortionists who exploited Jewish misfortunes, informers who betrayed Jews to the Nazis, and extreme right-wing nationalists even willing to kill Jews. The insidious influence of Nazi anti-Semitic propaganda, the introduction of the death penalty for anyone caught helping the Jews, the sight of mass executions, and the general atmosphere of terror gradually numbed the moral responses of many people, prompting indifference, fear for their own skin, and even fanning old anti-Jewish sentiments. Reports that some Jews in eastern Poland had welcomed the Soviets in 1939 also strengthened the widely held stereotype of 'Judaeo-communism' which had been promoted by right-wing parties before the war. Contemporary accounts suggest that numerous Poles easily came to accept the dispossession of the Jews and their isolation in the ghettos. The observed willingness of many peasants to help the Jews, even in 1941, had definitely altered by the autumn of 1942. On the other hand, there were Gentile Poles willing to take the risk of offering sanctuary to the Jews, to which the Yad Vashem Institute in Israel today provides considerable testimony; religious convents were also able to save many Jewish children. Assimilated middle-class Jews had the best chance of survival outside the ghettos, while orthodox religious Jews were the easiest targets for the Nazis. The influential Catholic writer Zofia Kossak-Szczucka condemned the genocide in no uncertain terms. In August 1942 the Polish Underground established a separate council (known by the acronym 'Żegota') for co-ordinating assistance to the Jews; this came in the form of money, false identity papers and safe places of refuge. The Polish government in London provided an initially incredulous outside world in 1942 with details of the Nazi atro-

39   The Holocaust in art. *El Mole-Rachmim* from the series 'Kamienie krzyczą' ('The stones are screaming'), painted in 1946 by Bronisław Wojciech Linke (1906–62). 'El Mole-Rachmim' (God full of mercy) is sung at Jewish funerals and the Day of Atonement. Except for the period 1939–46, Linke spent most of his working life in Warsaw. He deployed a powerful surrealist form of art to attack cruelty, meanness and hypocrisy.

cities. In the circumstances, the saving of up to 45,000 Jews, including 12,000 within Warsaw itself until autumn 1944, could be seen as something of an achievement.

The absence of civilized norms of government during the Nazi occupation of Poland and the general brutalization of the population not only generated bitter Polish hatred of the Germans but created ripe conditions for the outbreak of other inter-ethnic conflicts, especially in the eastern areas of pre-war Poland. Polish underground fighters clashed with Lithuanian police units raised by the Germans and with Soviet-sponsored partisans. After 1942 terrible atrocities occurred in Volhynia, where local Ukrainian nationalists set out to 'cleanse' the area of its remaining Polish population, which brought about violent Polish retaliation.

The bestial nature of Nazi policies in Poland and the intensity of Polish nationalism ruled out any prospect of serious political collaboration with the Nazis; there was simply no scope for a Polish Pétain or a Polish Quisling. For General Sikorski's government there was no alternative but to continue the war effort. Polish troops displayed characteristic valour during the Allied expedition to Narvik in May 1940 and during the French campaign in which four Polish divisions took part. After the fall of France, the Polish government, with 20,000 soldiers, was evacuated to Great Britain. A Polish brigade helped to defend Tobruk in late 1941. Initial British doubts about the competence of Polish airmen were rapidly dispelled, and Polish pilots (numbering 10 per cent of Fighter Command) showed their real mettle during the Battle of Britain when they downed over 200 German aircraft, one-seventh of the total. The Polish navy acquired additional ships, and participated alongside the Royal Navy in most operations in the Atlantic and the Mediterranean. A particularly significant contribution to the Allied cause was the transfer by Polish military intelligence to the French and British, in August 1939, of a replica of the German 'Enigma' machine, the coding system of which had been cracked by Polish cryptologists. Out of this grew Station X at Bletchley Park, where British cryptographers were able to decipher German military communications. Polish intelligence networks in occupied Europe provided other useful information, including details of the German V1 flying bomb and V2 rocket.

The Polish tradition of conspiracy and resistance, reinforced now by the legacy of inter-war independence, found full expression again. Diverse resistance groups began to emerge spontaneously as early as September 1939; their activities were gradually co-ordinated by General Stefan Rowecki, appointed commander of the underground forces by General Sikorski in June 1940. By mid-1944, when it reached its maximum size of 400,000 members, the so-called Home Army (Armia Krajowa or AK) formed the largest underground organization in the whole of occupied Europe; it embraced within its structure all Polish resistance groups with the notable exception of the smaller communist-led People's Army (AL) and the ultra-nationalist 'National Armed Forces' (NSZ). Although officers of the pre-war army who had evaded capture provided much of its cadres, the Home Army drew on all sections of the Polish population and represented a veritable citizen army on a scale hitherto unknown in Polish history. Its main area of activity was the General Government, but it also established sizeable units in the Wilno-Nowogródek region and in Volhynia. At first the AK concentrated on intelligence gathering, organizing propaganda, punishing collaborators, bandits and extortionists, and on organizing numerous acts of sabotage, especially along German lines of communication to the eastern front. It increased its military activity in early 1943, and, although woefully under-equipped, prepared for a nationwide insurrection in propitious circumstances.

The AK was the military wing of an extensive 'underground state' led since autumn 1940 by a Delegate appointed by the government-in-exile in London. The Polish Underground State was endorsed by the four main Polish political parties which continued to function clandestinely and which in February 1940 managed to overcome their pre-war rivalries to form a broad coalition committed to the creation of a genuine parliamentary democracy after the war: the Polish Peasant Party (PSL), the Polish Socialist Party (PPS), the National Party (SN) as the successor to the National Democrats, and the Catholic centrist Party of Labour (SP). The supporters of the pre-war Sanacja, humbled by the defeat of 1939, were mostly absorbed into the main resistance movement. Only the communists, who remained relatively inactive until the Nazi invasion of the USSR in 1941, and the right-wing extremists did not join the broad national coalition, nor recognize the authority of the Government Delegate.

Within the limits imposed by conspiratorial activity, the Underground State maintained the continuity of Polish statehood and carried out a remarkable number of the functions of a regular government. It possessed a civil service with quasi-ministries, a judicial system, and it promoted educational and cultural activities as a counter-measure to the Nazi policy of debasing the cultural life of the population. Clandestine university teaching and secondary schooling took place in many cities and towns, at great risk to those participating, and ensured the survival of a core of educated people. Works of art were hidden; textbooks, journals and newspapers appeared off secret printing presses; banned Polish classics were staged in covert dramatic theatres and at poetry readings. Indeed, much of Polish organized cultural, social and sporting life, from trade unions to the scouts, operated underground. Charitable institutions allowed by the Germans, such as the Polish Red Cross, also provided cover for conspiratorial activity. Street ballads, mocking the Germans, helped to maintain popular morale, while intentionally slow and shoddy 'tortoise' work in German-run armaments factories damaged the Nazi war effort.

The prospect of an early liberation of Poland was very bleak as the Axis Powers extended their control of mainland Europe. Britain by itself could not liberate Europe. It was the Nazi invasion of the Soviet Union on 22 June 1941, and Hitler's ultimate failure to destroy the USSR which dramatically altered the character of the war in Europe; it also changed Poland's prospects, although not necessarily in accordance with many Polish hopes. With the Japanese attack on Pearl Harbor in December 1941 the war became a global conflict, the outcome of which would be decided primarily by the USA and the USSR. The Poles were to make costly attempts to recover their independence, but once again, as in 1814–15, Poland's fate was ultimately to rest in the hands of the Great Powers.

In the wake of the British–Soviet alliance of 13 July 1941, Churchill pressed Sikorski to sign an agreement with the USSR (the so-called Sikorski–Maisky treaty) on 30 July 1941: diplomatic relations were restored, the Nazi–Soviet partition of Poland was annulled, Polish prisoners in the USSR were freed, and a Polish army was to be formed on Soviet territory. With all of pre-war Poland now under Nazi occupation Stalin could afford to make temporary concessions to the Poles. Sikorski hoped that a Polish army, under the jurisdiction of the Polish government in London and fighting on the eastern front alongside the Red Army, would help to liberate Poland, and that the USSR would respect Poland's future sovereignty. However, the absence of a precise Soviet commitment to respect the pre-war Polish–Soviet border split the Polish leadership and led to a government reshuffle which raised the profile of Stanisław Mikołajczyk, the leader of the Peasant Party (PSL). Nor was Stalin ultimately willing to nurture an independent Polish army that was being formed under the command of General Władysław Anders in Soviet Central Asia. Numerous Soviet bureaucratic obstructions, Moscow's refusal to recognize as Polish citizens all but ethnic Poles from eastern Poland, and finally the unexplained absence of thousands of Polish officers captured by the Soviets in 1939, all militated against Sikorski's strategy of co-operation with the USSR. The logical outcome was the evacuation of Anders' army of 70,000 men to Iran in the summer of 1942 to reinforce British and Commonwealth forces in the Middle East. With Anders left 40,000 emaciated civilians; hundreds of thousands of the original deportees remained behind in what the writer Józef Czapski, one of the freed prisoners, aptly labelled 'the inhuman land'.

Polish–Soviet relations continued to deteriorate just when the war on the eastern front, after Stalingrad, began to turn in Stalin's favour. Any Polish hopes that there might be a repetition of the outcome of the First World War were to be mere illusions. It is clear that, as a consequence of the Nazi attack on the USSR, Stalin had revised his earlier, inimical, views on Polish statehood; yet he was adamant that he would be the arbiter of the territorial and political configuration of a restored Polish state. Since the Polish government in London remained equally resolved in pressing for full Polish sovereignty and the restoration of the pre-1939 eastern border, there was ultimately to be no scope for a genuine compromise between the two sides. Stalin therefore set to work to create rival institutions to those of the Polish government in London and of the Polish Underground State.

To promote his influence within Nazi-occupied Poland, Stalin had already encouraged the establishment, in January 1942, of a revived Polish communist party under the modified name of the Polish Worker Party (PPR). Led after autumn 1943 by Władysław Gomułka, a Moscow-trained Polish communist, and by Bolesław Bierut, a former Comintern agent and member of the NKVD, the PPR not only refused to subordinate itself to the underground Government Delegature but began to lay a rival claim to represent the 'real' interests of the Polish nation. In early 1943 Stalin sanctioned the activities of a Union of Polish Patriots, led by Polish communists and fellow-travellers, and the formation of a Polish army under Soviet control commanded by Colonel Zygmunt Berling, a former prisoner now willing to collaborate with the USSR. Into this army, which was to taste action at Lenino in Belorussia in October 1943, flocked thousands of Poles who had failed to reach Anders. The discovery by the Germans of the mass grave with the corpses of 4,000 Polish officers at Katyn in April 1943, followed by Sikorski's request to the Red Cross to investigate, amid justified suspicions that the Soviets had perpetrated the atrocity, provided Stalin with an excellent opportunity to 'suspend' diplomatic relations with the Polish government on 25 April 1943.

The year 1943 brought further blows to the Polish cause. The death of General Sikorski in a still not fully explained air crash off Gibraltar on 4 July deprived the Poles of an internationally respected leader. Stanisław Mikołajczyk, the new prime minister, was shrewd and able but lacked his predecessor's authority, and was on bad terms with General Sosnkowski, the new commander-in-chief, who had opposed the Sikorski–Maisky treaty. Secondly, unknown to the Poles, at the Allied conference in Teheran on 28 November to 1 December 1943 both Roosevelt and Churchill expressed their broad agreement with Stalin's request that the Curzon Line should form Poland's future eastern border, thus leaving Wilno (Vilnius) and probably Lwów (L'viv) in Soviet hands, and that Poland should be compensated in the west at Germany's expense. For the Western Powers the Poles were a gallant and useful ally, but in the cold realities of the global Allied strategy after 1941, and at a time when the Red Army was bearing the brunt of the land fighting against Nazi Germany, the Soviet alliance was inevitably given precedence over Polish interests and sensibilities.

To weaken communist influence, the coalition parties of the Underground State announced their commitment, in August 1943 and March 1944, to a sweeping land reform and to the nationalization of the industrial base, the re-establishment of the pre-1939 eastern border, and territorial compensation from Germany for the human losses and material damage inflicted on Poland. What at this stage distinguished the non-communist Underground State and the crypto-communist PPR, which avoided any dogmatic posturing and presented itself in patriotic garb, was not so much the radical social and economic reforms advocated by both sides, but their attitudes towards national sovereignty, the frontier issue and the nature of future Polish–Soviet relations. The PPR attracted a variety of splinter groups from the peasant and socialist parties, but it remained for the moment a small player in Polish politics; its armed wing, the People's Army, was still only a fraction of the size of the AK. All this was to change with the approach of the Red Army.

In 1944 the Polish armed forces in the west were at last making a significant contribution to the Allied war effort: in May the Second Corps under General Anders stormed the heavily defended Monte Cassino and opened the road to Rome; in August General Maczek's 1st Armoured Division distinguished itself at the battle of Falaise; while in September General Sosabowski's Parachute Brigade fought hard at Arnhem. All these men were fighting for Poland's freedom, but they were to be cruelly deceived by the wider course of events. The ground was rapidly slipping from under the government-in-exile. On the one hand Churchill pressed Mikołajczyk to come to terms with Stalin and to give way on the frontier issue; on the other hand, Stalin now demanded not only the explicit recognition of the Curzon Line but the exclusion from the Polish government of elements 'hostile to the Soviet Union', that is, the resignation of none other than President Raczkiewicz himself, General Sosnkowski, and other prominent ministers.

Nor was the Polish Underground State able to prevent Stalin, with his overwhelming power and ruthless methods, from imposing Soviet control on the ground. The attempt in the summer of 1944

40   Polish tanks in Normandy, early September 1944. Sherman tanks of the 24th Lancers of General Maczek's Polish 1st Armoured Division passing through the hamlet of Sommery, north of Rouen, in pursuit of the retreating Germans. The division's battle route took it from Caen, through Belgium and Holland, to Wilhelmshaven on the North Sea coast of Germany.

to establish Polish authority in the former eastern territories of Poland in the path of the Soviet advance ended in tragedy. Initially joint action between the AK and the Red Army proved successful, as in the battle for the liberation of Wilno in July 1944. But once the front had moved on to the west, the Soviets arrested the local Polish leaders and demanded that the AK soldiers join the Soviet-sponsored Berling army; most refused and found themselves dispatched to the Gulag.

On 21 July 1944 the Red Army crossed the Bug river into what Stalin recognized as Polish territory. Yet even here he had no time for the independent Polish underground. On 22 July, in Chełm, a Soviet-backed Polish Committee of National Liberation (PKWN) laid its claim to be the effective government of liberated Poland. The PKWN announced its commitment to the democratic constitution of 1921, to radical reforms, and to Poland's expansion in the west at Germany's expense. It presented itself as a broad left-wing and democratic body of a Popular Front type, although none of the major Polish political parties was represented. Its chairman, Edward Osóbka-Morawski, was a hitherto unknown member of a socialist splinter group. Security, propaganda and military affairs were all controlled by communists. On 26 July the PKWN was installed in Lublin, from which it began to extend its authority within the areas occupied by the Soviet forces, and to conscript men for its armed forces.

In the summer of 1944 there were therefore two rival centres claiming authority in Poland. On one side, there was the non-communist Underground State with the AK, enjoying the support of most Poles, and owing allegiance to the legitimate Polish government in London, which was still recognized by the Western Allies; and on the other, the Soviet-sponsored PKWN which, despite its feeble roots among the Polish population, enjoyed the full material support of the Red Army and of the Soviet security forces in the creation of structures of government behind the Soviet front line.

The approach of the Red Army to Warsaw heralded the final tragedy of the Polish Underground State. On 1 August the AK in Warsaw launched a wholescale attack on the Germans with a view to establishing an independent Polish administration in the city before the arrival of the Soviets. Expecting to seize control of the city from the retreating Germans within several days, the poorly equipped AK found itself fighting for two months. The Germans turned some of their most vicious units on the city. Desperate street fighting was accompanied by large-scale massacres of the civilian population. The Red Army halted its operations on reaching the Vistula, while Stalin delayed granting permission to Allied aircraft bringing supplies to the insurgents to use Soviet airfields. He simply had to wait while the Nazis annihilated the last Polish obstacle to his control of Poland. A late attempt by Soviet-sponsored Polish troops to cross the Vistula in September received little Soviet help, and failed.

While Paris was liberated in August with limited loss of life and little material damage, Warsaw was the scene of one of the most desperate and savage urban battles of the Second World War. The city's agony ended with capitulation on 2 October. Military losses on each side numbered about 17,000, but up to 200,000 civilians also perished. The remaining population was driven from the city, which, in a barbaric act of vengeance, was then systematically destroyed; in Hitler's words, Warsaw was henceforth to be no more than 'a point on a map'. While the rising's heroism might have impressed on Stalin the strength of Polish nationalism, the heart of the Polish Underground State had been torn out and the AK effectively decapitated. The final concerted bid to assert Poland's independence had failed.

In the areas of Poland cleared of the Germans the PKWN deployed a carrot-and-stick policy. On the one hand, its security forces and the NKVD mercilessly hounded surviving units of the 'counter-revolutionary' AK; on the other hand, the PKWN moved deftly to win wider support among a sceptical population. The new, largely Soviet-officered Polish army, formed out of the fusion of General Berling's forces and the communist People's Army (AL), retained all the trappings of a national army. Indeed, this army was to expand to 400,000 men and was to participate in the subsequent Soviet drive into Germany and in the final assault on Berlin. Other gestures were made to patriotic sentiment. The authorities in Lublin sponsored cultural activities, for which there was a powerful thirst after five years of occupation, and thereby attracted the collaboration of many actors and writers. And, in a highly effective

41 The Warsaw Rising, 1944. One can only speculate as to the fate of these young girls who, with many others, served as liaison officers for the Home Army (AK). To the present day, most Poles are united in their homage to the bravery of the fighters and the courage of the city in 1944. But they remain divided over the Rising's wisdom and objectives. The traumatic effect of the Rising's failure did much to instil greater political realism and restraint among the Poles when facing communist rule after 1945.

move urged by Stalin to win over the rural poor to the emerging new political order, a radical land reform of September 1944 inaugurated the distribution among poor peasant families of all private estates and farms with over 50 hectares (125 acres) of arable land; in 1944 alone over 100,000 such families benefited in this way. The remaining aristocracy and landed gentry were hounded out of their ancestral homes.

Most of the cards were now neatly stacked in Stalin's favour: his control of Polish territory was growing every day, and he was now less interested in securing changes in the Polish government-in-exile than in using the PKWN as the basis for a new Polish government to which acceptable 'democratic elements' from the London government might be added. Although more concerned about Poland and more realistic in his attitude to the USSR than Roose-

velt, Churchill felt that if genuinely free democratic elections could
be built into a deal with Stalin then Poland, within new frontiers,
could be assured of a degree of internal freedom. But ultimately,
neither the United States nor Britain (increasingly dependent on its
transtlantic ally) was prepared to damage their relations with the
USSR over Poland. On the contrary, Roosevelt was anxious to
secure Soviet help in the war with Japan and Soviet co-operation in
the building of a new post-war order, symbolized by the creation of
the United Nations Organization in 1945.

Having failed to secure his ministerial colleagues' agreement to
Stalin's territorial and political demands, Mikołajczyk resigned
from the premiership on 24 November 1944, taking the Peasant
Party (PSL) out of the coalition government. For Stalin the games
with the London Poles were over. On 31 December 1944, the
PKWN declared itself the Provisional Government of the Republic
of Poland; as such it received formal Soviet recognition in January
1945. The Polish government-in-exile, now led by the veteran
socialist Tomasz Arciszewski, was still recognized by the United
States and Britain, but to all intents and purposes it was no longer
relevant in the settlement of the Polish Question. On 17 January
1945 Soviet-sponsored Polish troops entered the ghostly ruins of
Warsaw.

At the end of the First World War Poland's western border had
been decided with Polish participation at Versailles, while the
eastern border had been secured after a victorious war with
Bolshevik Russia. The scenario in 1945 was dramatically different;
if anything, it resembled the settlement of the Polish Question at
the Congress of Vienna in 1815. At the Yalta conference of
February 1945 Stalin, Roosevelt and Churchill agreed to the establishment of 'a strong, free, independent and democratic Poland'; its
eastern border was roughly to follow the Curzon Line, while in the
west Poland was to obtain substantial but still unspecified territory
from Germany. The western leaders also secured Stalin's agreement
to broaden the Provisional Government in Warsaw with the inclusion of 'democratic leaders from Poland itself and from among
Poles abroad'; this government would pledge to hold early and free
democratic elections. For many Poles Yalta was the ultimate
betrayal by their western allies. For the Western Powers it seemed,

in the circumstances, a practical resolution of the Polish issue with plausible safeguards against the total Soviet control of Polish internal affairs. Mikołajczyk expressed his willingness to return to Poland on that assumption. It all depended, of course, on whether such free elections would take place and whether their results would be respected.

Two events in Moscow on 21 June 1945 demonstrated the new realities of power in Poland. In the Kremlin, Stalin graciously concluded a conference establishing the new Polish Provisional Government of National Unity. In accordance with the Yalta agreement, Mikołajczyk and five other non-communists joined a twenty-man cabinet dominated by the PPR and its allies, and led by the pro-Soviet socialist Osóbka-Morawski. Mikołajczyk was offered the agriculture portfolio and was made one of two deputy prime ministers, the other being the communist Gomułka. Meanwhile, a few hundred yards away, in the Hall of Columns of the trade union headquarters, the show trial ended of the sixteen military and civilian leaders of the non-communist Underground State, including the Government Delegate Jankowski and the last commander of the AK, General Okulicki, who had all been kidnapped by the NKVD outside Warsaw in March 1945. They were convicted, and in most cases imprisoned, on charges of belonging to illegal organizations and, what was most grotesque, of collaborating with the Germans. The tragedy that befell these men, and indeed many members of the now-dissolved AK, who for five years had struggled against the Nazi oppressors and more recently had defied Soviet designs on their country's independence, vividly symbolized some of the moral ambiguities of the Second World War. On 5 July Britain and the United States finally withdrew their recognition of the Polish government-in-exile in London. It was to continue its phantom existence until 1990, as a symbol of constitutional legitimacy, bearing witness before the world of the violence inflicted on its nation.

Of all the countries of Nazi-occupied Europe the Poles had fought the Germans the longest, and had suffered appalling human and material losses. It is estimated that Poland's total wartime losses (including both Gentiles and Jews) amounted to a fifth of the country's population. The Poles also had good reason to distrust

------- Poland's boundaries in 1939

Territories re-incorporated by the USSR, 1945

German territories (and Danzig/Gdańsk) transferred to Poland, 1945

Restored to Czechoslovakia, 1945

Poland's boundaries since 1945

Minor modifications made in 1951: ① to the USSR ② to Poland

Boundaries of individual republics within the USSR (1945)

LATVIAN SSR Names of Soviet republics (1945)

Map 11 Poland's 'move to the west', 1945.

TVIAN   SSR

HUANIAN
SSR

Kaunas

USSR

Dvina

Vilnius
(Wilno)

Hrodna
(Grodno)

Niemen

Minsk

Navahrudak
(Nowogródek)

k

BELORUSSIAN
SSR

Brest
(Brześć)

Pinsk

Pripet

Bug

Chełm

Lutsk
(Łuck)

① UKRAINIAN
SSR

Kiev

L'viv
(Lwów)

Ternopil
(Tarnopol)

Dnieper

Ivano-
Frankivsk
(Stanisławów)

lovakia
(1945)

Dniester

the Soviets. Yet Poland's tragedy again was its geography. The
country lay directly on the Soviet route to Berlin and to what was
to become the Soviet zone of occupation in Germany; in that
critical sense Poland was of greater strategic concern to the USSR
than Hungary, Romania, or even Czechoslovakia, not to mention
Finland. Soviet territorial demands from the latter three states were
also relatively limited when compared to the Soviet annexation of
over two-fifths of pre-war Poland. Despite the fears of some Poles,
Stalin had no intention after 1941 of incorporating the rest of
Poland as an integral part of the USSR, in contrast to the Baltic
States. Nevertheless, Soviet imperial interests demanded that, even
if allowed nominal statehood, Poland had to be under total Soviet
control. Any resistance to Soviet domination therefore had to be
quashed, while the admission of Mikołajczyk to the 'Provisional
Government of National Unity' provided a democratic fig-leaf to
cover the reality of communist control, and the price for western
recognition.

At the Potsdam conference in July–August 1945, the United
States and Britain reluctantly agreed to the Oder–Neisse (Odra–
Nysa) Line as the western limit of Polish administration, prior to a
final peace conference, and to the expulsion of the remaining
German population in the areas under Polish control. Transferring
to Poland extensive ex-German lands was bound to make Poland
dependent on Soviet support in the face of any future German
demands for the restoration of these lands. The non-communist
Underground State had certainly envisaged some territorial acquisi-
tions in the west at Germany's expense, but the push for the whole
of Silesia and Pomerania as far as Stettin (Szczecin) came at first
primarily from the pro-Soviet communist leadership which proudly
proclaimed Poland's return to the frontiers of Piast Poland of the
tenth century.

Over 6 million Silesian, Pomeranian and East Prussian Germans,
including those who had already fled before the Red Army and
those who were now evicted by the Poles, paid a tragic price for the
bankruptcy of Nazi dreams of *Lebensraum* in the east. Nazi ethnic
cleansing in Poland was now reversed with a vengeance. In the
place of the departing Germans there arrived in 1945–6 about 2
million settlers from central Poland and 1.5 million Poles uprooted

and 'repatriated' from the eastern provinces annexed by the USSR. Most of the Polish population of Lwów (L'viv), for instance, found new homes in the largely ruined ex-German city of Breslau, now renamed Wrocław. A communist-run Ministry for the Recovered Territories had the monopoly of allocating to the new settlers former German homes and land. The so-called 'autochthonous' Polish-speaking inhabitants of East Prussia and former German Silesia were allowed to remain, but were discriminated against by outsider bureaucrats ignorant of local conditions; their future in communist Poland was not to be a happy one. Between 1945 and 1947 over 1.5 million Polish forced labourers and prisoners returned from Germany. Much of the new Poland in those years was like a vast railway station, with hundreds of thousands of people on the move. On the other hand, about 500,000 Poles, including a half of the Polish armed forces in the West, chose political exile and ultimately a new life in the West: primarily in Britain, North America and Australia.

In Poland thousands of ex-AK guerrillas and other armed groups hostile to the new regime continued a desperate struggle against Soviet security forces and those of their Polish allies. But for millions of ordinary Poles, exhausted, impoverished, mourning the deaths of their loved ones, and forced to survive by barter or on the black market, the end of the war naturally brought profound relief; there was an overwhelming desire for reconstruction and for a return to a normal everyday existence. The early pragmatism of the new pro-Soviet government, with its appeal to many young radicalized peasants and workers, and to some intellectuals dreaming of careers in the shaping of a better world, appeared to respond to those expectations. At the same time, the presence of Mikołajczyk and the legal activity of his large Peasant Party seemed to indicate that the cause of freedom and democracy within Poland's imposed borders might perhaps not be lost. In reality, however, the next few years proved to be merely a transitional phase between one totalitarianism and another.

7

Communism and beyond, 1945–?

Out of the ordeals of the Second World War emerged a new Polish state starkly different from the pre-war republic in terms of its territory, the size and composition of its population, its political and social order, and its relations with its neighbours. Poland's territorial losses in the east and its compensatory expansion in the north and west dramatically altered the country's shape and position on the map of Europe. The new Poland was 20 per cent smaller, but it was more compact and it had acquired a 300-mile-long Baltic coastline. Although much devastated, the ex-German lands were more developed than the provinces lost to the USSR. The demographic changes were also conspicuous. The new Poland had just under 24 million inhabitants in 1946, as opposed to 35 million in 1939, but it now contained an overwhelmingly ethnic Polish population. Death, displacement and dispossession had all but obliterated the country's pre-war political and social elite. With wartime material destruction estimated at two-fifths of its productive capacity, Poland was the most devastated country in Europe. Accompanying this were malnutrition, acute shortages of housing, and the widespread incidence of tuberculosis and venereal diseases. The war had also left thousands of invalids and orphans.

The new Poland was also firmly under Soviet military and political control. All the key levers of power within the country rested in communist hands, while a Ministry of Public Security directed by the NKVD-trained Stanisław Radkiewicz, and backed ultimately by the Red Army and the notorious NKVD itself,

42   A queue for water in ruined Warsaw, spring 1945. Although over 80
per cent of Warsaw had been devastated, many former inhabitants who
had survived the Warsaw Rising of 1944 soon started to return to the city,
despite the primitive conditions of existence. By July 1945 the population
had reached nearly 400,000, a third of its pre-war size. The rebuilding of
Warsaw was an undeniable achievement of the post-1945 regime.

tightened its grip over the country. On the other hand, lacking
genuinely popular leaders, the communist PPR was more than
aware that it needed time to consolidate its position and to build up
a mass membership. To mobilize the population in the awesome
task of post-war reconstruction and to win for itself a degree of
legitimacy, the regime had to make a broad patriotic appeal, not
least by depicting the post-1945 frontiers, within which a purely
Polish nation-state could at last be created, as representing a return
to the original Poland of the Piasts. Furthermore, the decisions
taken at Yalta and Potsdam demanded a limited gesture to pluralism. And so, while brutally destroying the remnants of the anti-
communist underground, the Temporary Government of National
Unity pursued pragmatic and flexible policies in the realms of
economic reconstruction, culture and religion.

All industrial enterprises employing over fifty workers per shift
were nationalized in January 1946, but much economic activity,

notably in the retail trade and in agriculture, remained outside direct government control. Indeed, the moderate *étatiste* proposals emanating from the newly created Central Office of Planning, where non-Marxist socialists and experts held sway, envisaged the continuation of a mixed economy. Current political issues were subject to strict censorship, but otherwise a broad range of publishing and artistic work, including films and radio broadcasts, was permitted. There was still no ideological supervision of teaching in the rapidly growing network of schools or in the hurriedly restored universities.

Although the 1925 Concordat was annulled by the government in September 1945, the Church recognized the need for compromise with the new political order. It retained full freedom of worship, and proceeded, not without a touch of triumphalism, with the creation of new parochial structures for the millions of Poles settling in the so-called 'Recovered Lands' and with taking over the ruined churches of the departing, mostly Protestant, German population. Indeed, as a result of the frontier and population changes, and for the first time since the fourteenth century, Poland was now an overwhelmingly Catholic country. The sufferings endured by the clergy during the war had enhanced the Church's status in Polish society and contributed to an even closer identification of the Church with the nation than had been the case before 1939. Little wonder that the authorities moved cautiously in their relations with the Church; the Stalinist Bierut even used the traditional formula 'So help me God' at his presidential inauguration in 1947.

However, the struggle for political power went on unabated, generating in many regions an atmosphere of insecurity and violence, even of civil war. Illusions that an armed conflict between the Western Powers and the USSR was imminent, and that it would reverse the Soviet domination of Poland, encouraged the survival until the end of 1947 of many armed anti-communist guerrilla groups or 'forest battalions'. Anti-Semitic outbursts against Jews who had survived the Holocaust, the most notorious in Kielce in July 1946, were also a grim feature of this unsettled period. And in the extreme south-east of the country the forcible eviction of the local Ukrainian population resulted in a brutal counter-insurgency campaign against nationalist Ukrainian partisans who waged a forlorn struggle against communist-led Polish and Soviet forces.

Far more dangerous for the PPR was the newly reconstituted Polish Peasant Party (PSL), led by Mikołajczyk; with its million members at the end of 1945 it was more than twice the size of the PPR. The PSL enjoyed widespread support in the villages and, in the absence of the main pre-war centrist and right-wing parties, it also became the focus for many elements in Polish society opposed to the communists. Conscious of its weakness, and desperate to avoid the kind of electoral disaster that befell Hungary's communists in November 1945, the PPR resisted Mikołajczyk's insistence on the free elections promised for Poland by the Yalta agreement.

Using intimidation, violence and electoral fraud, it took the communists just over two years to eliminate the PSL from public life. To delay an electoral contest the communists resorted to the ploy of a national referendum on 30 June 1946, with three questions relating to the abolition of the Senate, approval of the government's economic policies, and endorsement of the Oder–Neisse frontier. It was hoped that all voters would vote unanimously for the government propositions and thus endow the authorities with a degree of legitimacy. To assert their independence, the PSL recommended a 'no' vote to the first question; the anti-communist underground called for two or even three 'no' votes. The communists, who retained sole control of the electoral commissions, claimed that 68 per cent of the voters had endorsed all three of their proposals; the real figure, as revealed by confidential PPR records, was only 27 per cent. The final confrontation with the PSL occurred during the general election which finally took place on 19 January 1947. The PSL refused to join a single electoral list under PPR auspices, and stood as a distinct rival party. Thousands of PSL activists and over 100 PSL candidates were detained by the authorities; the number of polling stations was drastically reduced; over a fifth of the electorate was disenfranchized for alleged right-wing sympathies. The officially announced outcome of the rigged election was hardly surprising: the PPR-led bloc obtained 80 per cent of the votes, and the PSL only 10 per cent. Recent fragmentary studies suggest that even with this heavy intimidation the PSL received between 60 and 70 per cent of the popular vote. The free elections promised at Yalta were little more than a farce. American and British protests had no effect, but the nature of the communist take-over in Poland contributed to the widening of the rift between the Western Powers and the USSR.

The new government formed in February 1947 (no longer 'provisional') was led by the pro-communist socialist Józef Cyrankiewicz, while the key ministries continued to remain in communist hands. In October 1947 Mikołajczyk fled the country. The PSL was reduced to impotency and its rump taken over by communist sympathizers; in November 1949 it was formally absorbed into the pro-communist United Peasant Party (ZSL). Despite the inauguration of a superficially democratic 'little constitution' in 1947, effective power lay with the Politburo of the PPR, whose general secretary owed his position directly to Stalin.

On the political scene there remained for the communists the awkward problem of the Polish Socialist Party (PPS) whose wartime leaders, both in Poland and abroad, had little time for Soviet communism. Although the PPS had been reconstituted in Poland after the war under a left-wing faction which collaborated with the PPR, many rank-and-file socialists expected full equality for their party (whose membership exceeded that of the PPR until 1947) and the avoidance of sovietization. They hoped that Poland would retain a pluralism of autonomous social organizations, trade unions and co-operatives. Yet by associating themselves with the iniquities of the PPR and by co-operating with the PPR during the 1947 election, the PPS had allowed themselves to be tarred with the same brush.

In 1947 and 1948, in the ever-worsening climate of the Cold War, Moscow tightened its grip over its satellites. Not only were they obliged to abandon any involvement with the Marshall Plan but they were also forced to accelerate the adoption of the Soviet model of political, economic and social control. In 1948, after Stalin's split with Tito, steps were taken to eliminate all so-called 'Titoist' or 'nationalist' deviations within the communist parties of the Soviet bloc. In September 1948 Władysław Gomułka, the advocate of a 'Polish' road to socialism, was dismissed from his post as deputy prime minister and was replaced as secretary of the central committee of the PPR by Bierut. In December 1948 a thoroughly purged and browbeaten PPS agreed to unite with the PPR to form the PZPR (Polish United Workers' Party), under which appellation the communists were to rule Poland until 1989.

All of Poland's large pre-war political parties had either been banned, obliged to dissolve themselves, absorbed by the communists, or transmogrified into mere appendages of the PZPR; the latter were useful to demonstrate to foreigners as evidence of political pluralism. The PZPR had achieved hegemony. There was no room for any independent political or social movements in the 'brave new world' of Stalinist Poland in which the communist PZPR controlled all state institutions through the exercise of the patronage of jobs (the so-called *nomenklatura*) and the establishment of party cells at every level of public employment. For many opportunists and 'realists' membership of the PZPR offered prospects of careers. In July 1952 a new constitution, amended personally by Stalin, enshrined the industrial workers as 'the leading class in society', and proclaimed the creation of the Polish People's Republic. Elections after 1952 became a collective ritual in which over 99 per cent of the electorate voted unanimously for a single list of candidates of the so-called Front of National Unity dominated by the PZPR. Consequently the Sejm was reduced to the role of a rubber-stamp on all Party decisions. The communist-controlled system of government was never to enjoy legitimacy based on a freely expressed and genuine democratic mandate.

A vast and repressive police and security apparatus (by 1953 numbering over 200,000 functionaries, or nearly sixfold the size of the pre-war police force) kept a vigilant eye on the population, which was intimidated by a continuous atmosphere of tension and fear, and mobilized in carefully staged public processions and other artificial expressions of joyful togetherness. Between 1945 and 1956 5,000 death sentences were passed for political reasons; half of them were carried out. Tens of thousands of people suffered longer or shorter periods of arbitrary detention; files were kept on nearly a third of all Polish adults. The judicial system, all trade unions, youth and student organizations, and the press came under Party control. Nor did Stalin trust the Polish army, whose native officer corps was purged and then in November 1949 placed under the command of the Soviet Marshal Rokossovsky, an appointment strikingly analogous to that of Grand Duke Constantine in the Congress Kingdom of Poland in 1815 to 1830. By the end of 1952 three-quarters of all active generals in the Polish army were Soviet citizens.

A Soviet-style planned economy was imposed. In 1950, Hilary Minc, the hard-line Stalinist chairman of the state planning commission who had already destroyed the private retail sector and deprived all co-operatives of their autonomy, launched the Six Year Plan, an ambitious programme of rapid heavy industrialization. Its triumphal showcase was the Lenin steel mill in Nowa Huta, a new 'socialist' town that was intended to dwarf the neighbouring ancient city of Kraków, that bastion of Polish conservatism. As international tension heightened during the Korean War, much of the industrial expansion, brought about at the expense of real wages and of consumption but accompanied by Stakhanovite propaganda, was geared to the production of armaments. Hundreds of thousands of young, mostly poor, peasants were uprooted from their village communities, lodged in workers' hostels at the industrial sites, and promised a share in a glorious proletarian future. Their often genuine enthusiasm was dampened by drunkenness, low productivity, and a sense of dislocation. The state provided a basic welfare system, although it favoured those who were economically active in the industrial sector at the expense of the elderly and the rural population. Nevertheless, the pre-war curse of unemployment seemed to have gone for good. For thousands of peasants and workers there was the prospect of social advancement in the new urban centres, and in the new vast economic and administrative structures created by the state. But while industry mushroomed at breakneck speed, agriculture suffered. Having handed over to the peasants most arable land in 1944 and 1945, the communists began slowly in 1949 to enforce collectivization. By 1955 nearly a quarter of all arable land belonged to collective or state farms, although most of the latter were to be found in the still sparsely settled ex-German territories. Food production inevitably fell, which in turn led to compulsory requisitioning (especially in 1950 and 1951) and food rationing.

The methods of social engineering and Marxist indoctrination were applied also in educational policy and in the creation of a new intelligentsia. Youngsters from peasant and proletarian homes were encouraged, through positive discrimination, to enter higher education, while opportunities were narrowed for children with 'bourgeois' or 'reactionary' backgrounds. Syllabuses were revised in a Marxist spirit, many Soviet textbooks were translated for Polish use, and the teaching of Russian became compulsory in schools. All youths and young adults between the ages of 14 and 25 were drafted into Soviet-style pioneer and Komsomol organizations, while army conscripts received a two-year dose of ideological instruction. Culture was made available to the masses on an unprecedented scale through the heavily subsidized expansion of publishing, of the cinema, the theatre and of concert halls. By 1957 Poland could boast twenty-seven symphony orchestras and nine major operas houses. But the content of this cultural diet was strictly controlled; anything deemed religious, anti-Russian, or 'decadent' was excluded. In 1951 all university departments of English were closed, except in Warsaw, as potential centres of ideological contagion.

The main thrust of cultural policy as directed by the cultural commissar Włodzimierz Sokorski was socialist realism, defined many years later by Andrzej Wajda, one of Poland's most distinguished film directors, as the 'representation of reality not as it is, but as it ought to be'. Novels about the achievements of socialism, or about heroic workers who exceeded production targets and foiled the wicked schemes of imperialist spies and native counter-revolutionaries were the order of the day from 1949 to 1953. Poets and writers such as Zbigniew Herbert or Stefan Kisielewski, who refused to join the 'Stalinist choir', were pushed aside. The other officially approved theme in books and films was the horrors of the Nazi occupation. Academic research in the arts and social sciences had to bend to the ideological requirements of Marxism-Leninism; even in the sciences the Stalinist condemnation of the 'bourgeois' theories of genetics and relativity had to be endorsed. The first incisive attempt to analyse the illusions of the Polish intelligentsia and its vulnerability to Stalinism was provided by Czesław Miłosz in *The captive mind*, published abroad in 1953 after his defection to the West.

As the upholder of an alternative spiritual and ethical system of

43 Socialist realism: bringing culture to the masses. *Chopin's Polonaise in A-major in the forge of the Kościuszko mill*, in Chorzów, Upper Silesia. Painted in 1952 by Mieczysław Serwin-Oracki (1912–77). At the piano is the pianist Władysław Kędra who, like other artists, frequently performed in places of work. Until the construction of Nowa Huta in the 1950s, Chorzów possessed the largest steel mill in Poland.

values and the only remaining autonomous all-national institution, the Roman Catholic Church could hardly escape the onslaught of Stalinist atheism. The fact that in 1949 Pius XII had excommunicated all members of communist parties, and that the Vatican had not formally recognized Poland's new western border and continued, until 1956, to recognize the exiled Polish government in London, provided convenient ammunition for attacking the Church. Despite an understanding between the Catholic hierarchy and the authorities in 1950 whereby the Church's loyalty to the state was rewarded with a degree of independent activity, many church-run organizations and charities were dissolved, religious activities were banned from schools, hospitals and the army, and church attendance was discouraged; priests and bishops were harassed. Diverse ploys were used to split the Church from the inside; schemes were even hatched to sever the Polish Church's links with Rome and to create a state-controlled national church. Bierut's grotesque plan to secularize Warsaw's skyline by cutting off all church spires was fortunately never implemented, but in 1951 there arose in the centre of the city a Palace of Culture and Science, Stalin's 'gift' to Poland and a towering symbol of Soviet domination.

The height of the anti-Church campaign was reached in 1953 when the state unilaterally assumed the power to control all church appointments and demanded an oath of loyalty to the state from all clergy. The new primate, Archbishop Stefan Wyszyński, eventually advised compliance but himself publicly and symbolically refused: 'We are not permitted to place the things of God on the altar of Caesar. Non possumus!' His resultant detention was followed by large-scale arrests of bishops and clergy, and the closure of numerous monasteries and churches. The leading Catholic weekly, *Tygodnik Powszechny* of Kraków, was banned for refusing to publish a panegyric upon Stalin's death on 5 March 1953. While Wyszyński remained isolated in detention, the episcopate bowed in September 1953 to the state's demands.

Despite its totalitarian features, Stalinist rule in Poland never became a clone of its Soviet model and avoided some of the excesses witnessed in other satellite states, such as the purge trials of communist leaders in Czechoslovakia and Hungary between 1949 and 1952. But the post-Stalinist political thaw was a slow process, limited at first to the PZPR. It started with discreet purges in 1953 within the Polish security apparatus. The defection to the West in December 1953 of Józef Światło, a high-ranking officer in the security police (the UB), and his revelations on the airwaves of Radio Free Europe in autumn 1954 about the iniquities of the UB, aroused widespread ferment within the Party. Scapegoats were sought for the now admitted illegalities of the security police. In December 1954 the Ministry of Public Security was restructured and its notorious chief Radkiewicz transferred, in a mild post-Stalinist manner of demotion, to the ministry for state farms. Gomułka, who had been under arrest since August 1951, was quietly released from jail. In January 1955 the central committee of the PZPR publicly condemned the repression of the Stalinist period. It proved increasingly difficult for the Party leadership to contain its internal critics, many of them young communists associated with the weekly *Po prostu* (Straight Talk) and a host of discussion clubs that appeared all over the country. An attack on socialist realism in literature was launched by Marek Hłasko, a young rebellious exponent of black realism, while the poet Adam Ważyk questioned the price paid for 'the great building of socialism' in his published 'Poem for adults'. Khrushchev's denunciation of Stalinism at the twentieth Congress of the Soviet Communist Party on 25 February 1956 was a clear message that the old style of repression had to go; in Poland and Hungary it provided a powerful boost for change.

The death of Bierut in Moscow on 12 March 1956 increased the pressure on the beleaguered Stalinists. It also provided the dispirited PZPR, now led by Edward Ochab, with a timely opportunity to break with the euphemistically labelled period of 'errors and distortions', for which Bierut could be blamed. But an amnesty for thousands of political prisoners could not by itself appease the growing demand for change. The lowering of the threshold of fear across the country and the continuing low living standards contributed to the outbreak of mass demonstrations in the city of Poznań on 28 June 1956. Crowds carrying national flags and singing religious hymns demanded 'bread and freedom'; security police and PZPR headquarters were attacked. Although quelled by troops with tanks, the protests in Poznań were a sharp warning that the communist system in Poland was facing a profound crisis. The participation of over a million pilgrims at the shrine of the Black Madonna in Częstochowa on 25–26 August 1956 to commemorate the 300th anniversary of the deliverance from Swedish invaders indicated that powerful national emotions were at play.

Within the Party, whose leaders had become isolated from the mass of the population, two rival strategies were proposed for dealing with the crisis. Advocates of reform called for the controlled liberalization of the system; the hardliners tried to channel discontent against scapegoats, including Jewish members of the now discredited security apparatus. Both groups were looking for a new leader with clean hands. Gomułka, the recently freed victim of Stalinist repression, appeared the ideal choice. The reformist grouping succeeded in winning over many workers and Party intellectuals, and in making common ground with Gomułka. The Party boss, Ochab, also wisely showed willingness to step down. But Moscow was not consulted. And so when on 19 October 1956 the central committee of the PZPR met at its VIIIth plenary session to resolve the internal crisis, Soviet forces stationed in Poland started converging on Warsaw. The scent of a national revolution was in the air and preparations were made for resistance. At that juncture a furious Khrushchev, accompanied by most of the Soviet leadership, made an unexpected appearance in the Polish capital. In a dramatic nocturnal talk, Gomułka succeeded in persuading the Soviet leader that the undertaking of repairs would not undermine the principles of the system or deflect Poland from the road to socialism. Mao Tse-Tung's support for Gomułka also carried weight in Moscow. In a major speech on 20 October, Gomułka attacked the Stalinist illegalities, the misconceived methods used in collectivization, and the excessive dependence on the USSR. On 21 October a new Politburo, with Gomułka as first secretary, was elected. While anxious to allay Soviet fears, Gomułka at the same time had to mollify the enthusiastic expectations of a population that saw in him a national leader against Soviet domination. The sobering effect of the brutal Soviet suppression of the Hungarian Revolution in November 1956 played well into Gomułka's hands. Hungary demonstrated to the Poles the limits of Soviet tolerance.

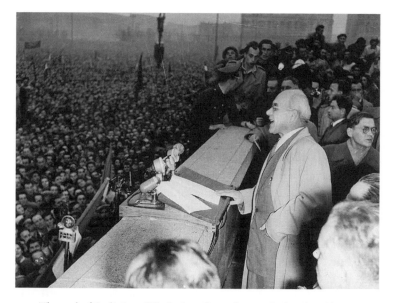

44   The end of Stalinism. Władysław Gomułka, at the height of his
popularity, addressing hundreds of thousands of Varsovians on 24 October
1956. He appealed for an end to demonstrating and for a return to work.
'United with the working class and with the nation,' he concluded, 'the
Party will lead Poland along a new path to socialism.' Gomułka's
popularity in October 1956 probably equalled that of Piłsudski in May
1920 and of Lech Wałęsa in 1980–1. Disenchantment was soon to follow.

Poland remained within the Soviet bloc and the Party retained its
monopoly of power. Yet the changes following Gomułka's appointment marked a radical break with the Stalinist past, and opened the
road to a milder form of communist rule. It was a turning-point in
the history of post-war Poland. Rokossovsky was deprived of the
command of the Polish army and returned to the USSR, the security
police was tamed, some of the worst Stalinist torturers were put on
trial, and Party bosses were changed at every level. The most hated
factory directors found themselves removed by the workers in
wheelbarrows, while workers' councils were established in many
factories as an antidote to rigid bureaucratic methods. Nearly all
collective farms were dissolved. Cardinal Wyszyński was freed, his
moral authority enhanced. A compromise was reached with the
Church which in turn helped to restore stability within the country.

Religious education returned to the schools and five Catholic deputies of the Znak group were allowed to sit in the Sejm. Gomułka successfully renegotiated in Poland's favour a number of military and economic agreements with Moscow; the USSR was no longer to buy Polish coal at paltry prices. The repatriation of over 200,000 Poles still detained in the USSR was secured. Foreign travel was eased, as was contact with Poles living in the West.

The regime acquired the qualified acceptance of much of the population, while the relative stability in the country obviated the need for preventive repression. In the field of culture, freed from ideological restraints, there was renewed vigour after 1956. The innovative musical compositions of Witold Lutosławski and Krzysztof Penderecki quickly acquired an international renown, while Andrzej Wajda's epic war films marked a breakthrough in the post-war Polish cinema. Sławomir Mrożek published his first satirical works, while Stanisław Lem began his long career as Poland's most famous science-fiction writer. New student cabarets introduced a breath of fresh air in the arts. Greater pluralism was tolerated in the academic world. Even Poland's Olympic successes in Rome in 1960 enhanced the country's reviving national pride.

But there was only disappointment for those who expected further liberalization of the system. For all his courage in 1956, Gomułka remained adamantly hostile to revisionism, that is democratization within the Party and worker self-rule. In October 1957 the journal *Po prostu* was closed down, and in 1958 the workers' councils were dissolved and replaced by supine Party-led groups. The authorities' attack on revisionist communist intellectuals gradually widened into a general campaign to force all the country's writers and intellectuals to toe the Party line: in 1963 Mrożek left Poland, while the highly popular writer Melchior Wańkowicz, who had returned from exile after 1956, received a three-year sentence in 1964 for including in a private letter information 'liable to damage the interests of the Polish People's Republic'. In 1965 the young revisionists Jacek Kuroń and Karol Modzelewski were expelled from the Party, to be followed the next year by the eminent philosophy professor Leszek Kołakowski.

Expectations of economic reform led nowhere. The retention of rigid planning and Gomułka's incompetence in economic matters allowed only a modest improvement in living standards in the late 1950s and the 1960s. Polish agriculture continued to stagnate: obstacles were placed in the way of the modernization of private farming, while the highly subsidized state farms remained grossly inefficient. Food shortages, especially of meat, continued to plague the Polish scene for decades.

There was also a retreat from the concessions made to the Catholic Church. By 1961 religious instruction in schools had ended and drastic official limits had been placed on the building of new churches. The nadir in church–state relations occurred between 1965 and 1966. In November 1965 Poland's bishops sent a formal letter to the German Roman Catholic episcopate seeking reconciliation between the two nations. While reminding the Germans of Nazi atrocities in Poland, the letter also acknowledged the sufferings inflicted by the Poles on the Germans. For Gomułka this was an unacceptable interference by the Church in foreign affairs, all the more resented since the communist authorities had used the threat of West German revanchism as one of their key arguments in defence of communist rule in Poland and of Poland's alliance with the USSR. But whatever points the government was able to score from the ensuing propaganda attack on the Church were lost the following year. The celebrations organized by the Church in 1966 to commemorate the millennium of Christianity in Poland (the baptism of Mieszko I in 966) confirmed the loyalty of the faithful to the Church. The authorities' attempt to hold rival celebrations of the millennium of Polish statehood introduced an element of theatrical farce and only weakened their standing among the population. Bruised, the communist party withdrew from any further direct confrontation with the Church, whose position in the country was gradually but remorselessly strengthened by the implacable Cardinal Wyszyński.

Within a year the country lurched into another phase of turmoil. For while Gomułka was able, for the moment, to silence the revisionists, a far stronger and more sinister threat was emerging within the Party apparatus in the form of an anti-intellectual communist grouping which was to make a bid for power by riding the nationalist tiger. Led by Mieczysław Moczar, the deputy minister of the interior and a shady wartime communist guerrilla

45   Cardinal Wyszyński at the Jasna Góra monastery in Częstochowa
during the celebration of the millennium of Christianity in Poland, 3 May
1966. Unlike the conservative Cardinal Mindszenty of Hungary,
Wyszyński was receptive to ideas of social and cultural progress, and was
politically more astute. The Polish communist authorities failed to break
the moral authority of the Catholic Church, whose strength grew under
Wyszyński's primacy.

fighter, the so-called 'Partisans' espoused a crude nationalism that
was anti-German, anti-Ukrainian and anti-Semitic. They targeted
liberalizing pro-reformers within the Party, as well as 'cosmopoli-
tan' writers and film-makers. The tensions within the Party
between Moczar's Partisans on the one hand, and the remaining
reformers on the other, came to a dramatic head in 1967–8. The
condemnation of Israel and Zionism by the USSR and most of its
east European satellites during the Arab–Israeli war of June 1967
was not shared by Poland's small number of Jews or indeed by
many young Poles. Gomułka personally had no record of anti-
Semitism (and his wife was of Jewish origin), but his public
condemnation of Polish 'Zionists' who had rejoiced in Israel's
victory as a potential 'fifth column' provided an excellent opportunity for Moczar and his followers to exploit anti-Semitism in

their bid for power. In a climate of political hysteria, tantamount to a witch-hunt, old Party members of Jewish origin were expelled from their posts. An attack was also launched on the young radical revisionists (Kuroń, Modzelewski and the student activist Adam Michnik) whose support for Dubček's reform movement in Czechoslovakia further enraged the Party authorities.

The final push by the Partisans to topple Gomułka took place after students cheered all liberal and anti-Russian statements in Mickiewicz's play *Forefathers' eve* staged in Warsaw's National Theatre in January 1968. In an inept move of cultural censorship, probably inspired by Moczar to provoke disturbances, Gomułka ordered the play's suspension. The ensuing student protests, first in Warsaw and then in most university towns in March 1968, were met with a violent police response and thousands of arrests. All over the country, orchestrated demonstrations of hatred, endorsed by the Moczar-controlled press, were staged against 'Zionists', students and 'Stalinist criminals'. Protests against this came from the Church, the Union of Polish Writers, and the small Catholic Znak parliamentary group. Gomułka next tried to limit the wild anti-Semitism, but the damage was done: up to 20,000 people of Jewish descent, in the main fully assimilated and almost all belonging to the intelligentsia, and some non-Jewish intellectuals were pressured into leaving the country. Gomułka survived Moczar's onslaught, but serious damage had been inflicted on the international reputation of the communist regime in Poland. Gomułka's relentless hostility to all forms of revisionism, whether of the Polish or Czechoslovak variety, and a desire to maintain his credit in Moscow led him to support militarily the Soviet-led invasion of Czechoslovakia in August 1968.

For the moment the Party apparatus was triumphant, but it had alienated an entire generation of young educated people by its brutal police methods and mendacious propaganda. Convinced that the communist system could not be reformed from within, the revisionists began to turn their backs on Marxism and to seek collaboration with non-Marxist student activists and the liberal Catholic intelligentsia. The deteriorating economic situation and continuing food shortages brought Gomułka no credit either. Nor did his apparent foreign policy success, in the shape of a treaty with the West German government of Willi Brandt on 7 December 1970, which recognized *de facto* Poland's post-war western border, enhance his domestic position.

Whatever self-satisfaction Gomułka's team may have felt at the signing of the treaty with Bonn evaporated a week later with the outbreak of strikes in the shipyards of Gdańsk and Gdynia. A programme of modest economic reform, intended to give some autonomy to factories and to introduce a system of wage incentives, went badly wrong when its first phase, a large increase in food prices, was introduced without warning on 12 December. It was a blow for many working-class families, who often spent about three-fifths of their budget on food. The timing of the measure, a fortnight before Christmas when Polish families make considerable and costly preparations for the festivities, was nothing short of crass stupidity.

The authorities' inept and bloody response to the strikes on the coast, especially the gunning down in Gdynia on 17 December of scores of workers on their way to work, led to a veritable workers' revolt across much of northern Poland. To economic demands was now added the demand for the creation of independent trade unions, in complete contravention of the Leninist principle that trade unions under communism were merely to serve as 'transmission belts' of Party orders to the masses. Faced with the prospect of a general destabilization of the entire country, Moscow agreed to the dismissal of Gomułka, taken ill after a mild cerebral stroke, and the appointment of Edward Gierek as first secretary of the Party on 20 December. As Party boss in Upper Silesia, Gierek had acquired a reputation for efficient management and had been the Party's rising star since 1968.

New strikes broke out in January 1971 and a general strike paralysed the port city of Szczecin on 23 January. Gierek's direct personal appeals to the workers of Szczecin and Gdańsk, his promises of reform and improvement of workers' living standards, and the freeing of detained workers, coupled with further personnel changes at ministerial and top Party level, finally helped to ease the situation. But it took a further strike by the textile workers of Łódź, a city much neglected by the authorities since the war, before the price rises were withdrawn on 15 February.

Although Gierek's team emerged from the crisis with some degree of public confidence, an end was put to all attempts to endow trade unions with greater autonomy. The workers remained cautious even if very much aware of their strength. The nationalist-communist Moczar, who had challenged Gomułka in 1968, was eased out of the interior ministry in the spring of 1971, after which Gierek skilfully kept ambitious colleagues away from the levers of power. Relations with the Church, now respected by the state as a key bastion of social peace in the country, improved. In June 1972 Pope Paul VI finally recognized the post-war ecclesiastical administration in the ex-German territories. There was a marked liberalization in cultural policy, especially evident in the realm of experimental theatre and in film-making. Repression was eased and government propaganda now emphasized the 'moral-political unity of the Polish nation'. The decision to rebuild the Royal Castle in Warsaw, which had been destroyed by the Nazis, was welcomed by Poles at home and abroad. On the other hand, the continuing emigration to West Germany of many Mazurians, Upper Silesians, and even Kashubians, who had been alienated from Polishness over the years by an insensitive administration, was a shameful indictment of the communist regime.

The key to the early buoyancy of Gierek's regime was the rapid expansion of the economy, fuelled by western credits amounting to 24 billion dollars, and the introduction of modern technology with a view to increasing Poland's role in international trade. Gomułka's policy of economic autarky was abandoned. There was a marked improvement in the general standard of living. Emphasis was put on reversing the chronic housing shortage, and motor-car production under licence increased (notably of the Fiat 125p), while the easing of foreign currency restrictions gave many Poles access to otherwise rare western consumer goods. At the same time the state continued its heavy subsidy of housing, transport, holidays and of the health service, and even brought independent peasant farmers within the social security system. In the new climate of East–West detente, Gierek paid official visits to several western countries, and in return played host to the French president Giscard d'Estaing, and the American presidents Nixon and Ford in Warsaw.

But Gierek's 'economic miracle' rested on flawed foundations.

46 Comrade Edward Gierek, the ex-miner, meets the miners of
Rydułtowy in Upper Silesia, September 1974. Despite the disastrous failure
of Gierek's economic policies, an opinion poll of October 1999 found that
most Poles who had reached maturity in the early 1970s, as well as those
least well off in the Third Republic, retain a favourable image of the 'good
times' under Gierek.

The centralized economy, run inefficiently by a privileged and venal
Party leadership, still revolved round heavy industry which underwent no structural reform. Many of the investments were misdir-
ected and indeed wasted. Many new Polish products intended for
export proved to be of shoddy quality and failed to win foreign
markets. External factors, such as the 1974 oil price rise (following
the 1973 Arab–Israeli war) and rising western interest rates, com-

pounded the economic difficulties. By 1974 the economy was over-heating, inflation was growing, and there was a return of food shortages; in 1976 sugar was rationed. Gierek's honeymoon with the nation was coming to an end. There were also serious squalls on the political front. As a price demanded by Moscow for Poland's greater diplomatic activity, the government proposed in mid-1975 to include in the text of the Polish constitution clauses stipulating that the Party held the 'leading political role in society' and, in a manner reminiscent of Poland's relations with Catherine the Great in the eighteenth century, that the alliance with the USSR was 'permanent'. A campaign of indignation and protest, backed by the Church, did not prevent the inclusion of the first amendment, but did succeed in watering down the second. The socialist character of the Polish state and the ideal of full collectivization were also enshrined in the constitution. However, the whole affair consolidated a wide opposition movement, ranging from the Catholic intelligentsia to the former communist revisionists, with significant implications for the future.

The government was further discredited when, faced with mounting foreign debts and growing inflation, it announced price rises on 25 June 1976. Widespread strikes and protests forced the authorities to back down. Although the authorities did not use fire-arms (unlike in 1956 and 1970), they meted out brutal punishments against the demonstrators. In September 1976 a Committee for the Defence of Workers (KOR) was formed which organized quick and effective material assistance to the victims of repression. KOR's early members came from diverse backgrounds, but among the most active were the former revisionists Jacek Kuroń and Adam Michnik, and the veteran socialist Jan Józef Lipski. Highly augural was the link which KOR provided between the intellectual opposition and the disaffected workers, something that had been lacking in 1968 and 1970 when both groups had fought their separate battles. In September 1977 KOR broadened its aims by becoming a permanent institution committed to the defence of human and citizen rights, and by stating as its aim the 'self-organization of Polish society'. Despite police harassment, KOR became an important focus for the opposition, publicizing acts of illegality committed by the state, and successfully assisting with the founding in

1978, in Gdańsk, of an independent (and of course illegal) trade union movement. Other dissident groups, some even demanding independence for Poland, also appeared.

In the less repressive climate of Gierek's Poland, and in marked contrast to the rest of the Soviet bloc, there was a burgeoning of unofficial cultural and publishing activity beyond the reach of the censor. The works of exiled writers like Czesław Miłosz and Witold Gombrowicz, as well as translations of hitherto banned foreign writers such as Orwell saw the light of day; outstanding among the illegal publications of authors living in Poland was Tadeusz Konwicki's *Small apocalypse* (1979) with its entertaining yet disturbing caricature of life in People's Poland. A so-called 'flying university', drawing on the services of many academics and publicists, and very reminiscent of unauthorized teaching during the tsarist period, organized lectures in private homes on officially forbidden historical and political subjects. Emigré publications, such as the Paris-based *Kultura*, and Polish-language radio stations abroad, especially the American-financed Radio Free Europe in Munich, also contributed to this effervescence of ideas. At the same time the relaxation on foreign travel and the spread of television increased popular awareness of the ever-widening gulf between Polish and western living conditions. Dependent on western loans and being a signatory to the Helsinki Final Act of 1975 with its emphasis on human rights, the Polish government was unable to root out the vigorous and pluralist world of dissent which now flourished behind the increasingly sterile official political order.

The Catholic Church contributed significantly to the creation of a broad-based movement in defence of human rights, which embraced Catholic and secular intellectuals active in the opposition. The Church had already been strengthened by Cardinal Wyszyński's deft, yet relentless, extension of its influence as a mass organization firmly rooted in the national tradition. Its prestige soared to unexpected heights when Karol Wojtyła, the archbishop of Kraków, was elected pope on 16 October 1978, assuming the name of John Paul II. For the authorities it came as a shock: 'By God's wounds, what are we going to do now?' Gierek was supposed to have exclaimed on hearing the news from Rome. The pope's triumphal pilgrimage to Poland from 2 to 10 June 1979

47 A walking time-bomb. Karol Wojtyła, the archbishop of Kraków, inspects a guard of honour on his return to Poland as Pope John Paul II, on 2 June 1979. On the left is Cardinal Wyszyński, and in the centre is Professor Henryk Jabłoński, the communist head of state. During his eight-day pilgrimage, 6 million Poles came out to greet the Polish pope. Wojtyła's election to the pontificate and his visit had a catalytic effect on the country.

confirmed not only the adherence to the faith of the bulk of the Polish population, which turned out in hundreds of thousands to greet the pontiff, but also the enormous capacity for 'self-organiza-tion' of Polish society. The pope's frequent references to human and national rights, and his appeal for courage and for change did not fall on deaf ears.

The papal visit had a powerful liberating impact on the national psyche at a time when, despite official propaganda to the contrary, the economic situation continued to deteriorate; in 1980 over four-fifths of Poland's income from exports went to service the foreign debt. Yet the scale and intensity of the strikes that swept across the country in July 1980, after the government had introduced minor meat price rises in factory canteens, took the government and the opposition by surprise. And this time, unlike 1970 or 1976, the strikers did not pour out into the streets or attack local Party

headquarters; they occupied factories and formed strike committees. Attempts to appease the strikers with pay rises and extra food
supplies failed to stem the tide of protest. The creation of an inter-
factory strike committee in Gdańsk on 16 August under the
chairmanship of Lech Wałęsa, a 37-year-old electrician, provided a
model for similar committees in other coastal cities, and proved to
be a turning-point. On 17 August the strike committee in Gdańsk
issued its twenty-one demands, which included the right to organize
independent trade unions, the right to strike, and the right to
freedom of expression. Members of the political opposition offered
their services as experts; individuals such as Tadeusz Mazowiecki, a
leading Catholic journalist, and Bronisław Geremek, a medieval
historian and doughty negotiator, joined Wałęsa's team.

Yet again a large section of the Polish working class, created by
the communist-led programme of post-war industrialization,
turned against its bureaucratic masters. When on 26 August the
strikes spread to the coal-mines of Silesia, Poland's industrial heartland, the government had little choice but to negotiate with the
strike committees. On 30 and 31 August, in Szczecin and Gdańsk
respectively, the floundering authorities capitulated over the central
demand for independent trade unions. To consolidate their position
against any future government intrigues, the trade union leaders
voted on 17 September to create a single national trade union
called 'Solidarity'. Under the leadership of Wałęsa, who displayed
a shrewd political instinct, combined with dynamism and a sense
of mission, Solidarity built up its internal democratic structures
and became a magnetic focus for a wide range of protest
groups. By mid-November it had 8 million members, roughly a
third of Poland's adult population; a year later its membership
exceeded 10 million. The discredited Gierek was removed from
office on 6 September and replaced by Stanisław Kania, an experienced apparatchik.

The developments in Poland made the headlines around the
world, while Miłosz's Nobel Prize for Literature in December 1980
also focused international attention on Polish affairs. In the West
there was considerable sympathy for Solidarity which also enjoyed
the support of the Polish pope. In Moscow and East Berlin there
was horror and alarm. President Carter's threat of sanctions against

48 Lech Wałęsa (with the giant pen) at the moment of signing the agreement which brought Solidarity into existence, in the Lenin shipyard in Gdańsk on 31 August 1980. On his immediate right is Mieczysław Jagielski, a deputy prime minister and member of the communist Politburo. Note the statue of Lenin, long since gone, in the right-hand corner.

the USSR, made to the Kremlin via the 'hot line' at midnight of 3–4 December 1980, may have dissuaded the Soviet leadership from ordering an imminent invasion of Poland. But Moscow remained unyielding in its hostility, and leant heavily on the Polish authorities to crack down on Solidarity. For Solidarity was not an ordinary trade union; it was evolving into a mass social movement committed to the democratization of political life, the dismantling of the command economy, and the introduction of autonomous production units. Although its leaders were realistic enough to hold back from seizing political power (Kuroń described it as 'a self-limiting revolution'), an effective state of 'dual power' was emerging. By its very existence, Solidarity represented a challenge to the communists' monopoly of political control within Poland, and ultimately to the Soviet empire in eastern Europe.

Under Wałęsa's leadership Solidarity not only withstood the

government's attempts to infiltrate its regional branches and to promote a split within its ranks but also grew in strength, most vividly demonstrated by the all-national four-hour general strike on 27 March 1981. In May Rural Solidarity of peasant farmers was legalized. The Polish authorities were not yet ready for a decisive confrontation. Indeed, under the impact of the euphoric expectations of greater freedom gripping the country, the Party itself was in turmoil and in a veritable state of decline. Of its 3 million members, about a third abandoned the Party altogether, while a further 700,000 members actually joined Solidarity. A reformist wing called for more democratic 'horizontal structures' within the Party, while the hardliners, encouraged by Moscow, urged decisive action against the 'counter-revolution'.

The Church's effective mediatory role in diffusing repeated crises between the authorities and Solidarity was temporarily blunted in May 1981 by the attempted assassination of the pope, probably instigated by the KGB, and by the death of Cardinal Wyszyński. The new primate Cardinal Józef Glemp did not have his predecessor's dominating prestige and had a hard act to follow. In any case, the day of reckoning was fast approaching, for the abnormal situation in Poland could not continue indefinitely. The appointment of the defence minister General Wojciech Jaruzelski as prime minister in February was an early indication that the Party leadership was bracing itself for action. Although of gentry origin and a young victim of Stalin's deportations, the aloof Jaruzelski was a loyal communist general with a long, successful military career behind him. At frequent meetings throughout the spring and summer of 1981, the Polish communist leaders assured the impatient Soviets of their resolve to end the crisis by their own means. At the extraordinary 9th Party congress in July, the first to be attended by democratically elected delegates, Kania succeeded in restoring some order within the Party. With the appointment in August of General Kiszczak, the head of military counter-intelligence, as interior minister, the authorities accelerated plans devised earlier for the introduction of martial law.

The drastic deterioration of food supplies triggered off further wage demands and deepened the weariness of the population. The hardening of the authorities' attitudes radicalized many Solidarity activists. At its national congress, held in Gdańsk in September, Solidarity overwhelmingly endorsed an appeal of fraternity to the workers of eastern Europe and of the USSR; it was a romantic gesture that only served as a red rag to the Soviet bull. The gravity of the situation and the high stakes involved were reflected when, on 18 October, the central committee of the Party replaced Kania with Jaruzelski as first secretary. Control of the state and Party apparatus and of the country's armed forces now rested in one pair of hands. The failure of General Jaruzelski, Cardinal Glemp and Wałęsa to secure a national compromise at a meeting on 4 November, followed by Solidarity's announcement of a great demonstration in Warsaw for 17 December, and continuing Soviet pressure, forced Jaruzelski's hand.

During the night of 12–13 December 1981, in a well co-ordi-nated and efficiently executed operation, observed closely by the Soviet Marshal Kulikov, and involving most of the Polish army and all the security forces, martial law ('a state of war') was imposed over the entire country. A so-called Military Council of National Salvation, headed by Jaruzelski, assumed supreme authority. Taken by surprise, 6,000 Solidarity activists, including Wałęsa, were arrested and interned. All social organizations were suspended, and all factories, transport and communications militarized. Force was used to crush the strikes that erupted over the country, but large-scale bloodshed was avoided; the worst incident was the killing of nine miners in the 'Wujek' coal-mine in Katowice.

The military crackdown restored a semblance of public order and drove people back to work, but did little to resolve Poland's fundamental political and economic problems. The Solidarity leaders who had escaped detention rebuilt the movement's struc-tures underground and prepared for a 'long march'. A propaganda war against the authorities was launched. Substantial amounts of printing and communication equipment, supplied by the CIA via American trade union organizations, was smuggled into Poland. Illegal 'samizdat' journals and books rolled off secret printing presses. Wałęsa's Nobel Peace Prize in October 1983 enhanced his international reputation and was a moral fillip to Solidarity.

There existed in Polish society a widely felt respect for the army, but Jaruzelski was unable to restore the badly damaged authority of the Party, despite extensive efforts to the contrary. Periodic amnesties were issued, Wałęsa was set free in November 1982 (but treated only as a private citizen), the pope was allowed to revisit his homeland again in June 1983, and martial law was formally suspended in July 1983. During the course of 1983–4 a new government-sponsored trade union was expanded as a counter-attraction to the banned Solidarity. Of limited effect were gestures to patriotic sentiment, such as the restoration of pre-war national feastdays or the festive commemoration of the 300th anniversary of King John Sobieski's victory over the Turks outside Vienna in September 1683.

With the dissolution of most social-political organizations, the role of the Church as the only publicly active autonomous focus of national life expanded in a manner highly reminiscent of earlier troubled periods in Polish history. Millions of people with Solidarity banners attended church services while the episcopate, although not directly involved in the political opposition, intervened on behalf of the repressed. During his second visit to Poland in June 1983, Pope John Paul II expressed his hope for the relegalization of Solidarity to the 10 million Poles who came out to greet him. The murder of Father Jerzy Popiełuszko, a vocal critic of the regime, in October 1984 by agents from the interior ministry backfired badly on the government. Several hundred thousand people attended the funeral of the martyred cleric, whose grave became a shrine.

By the mid-1980s there was political stalemate. Jaruzelski curbed the advocates of violent police methods and strove for moderation. But the government's inability to tackle the structural economic problems, compounded by the vast foreign debts ($40bn in 1988) and the West's unwillingness to advance further credits, not to mention US economic sanctions, continued to gnaw at the very sinews of national life. Industrial production and living standards continued to fall; prices rose; shops emptied; the state budget faced a dramatically growing deficit. Alarming effects of industrial pollution were observed in many areas of the country. Poland's prospects seemed hopeless and some half a million Poles, mostly young and enterprising, left the country or chose to remain abroad in this period. In 1986 the government released all remaining political

prisoners but the Solidarity leadership, although no longer prevented from acting openly, refused to participate in a government-
sponsored consultative assembly. Treated by visiting foreign politicians as the effective leader of the opposition and encouraged by
the pope's third visit in June 1987, Wałęsa continued to insist on
the restoration of political pluralism as a precondition for any all-
national action to deal with the economic crisis.

Jaruzelski's government and the Party sought other measures to
break out of the impasse without having to surrender their monopoly of power. A referendum, held on 29 November 1987, to seek
the nation's endorsement of the government's hesitant attempt at
economic reform, was a resounding defeat for the authorities.
Nevertheless, the government refused to give way to Solidarity
demands and responded with force against widespread strikes in
April and May 1988. A second wave of strikes enveloped the
country in August 1988. Fearing that the country was on the edge
of an uncontrolled major explosion, the authorities drew back from
reintroducing martial law.

Of decisive significance for the situation in Poland was now the
dramatic reversal of the policy of the USSR towards its satellites.
Forced by the stress of renewed military rivalry with the USA into a
radical overhaul of the Soviet economic and political system, the
new Soviet leader Gorbachev was no longer prepared to underwrite
the unreformed communist regimes of eastern Europe. Disoriented
by the changes in the USSR, and no longer able to justify a
restoration of martial law as preferable to a Soviet invasion (as had
been the case in 1981), the Polish communists now faced two stark
choices: to maintain control by force over a restless population and
a degraded economy, or retain some degree of power and the
benefits of wider economic reform by an accommodation with the
opposition which would secure for the regime popular legitimacy
and international respectability.

In a televized broadcast on 26 August 1988 the interior minister
General Kiszczak proposed 'round table' talks between the govern-
ment and the opposition. Emerging as a level-headed politician,
Wałęsa next succeeded in bringing to an end the strike campaign
that was destabilizing the country. On 31 August Kiszczak met
Wałęsa privately for the first time. Extremists in both camps

opposed the talks, and it took five months of complex political manoeuvring before they got off the ground on 6 February 1989. It was only by threatening to resign that Jaruzelski and Kiszczak secured the consent of the central committee of the PZPR to the relegalization of Solidarity.

The deliberations of the 'round table' ended on 5 April with a compromise agreement which heralded extensive changes to the constitutional order. The offices of the president and the Senate, abolished in 1952 and 1946 respectively, were restored; the former was to be chosen jointly by the Sejm and the Senate, and the latter was to be elected on the basis of fully free national elections. Both the president and the Senate would exercise the power of veto over the Sejm in which 65 per cent of the seats would be reserved for the PZPR and its allies, while 35 per cent of the seats would be decided by a free electoral contest. Solidarity and Rural Solidarity were relegalized on 17 and 20 April, respectively.

The semi-free elections took place on 4 June 1989. Although boycotted by a sceptical third of the electorate, they were an overwhelming disaster for the Party and exceeded all expectations of the architects of the 'round table' agreement. In retrospect, the Polish elections of 1989 proved to be the first key move in the dismantling of the communist system in east-central Europe. All but one of the hundred seats in the Senate and all the free seats in the Sejm were won by the Solidarity-backed Citizens' Committee, while only five government-backed candidates passed the 50 per cent vote needed to secure the reserved seats in the Sejm. A second round of voting was therefore needed on 18 June to enable the pro-government parties to fill their guaranteed places. On 3 July Gorbachev's envoy made the momentous announcement that Poland was free to determine the shape of its own government. In another compromise arrangement, Jaruzelski was elected president on 19 July; ten days later he resigned from the Party secretaryship. On the other hand, Wałęsa skilfully wooed the the United Peasant Party (ZSL) and the Democratic Party (SD), hitherto communist-controlled parliamentary groupings but now eager to assert their independence, to prevent the creation of a coalition government led by General Kiszczak. On 19 August President Jaruzelski invited the respected Catholic intellectual

Tadeusz Mazowiecki to form a coalition government. With the almost unanimous support of the Sejm, Mazowiecki became the first non-communist prime minister in what was still formally communist eastern Europe. Wałęsa himself eschewed all public office for the time being. Although the PZPR retained the key ministries of the interior and of defence, in accordance with the 'round table' agreement and to reassure Moscow, its days as a 'Marxist-Leninist' party were over.

The forty-five-year period of communist rule in Poland cannot be simply dismissed as one in which nothing constructive or beneficial was achieved. And Poland's satellite status was certainly preferable to the fate of the Baltic States, which were incorporated in the USSR. But the forcible imposition of an ideology alien to most of its inhabitants, the cynical travesty of the concept of democracy, the decades of mendacity, the humiliating subservience to the USSR, and the sheer wastefulness of much economic activity all weigh heavily in any objective assessment of the communist legacy in Poland. In terms of living standards, communist Poland not only did not catch up with the West, but fell further behind. Impressive statistics of coal or steel production were no substitute for chronic shortages of basic goods.

Although many hardline Solidarity supporters resented the fact that there was no clean break with the communist past and no settling of scores with the communists, the constitutional changes and the elections of 1989 are now generally accepted as marking the birth of the Polish Third Republic. On 29 December 1989 Poland formally ceased to be a so-called 'People's Republic' and recovered the crowned white eagle as its emblem; references to the 'leading role' of the PZPR, to the Soviet alliance, and to socialism were expunged from the constitution. What made possible Poland's peaceful transformation in 1989–90 was the 'self-organization' of Polish society that had evolved since the 1970s and the self-restraint and sense of responsibility of the country's political leaders, whether communists or members of the former opposition. As a result a dangerous political vacuum was avoided and social peace was maintained. Indeed, the much greater political realism of the Poles in the second half of the twentieth century, as witnessed in 1956, in 1980–1, and now, marked a powerful contrast with the disastrous Romantic insurrections of the previous century and with the Warsaw uprising of 1944.

Mazowiecki's 'great coalition' showed exceptional energy in dragging Poland out of its economic marasmus. January 1990 saw the introduction of a wide-ranging programme of economic reform, the most radical in the whole of ex-communist Europe, prepared by the new finance minister Professor Leszek Balcerowicz. The resulting shock treatment halted the galloping inflation and propelled Poland fast towards a market economy, a process assisted by the favourable renegotiation of the country's vast foreign debts and by financial assistance from western financial institutions. The former dissident Jacek Kuroń, with his direct and engaging manner, did much as minister of labour to allay popular alarm at the painful social effects of the reform, which by the end of 1990 had generated 1 million unemployed. The dismantling of the socialist planned economy and the restoration of free enterprise inevitably created social divisions. Ironically, many former communist officials and managers gained materially from the privatization of state enterprises, while many workers who had helped to topple the communist system now found themselves the victims of economic rationalization. The appearance of new, well-stocked shops ended the chronic shortages of the 1980s and began to alter visibly the hitherto drab appearance of most Polish towns. The location of the new Warsaw stock exchange in the former central headquarters of the communist party added a nice touch of historical irony.

Under the direction of the new foreign minister, Professor Krzysztof Skubiszewski, an academic of no party allegiance, Poland carefully asserted its interests as a newly independent state. Of central importance for Poland's security and future association with western structures was the recognition by the united Germany of the Oder–Neisse frontier in November 1990 and the conclusion of a Polish–German treaty of friendship in June 1991. Relations with Moscow remained not only correct but improved dramatically with Gorbachev's official admission in 1990 of Soviet responsibility for the 1940 Katyn massacre, an act reinforced two years later in Warsaw by Yeltsin's personal gesture of apology. But as the USSR disintegrated, Poland was quick to recognize the independence of Ukraine, Lithuania and Belarus. While understandably interested

Map 12   Poland and its 'new' neighbours, 1989–2000.

LITHUANIA
(indep. 1990)

ЅIAN
ATION

VILNIUS •

PODLASKIE
Białystok
(29)

BELARUS
(indep. 1991)

E

ЅAW
ЅZAWA)

LUBELSKIE
• Lublin
(29)

• Rzeszów
KARPACKIE
(30)

UKRAINE
(indep. 1991)

Poland's boundaries since 1945

New provincial (Województwo) boundaries introduced in 1999

POMORSKIE Names of the new provinces (Województwa), with administrative centres e.g. Gdańsk

(40) Average per capita income in each province as a percentage of the average per capita income in the European Union (1999) The national Polish average was 37%

Provinces with 40% and above

Provinces with 30–39%

Provinces with under 30%

Boundaries of new states since 1989, following the dissolution of the German Democratic Republic, the USSR, and Czechoslovakia in the welfare of the Polish minorities in the states of the former USSR, independent Poland has accepted its post-1945 eastern frontier. By the same token, the absence of large national minorities within its borders (estimated now at about 1 million, with 300,000 Germans the largest group among them) has prevented the re-emergence of inter-ethnic and nationality conflicts which had bedevilled the Second Republic before 1939 and which now plagued some ex-communist states, most tragically in the case of Yugoslavia. In June and July 1991 the Comecon and the Warsaw Pact were dissolved, and the last Russian troops left Polish soil in the autumn of 1993.

Unexpectedly liberated from the Soviet yoke, Poland was entering a new era in its history. During the decade since 1989 a profound transformation of Polish political and economic life has occurred. A parliamentary democracy has been established with a popularly elected president and an accountable system of local government, and civil rights have been restored. In the realm of politics, the most striking phenomenon in the early 1990s was the disintegration of Solidarity as a broad social and moral movement of protest. Mazowiecki hoped to retain Solidarity unity and the 'round table' agreements during the difficult period of economic transformation. Wałęsa, on the other hand, argued that the collapse of the PZPR justified the acceleration of constitutional changes. His subsequent presidential ambitions only deepened the rift within the movement. The introduction in July 1990 of a generous system of proportional representation in parliamentary elections in its turn encouraged the proliferation of small parties. By 1991 the bulk of Solidarity had fragmented into several rival trade union organizations and a host of populist anti-communist and nationalist-Catholic groupings. Most remained suspicious of the free market economics propounded by Solidarity's liberal intelligentsia wing, represented by Mazowiecki and Geremek, which under the name of the Democratic Union (UD) and then the Freedom Union (UW), became the most successful post-Solidarity party.

The political parties of the communist era also underwent change. The communist PZPR dissolved itself in January 1990 and most of its members formed a disciplined social democratic party (SdRP) led by Aleksander Kwaśniewski, a young but experienced activist and sports minister in the last communist administration. In 1991 it allied with other left-wing groups to form the Left Democratic Alliance (SLD), one of the most important parties in Poland today. It is noteworthy that the post-communist left has respected the democratic process. The former pro-communist peasant party went through more traumatic upheavals, but eventually in May 1990 linked with other peasant groupings and adopted its pre-1947 label of the Polish Peasant Party (PSL). Attempts to revive the historic Polish Socialist Party (PPS) have so far failed.

Wałęsa won the 1990 presidential election and chose to receive his insignia of office not from the outgoing Jaruzelski but from Ryszard Kaczorowski, the last president-in-exile, thus establishing a symbolic constitutional link with the legitimist successors of the pre-war Second Republic residing in London since 1945. However, the parliamentary elections of October 1991, the first fully free since the Second World War, produced a fragmented Sejm and a series of short-lived centre-right coalition governments between 1991 and 1993. The growing demands from the right for the 'de-communization' of public life and for the 'lustration' or purging of politicians who had collaborated with the communist security services, and Wałęsa's increasingly confrontational style and head-strong attempts to strengthen presidential authority all contributed to an atmosphere of political acrimony.

The parliamentary elections of September 1993, based on a reformed electoral system aimed at eliminating the smallest political groupings from the Sejm (5 per cent minimal threshold for parties), produced unexpected results. Despite winning over a third of the popular vote, the right-wing parties paid for their internecine divisions by being virtually wiped out from the parliamentary scene. The post-Solidarity liberals (UD) fared moderately well. But the largest number of seats went to the post-communist SLD (171 seats) and the peasant PSL (132 seats), who formed a coalition that survived until 1997. Wałęsa's narrow defeat in the 1995 presidential election at the hands of the more tactful and urbane SLD leader Kwaśniewski confirmed the ascendancy of the left, ironically at a time when the population was beginning to feel the benefits of economic reform.

The fragmented post-Solidarity right had to learn the lessons of its electoral disaster. Under Marian Krzaklewski, a 41-year-old cybernetician from Silesia, it consolidated itself into the so-called Electoral Action Solidarity (AWS) and successfully entered the hustings in 1997, gaining 34 per cent of the popular vote and emerging as the single largest grouping in the Sejm. A coalition with the liberal Freedom Union (UW), led now by Balcerowicz, produced a centre-right government. The coalition of the two main post-Solidarity parties was not an easy one, but until the resignation of the UW ministers in May 2000 it did provide a degree of stability in Polish parliamentary life. Indeed, the AWS prime minister Józef Buzek, a chemistry professor, remained in office from 1997 until 2001, a record so far in the Third Republic. That Buzek is a Protestant is also a telling comment on the openness of the Polish political system.

The status of the Roman Catholic Church, a powerful champion in the ideological struggle against communism and a key mediator in the transfer of power in 1989, remains high in Polish society. It is noteworthy that a quarter of all Catholic priests in Europe are Polish. The Church has also successfully lobbied for the tightening of legislation on abortion, one of the most explosive issues in Polish politics in the 1990s. Other events, however, have shown that in a democratic and pluralist Poland, the Church's political influence can no longer be taken for granted. The blatant intervention of the hierarchy and of many priests during the 1991 parliamentary election alienated many voters, including Catholics, and contributed to the victory of the left two years later. The episcopate's warnings failed to prevent both Kwaśniewski's presidential victory in 1995 and the endorsement by a popular referendum of a new liberal constitution in 1997. Although a vociferous fundamentalist Catholic wing continues to attract many followers, attempts to revive an effective Christian Democratic party have proved unsuccessful.

Despite all the interpersonal rivalries and acrimonious political infighting of the last decade, all the post-1989 governments have maintained a considerable degree of continuity in economic policy. After a short sharp recession in 1990 to 1991 the Polish economy has continued to expand. Real incomes have increased since 1994, foreign investment has grown rapidly, and by 1998 inflation had fallen to below 10 per cent. In the period 1993–9 the per capita GNP of the Polish population increased from 33 per cent to nearly 40 per cent of that of the European Union. Private firms now produce over two-thirds of Poland's GNP. The pursuit of education and professional qualifications among the younger generation is a marked feature of the meritocratic nature of Polish society today. However, the changes since 1990 have not been without pain for large sections of the population. The restructuring of heavy industry, especially coal-mining, has proved difficult. The bankruptcy of the Gdańsk shipyard, the home of Solidarity, and its recent acquisition by the neighbouring Gdynia shipyard dramatically symbolized the ongoing transformation process. The great city of Łódź, once known as 'the Manchester of Poland', has ceased to be a major textile centre and has had to diversify its economic activity. Manual workers, and especially those on former state farms, have keenly felt a fall in real wages and in status. The most backward sector of the economy remains agriculture with its low yields and small holdings. It is peasant farmers, still representing a quarter of Poland's labour force, who are most fearful of the country's move towards the European Union. High unemployment (15 per cent of the workforce in 2001), housing shortages, underfunding of the public health and education services, and the growth of corruption and crime represent the bleaker aspects of Polish reality today. Many former owners (or their descendants) still await satisfactory compensation for property nationalized during the early years of communist rule. Yet for all its difficulties, Poland remains one of the most stable and dynamic countries of the former Soviet bloc.

There has been remarkable continuity in foreign policy since the dissolution of the Warsaw Pact in 1991. Despite some earlier talk of neutrality, all Polish governments have pursued the goal of joining western institutions. The Polish armed forces have accordingly been depoliticized and placed under civilian control. On 12 March 1999 Poland, together with Hungary and the Czech Republic, formally joined NATO. For the Poles, conscious of their country's vulnerability over the centuries, it was a major political and psychological breakthrough. Preparations are now going ahead for Poland, with its 39 million inhabitants, to join the European Union, although the target date of 2003 may prove

49   President Aleksander Kwaśniewski ratifies Poland's treaty of accession
to NATO, 26 February 1999. It is one of those ironies of Poland's history
that an ex-communist and leader of the post-communist SLD was to lead
Poland into NATO. The ceremony took place in the same hall of the
presidential palace in which the Soviet-led Warsaw Pact had been created
in 1955. On 8 October 2000 Kwaśniewski was re-elected president for a
second five-year term.

unrealistic through Polish unreadiness as much as foot-dragging
within the EU.

Despite memories and resentments of past wrongs, Poland is
today at peace with all its seven neighbours and in close partnership
with most of them. Relations with Germany have been resolved,
and a breakthrough achieved in relations with Ukraine and
Lithuania. Suspicions of Russia, which had campaigned against
Poland's membership of NATO and whose future remains
uncertain, continue to linger. Nevertheless, at the beginning of the
twenty-first century the inhabitants of Poland have the opportunity
of tackling their problems in an atmosphere of national freedom
and security denied so many of their previous generations.

Poland's early inclusion in the EU was accepted in principle at the European conference in Nice in December 2000. It was also decided that, as a member, Poland would be entitled to twenty-seven votes in the European Council of Ministers, on a par with Spain, and only two votes fewer than Germany, Great Britain, France and Italy.

Chart I   Polish rulers: the Piast dynasty

NB Regnal dates only are shown
This is a highly simplified chart; not all rulers mentioned in the text are shown; dates for rulers between 1138 (death of Bolesław III) and 1320 (coronation of Władysław Łokietek) are only for guidance, since many of these rulers exercised authority over territories and principalities which might vary considerably at any one time.
Names in bold denote rulers formally crowned as king.
- - - - - - Broken lines indicate the elapse of more than one generation.

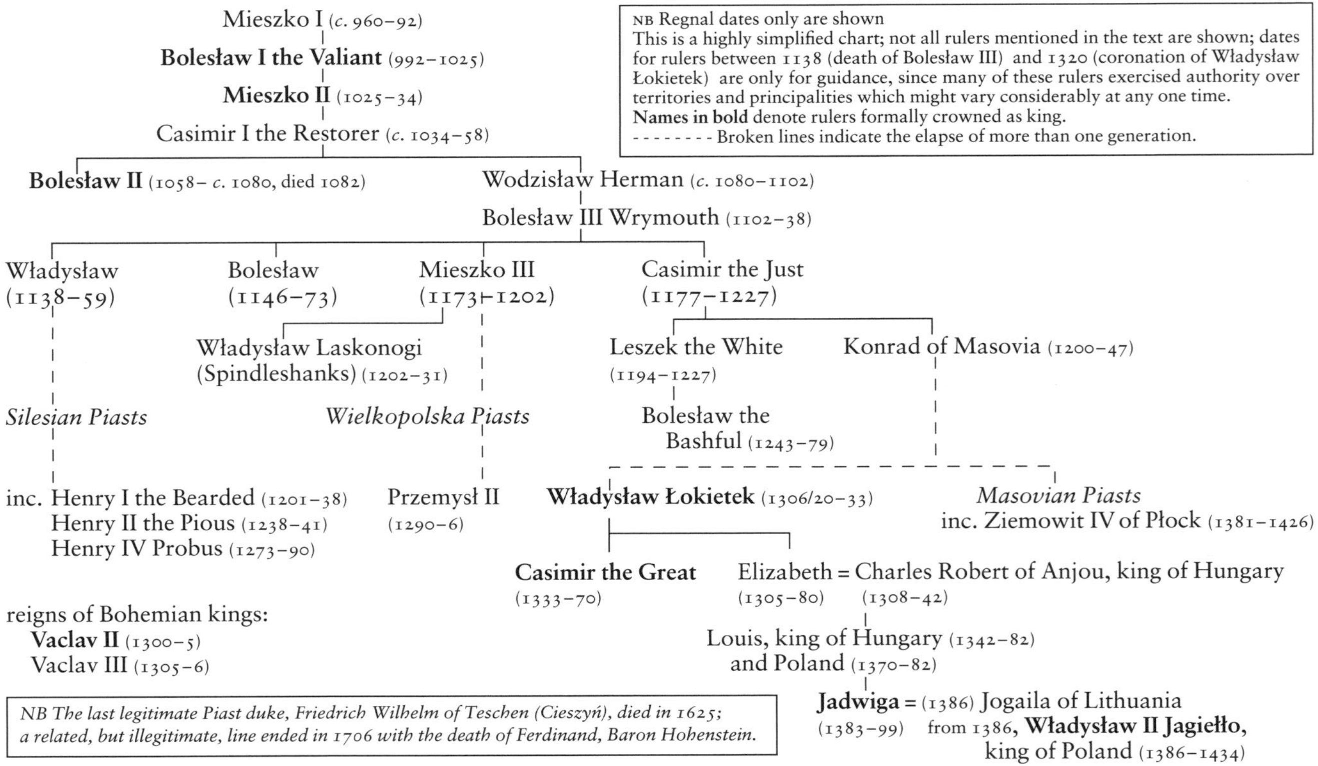

Mieszko I (c. 960–92)

Bolesław I the Valiant (992–1025)

Mieszko II (1025–34)

Casimir I the Restorer (c. 1034–58)

Bolesław II (1058– c. 1080, died 1082)

Wodzisław Herman (c. 1080–1102)

Bolesław III Wrymouth (1102–38)

Casimir the Just (1177–1227)

Leszek the White (1194–1227)

Konrad of Masovia (1200–47)

Bolesław the Bashful (1243–79)

Masovian Piasts
inc. Ziemowit IV of Płock (1381–1426)

Władysław Łokietek (1306/20–33)

Elizabeth = Charles Robert of Anjou, king of Hungary
(1305–80)   (1308–42)

Louis, king of Hungary (1342–82) and Poland (1370–82)

Jadwiga = (1386) Jogaila of Lithuania
(1383–99)   from 1386, **Władysław II Jagiełło,**
king of Poland (1386–1434)

Casimir the Great (1333–70)

Władysław (1138–59)

Bolesław (1146–73)

Mieszko III (1173–1202)

Władysław Laskonogi (Spindleshanks) (1202–31)

Wielkopolska Piasts

Przemysł II (1290–6)

Silesian Piasts

inc. Henry I the Bearded (1201–38)
Henry II the Pious (1238–41)
Henry IV Probus (1273–90)

reigns of Bohemian kings:
Vaclav II (1300–5)
Vaclav III (1305–6)

NB The last legitimate Piast duke, Friedrich Wilhelm of Teschen (Cieszyn), died in 1625; a related, but illegitimate, line ended in 1706 with the death of Ferdinand, Baron Hohenstein.

Chart II   The Jagiellonian dynasty: kings of Poland and grand dukes of Lithuania

Gediminas, prince of Lithuania (c. 1316–42)

Algirdas (1345–77)

Kestutis (1337–82)

Jogaila; 1377–1434 grand duke of Lithuania
from 1386, **Władysław II Jagiełło**, king of Poland (1386–1434)
= (1) 1386 Jadwiga of Poland (1383–99)
= (4) 1422 Sonia of Gol'shany

Vytautas,
grand duke of Lithuania 1392–1430

Władysław III 'of Varna'
king of Poland, 1434–44
king of Hungary, 1440–4

Casimir IV grand duke of Lithuania, 1440–92 = 1454 Elizabeth of Habsburg
king of Poland, 1446–92

John I Albert
king of Poland, 1492–1501

Alexander
grand duke of Lithuania, 1492–1506
king of Poland, 1501–6

Sigismund I 'the Old'
king of Poland and grand duke
of Lithuania, 1506–48
= (1) 1495 Barbara Zápolya
= (2) 1518 Bona Sforza

Władysław: King Vladislav II of Bohemia, 1471–1516
King Ulászló II of Hungary, 1490–1516

Louis II, king of
Bohemia and Hungary, 1516–26

Anna (1503–47)

= 1527

Ferdinand I of Habsburg
Holy Roman Emperor
1556–64

Isabella (1519–59)
= 1539 John Zápolya of Hungary

Sigismund II Augustus
reigned in Poland and
Lithuania 1548–72

Anna (1523–96)
= 1576 Stefan Batory
elective king of Poland,
1575–86

Catherine (1526–83)
= 1562 John III Vasa,
duke of Finland, king
of Sweden 1569–92

Sigismund III Vasa,
elective king of Poland, 1587–1632
king of Sweden, from 1592
deposed, 1599

Chart III   Elective rulers of the Polish-Lithuanian Commonwealth (and others)

Sigismund I 'the Old' 1506–48

(The Swedish Vasa line)

Henry I, duke of Anjou
elective king of Poland, 1573–4
King Henri III of France, 1574–89

Catherine Jagiellon	=	John III Vasa	Charles IX
(1526–83)		king of Sweden 1569–92	regent of Sweden 1599–1607
			king of Sweden 1607–11

Stefan Batory = (1576) Anna Jagiellon
prince of Transylvania   (1523–96)
elective king of Poland, 1575–86

Anna of Habsburg (1592) 1. = **Sigismund III Vasa**   2. = (1605) Constance of Habsburg
elective king of Poland 1587–1632
king of Sweden, 1592–9 *(deposed)*

Władysław IV   **John II Casimir**   **Karol Ferdynand**
elective king of Poland, 1632–48   elective king of Poland   (1613–55)
1648–68 *(abdicated; died 1672)*

Prince Sigismund Casimir (1640–7)

Catherine = John
              Casimir of
              Zweibrücken

Gustavus II Adolphus   Charles X
king of Sweden, 1611–32   king of Sweden, 1654–70

Christina   Charles XI
queen of Sweden, 1632–54   king of Sweden, 1660–97

Charles XII
king of Sweden, 1697–1718

Michael I Wiśniowiecki, elective king of Poland, 1668–73

John III Sobieski, elective king of Poland, 1673–96

Friedrich August I, elector of Saxony (1694–1733) ;
also **Augustus II**, elective king of Poland, 1697–1733

Stanisław Leszczyński: elective anti-king, 1704–10; elective king, 1733–5; *titular king of Poland and duke of Lorraine to his death in 1766*

Friedrich August II, elector of Saxony (1733–63);
also **Augustus III**, elective king of Poland, 1733–63

Stanisław August Poniatowski, elective king of Poland, 1764–95 *(abdicated; died, 1798)*

(Frederick Augustus, duke of Warsaw, 1807–15
also Friedrich August III, elector of Saxony, 1763–1806
then King Friedrich August I of Saxony, 1806–27)

Chart IV Rulers of the partitioned Polish territories (regnal dates only are shown)

Romanov emperors of Russia (bearing the title of 'Polish king' after 1815)	The Habsburgs of Austria (Holy Roman Emperors until 1806; emperors of Austria 1804–1918)	The Hohenzollern kings of Prussia (also grand dukes of Posen after 1815; German emperors after 1871)	The Wettins of Saxony (electors of Saxony until 1806; kings of Saxony after 1806)
Catherine II 'the Great' (1762–96)	Maria Theresa (1740–80)	Frederick II 'the Great' (1740–86)	Frederick Augustus, duke of Warsaw (1807–15)
Paul I (1796–1801)	Joseph II (1765–90)	Frederick William II (1786–97)	
Alexander I (1801–25)	Leopold II (1790–2)	Frederick William III (1797–1840)	
Nicholas I (1825–55)	Francis (II) I (1792–1835)	Frederick William IV (1840–61)	
Alexander II (1855–81)	Ferdinand I (1835–48)	William I (1861–88)	
Alexander III (1881–94)	Francis Joseph (1848–1916)	Frederick III (1888)	
Nicholas II (1894–1917) (abdicated)	Charles I (1916–18) (abdicated)	William II (1888–1918) (abdicated)	

Heads of state, presidents, Communist Party leaders (1918–2000)

The Second Republic (1918–1939)

HEAD OF STATE

Józef Piłsudski (November 1918–December 1922)

PRESIDENTS

Gabriel Narutowicz (December 1922)
Stanisław Wojciechowski (December 1922–May 1926)
Ignacy Mościcki (June 1926–September 1939)

Governments-in-exile (1939–1990)
maintaining constitutional continuity with the Second Republic

PRESIDENTS

Władysław Raczkiewicz (September 1939–June 1947)
August Zaleski (June 1947–April 1972)
Stanisław Ostrowski (April 1972–April 1979)
Edward Raczyński (April 1979–April 1986)
Kazimierz Sabbat (April 1986–July 1989)
Ryszard Kaczorowski (July 1989–December 1990)

The Polish People's Republic (1944–1989)

HEADS OF STATE

President of the National Council (KRN)
Bolesław Bierut (November 1944–February 1947)

President and Chairman of the Council of State
Bolesław Bierut (February 1947–November 1952)

Chairmen of the Council of State
Aleksander Zawadzki (November 1952–August 1964)
Edward Ochab (August 1964–April 1968)
Marian Spychalski (April 1968–December 1970)
Józef Cyrankiewicz (December 1970–March 1972)
Henryk Jabłoński (March 1972–November 1985)
Wojciech Jaruzelski (November 1985–July 1989)

LEADERS OF THE POLISH UNITED WORKERS PARTY (PZPR)
Chairman of the Central Committee
Bolesław Bierut (December 1948–March 1954)

First Secretaries
Bolesław Bierut (March 1954–March 1956)
Edward Ochab (March–October 1956)
Władysław Gomułka (October 1956–December 1970)
Edward Gierek (December 1970–September 1980)
Stanisław Kania (September 1980–October 1981)
Wojciech Jaruzelski (October 1981–July 1989)
Mieczysław Rakowski (July 1989–January 1990)

The Third Republic (since 1989)

PRESIDENTS

Wojciech Jaruzelski (July 1989 –December 1990)
Lech Wałęsa (December 1990 –December 1995)
Aleksander Kwaśniewski (December 1995–)

BIBLIOGRAPHY OF WORKS IN ENGLISH

GENERAL WORKS

Davies, N. *God's playground: a history of Poland*, 2 vols., Oxford: Clarendon Press, 1981

Davies, N. *Heart of Europe: a short history of Poland*, Oxford: University Press, 1984

Jedruch, J. *Constitutions, elections and legislatures of Poland 1493–1977*, Washington, D.C.: University Press of America, 1982

Kloczowski, J. *A history of Polish Christianity*, Cambridge: University Press, 2000

Knab, S. H. *Polish customs, traditions and folklore*, New York: Hippocrene, 1999

Kridl, M. *A survey of Polish literature and culture*, The Hague: Mouton, 1956

Magocsi, P. R. *A history of Ukraine*, Toronto: University Press, 1996

Miłosz, C. *The history of Polish literature*, Berkeley: University of California Press, 1983

Subtelny, O. *Ukraine: a history*, Toronto: University Press, 1988

Wandycz, P. *The price of freedom: a history of east central Europe from the Middle Ages to the present*, London: Routledge, 1992

Zamoyski, A. *The Polish way: a thousand years' history of the Poles and their culture*, London: Murray, 1989

POLAND, PRE-1795

Barker, M. (ed.) *The military orders*, vol. I: *Fighting for the faith and caring for the sick*, Aldershot: Variorum, 1994

Bartlett, R. *The making of Europe: conquest, colonization and cultural change 950–1350*, Princeton, N.J.: University Press, 1993

Basarab, J. *Pereiaslav 1654: a historiographical study*, Edmonton: Canadian Institute of Ukrainian Studies, University of Alberta, 1982

Bogucka, M. *The lost world of the 'Sarmatians'*, Warsaw: Polish Academy of Sciences, Institute of History, 1996

Butterwick, R. *Poland's last king and English culture: Stanisław August Poniatowski 1732–1798*, Oxford: Clarendon Press, 1998

Carter, F. W. *Trade and urban development in Poland: an economic geography of Cracow, from its origins to 1795*, Cambridge: University Press, 1994

Christiansen, A. *The northern crusades*, London: Macmillan, 1980

Długosz, J. *The annals of Jan Długosz: Annales seu Cronicae incliti Regni Poloniae:* an English abridgement by H. Michael with a commentary by P. Smith, Chichester: IM Publications, 1997

Dolukhanov, P. M. *The early Slavs: eastern Europe from the initial settlement to the Kievan Rus*, London: Longman, 1996

Fedorowicz, J. K. (ed.) *A republic of nobles: studies in Polish history to 1864*, Cambridge: University Press, 1982

Fiszman, S. (ed.) *The Polish Renaissance in its European context*, Bloomington: Indiana University Press, 1988

Fiszman, S. (ed.) *Constitution and reform in eighteenth-century Poland: the Constitution of 3 May 1791*, Bloomington: Indiana University Press, 1997

Fletcher, R. *The conversion of Europe: from paganism to Christianity 371–1386 AD*, London: Harper Collins, 1997

Frost, R. *After the Deluge: Poland-Lithuania and the Second Northern War 1555–1660*, Cambridge: University Press, 1993

Frost, R. *The Northern Wars: war, state and society in north-eastern Europe 1558–1721*, London: Longman, 2000

Friedrich, K. *The other Prussia: Royal Prussia, Poland and liberty, 1569–1772*, Cambridge: University Press, 2000

Fuhrmann, H. *Germany in the High Middle Ages* c. *1050–1200*, Cambridge: University Press, 1986

Geremek, B. *The common roots of Europe*, Cambridge: Polity Press, 1996

Górecki, P. *Economy, society, and lordship in medieval Poland 1100–1250*, New York: Holme and Meier, 1992

Gudziak, B. A. *Crisis and reform: the Kievan metropolitanate, the patriarchate of Constantinople and the genesis of the Union of Brest*, Cambridge, Mass.: Harvard University Press, 1998

Hundert, G. D. *The Jews in a Polish town: the case of Opatów in the eighteenth century*, Baltimore: Johns Hopkins University Press, 1992

Kamiński, A. S. *Republic vs. autocracy: Poland-Lithuania and Russia, 1686–1697*, Cambridge, Mass.: Harvard University Press, 1993

Kaplan, H. H. *The First Partition of Poland*, New York: Columbia University Press, 1962

Kirby, D. *Northern Europe in the early modern period: the Baltic world 1492–1772*, London: Longman, 1990

Knoll, P. W. *The rise of the Polish monarchy: Piast Poland in east central Europe, 1320–1370*, Chicago: University of Chicago Press, 1972

Kochanowski, J. *Jan Kochanowski: Laments*, trans. S. Heaney and S. Barańczak, London: Faber, 1995

Levine, H. *Economic origins of antisemitism: Poland and its Jews in the early modern period*, New Haven, Conn.: Yale University Press, 1991

Lord, R. H. *The Second Partition of Poland: a study in diplomatic history*, Cambridge, Mass.: Harvard University Press, 1915

Lukowski, J. T. *Liberty's folly: the Polish-Lithuanian Commonwealth in the eighteenth century*, London: Routledge, 1991

Lukowski, J. T. *The Partitions of Poland 1772, 1793, 1795*, London: Longman, 1999

Mączak, A., Samsonowicz, H. and Burke, P. (eds.) *East-central Europe in transition: from the fourteenth to the seventeenth centuries*, Cambridge: University Press, 1985

Manteuffel, T. *The formation of the Polish state: the period of ducal rule, 963–1194*, Detroit, Mich.: Wayne State University Press, 1982

Musteikis, A. *The Reformation in Lithuania: religious fluctuations in the sixteenth century*, Boulder, Colo.: East European Monographs, 1988

Pasek, J. Ch. *Memoirs of the Polish baroque: the writings of Jan Chryzostom Pasek, a squire of the Commonwealth of Poland and Lithuania*, ed. C. S. Leech, Berkeley: University of California Press, 1976

Polonsky, A., Basista, J. and Link-Lenczowski, A. (eds.) *The Jews in Old Poland*, London: Taurus, 1993

Rosman, M. *The Lords' Jews: magnate – Jewish relations in the Polish-Lithuanian Commonwealth during the eighteenth century*, Cambridge, Mass.: Harvard University Press, 1990

Rowell, S. C. *Lithuania ascending: a pagan empire within east-central Europe, 1295–1345*, Cambridge: University Press, 1994

Sedlar, J. W. *East central Europe in the Middle Ages 1000–1500*, Seattle: University of Washington Press, 1994

Segel, H. B. *Renaissance culture in Poland: the rise of humanism 1470–1543*, Ithaca: Cornell University Press, 1989

Subtelny, O. *Domination of eastern Europe: native nobilities and foreign absolutism, 1500–1715*, Kingston: McGill-Queen's University Press, 1986

Sysyn, F. E. *Between Poland and the Ukraine: the dilemma of Adam Kysil*, Cambridge, Mass.: Harvard University Press, 1985

Tazbir, J. *A state without stakes: Polish religious toleration in the sixteenth and seventeenth centuries*, New York: The Kościuszko Foundation, 1973

Zamoyski, A. *The last king of Poland*, London: Cape, 1992
Zank, W. *The German melting-pot: multiculturality in historical
perspective*, Basingstoke: Macmillan, 1998
Żółkiewski, S. *Expedition to Moscow: a memoir*, London: Polonica
Publications, 1959

POLAND, POST-1795

Abramsky, C., Jachimczyk, M. and Polonsky, A. (eds.) *The Jews in
Poland*, Oxford: Basil Blackwell, 1986
Ascherson, N. *The Polish August: The self-limiting revolution*, London:
Allen Lane, 1981
Bethell, N. *Gomułka, his Poland and his communism*, London: Longman,
1969
Brock, P. *Polish revolutionary populism: a study in agrarian socialist
thought from the 1830s to the 1850s*, Toronto: University Press,
1977
Bromke, A. *Poland's politics: idealism vs. realism*, Cambridge, Mass.:
Harvard University Press, 1967
Brown, J. F. *Surge to freedom: the end of communist rule in eastern
Europe*, Durham, N.C.: Duke University Press, 1991
Brzeziński, Z. K. *The Soviet bloc: unity and conflict*, Cambridge, Mass.:
Harvard University Press, 1971
Ciechanowski, J. M. *The Warsaw Rising of 1944*, Cambridge: University
Press, 1974
Cienciala, A. M. *Poland and the Western Powers 1938–1939: a study in
the interdependence of eastern and western Europe*, London:
Routledge and Kegan Paul, 1968
Cienciala, A. M. and Komarnicki, T. *From Versailles to Locarno. Keys to
Polish foreign policy 1919–25*, Lawrence, Kans.: Kansas University
Press, 1984
Curry, J. L. and Fajfer, L. (eds.) *Poland's permanent revolution: peoples vs.
elites 1956–1990*, Washington, D.C.: American University Press,
1996
Davies, N. *White eagle, red star: the Polish–Soviet war 1919–1920*,
London: Orbis Books, 1983
Dawisha, K. *Eastern Europe, Gorbachev and reform, the great challenge*,
2nd edn, Cambridge: University Press, 1990
Dziewanowski, M. K. *The Communist Party of Poland. An outline of
history*, 2nd edn, Cambridge, Mass.: Harvard University Press, 1976
Eile, S. *Literature and nationalism in partitioned Poland, 1795–1918*,
Basingstoke: Macmillan, 2000
Eisenbach, A. *The emancipation of the Jews in Poland 1780–1870*,
Oxford: Basil Blackwell, 1992

Fejto, F. *A history of the people's democracies*, Harmondsworth: Penguin 1974

Fountain, A. V. *Roman Dmowski: party, tactics, ideology 1895–1907*, Boulder, Colo.: East European Monographs, 1980

Garliński, J. *Poland in the Second World War*, London: Macmillan, 1985

Garton Ash, T. *The Polish revolution: Solidarity*, London: Penguin, 1999

Gilbert, M. *The Holocaust: The Jewish tragedy*, London: Fontana/Collins, 1989

Gross, J. T. *Polish society under German occupation: the general gouvernement 1939–1944*, Princeton, N.J.: University Press, 1979

Gross, J. T. *Revolution from abroad: the Soviet conquest of Poland's western Ukraine and western Belorussia*, Princeton, N.J.: University Press, 1988

Hagen, W. W. *Germans, Poles, and Jews. The nationality conflict in the Prussian east, 1772–1914*, Chicago: University of Chicago Press, 1980

Hayden, J. *Poles apart: Solidarity and the new Poland*, Blackrock: Irish Academic Press, 1994

Howard, A. E. D. (ed.) *Constitution making in eastern Europe*, Washington, D.C.: Woodrow Wilson Center Press, 1993

Jaworski, R. and Pietrow-Ennker, B. (eds.) *Women in Polish society*, Boulder, Colo.: East European Monographs, 1992

Jedlicki, J. *A suburb of Europe: nineteenth-century Polish approaches to western civilization*, Budapest: Central European University Press, 1999

Jędrzejewicz, W. *Piłsudski: a life for Poland*, New York: Hippocrene Books, 1982

Kamiński, B. *The collapse of state socialism: the case of Poland*, Princeton, N.J.: University Press, 1991

Karski, J. *Story of a secret state*, London: Hodder and Stoughton, 1945

Karski, J. *The Great Powers and Poland 1919–1945: from Versailles to Yalta*, Lanham, Md: University Press of America, 1985

Kaser, M. C. and Radice, E. (eds.) *The economic history of eastern Europe 1919–1975*, Oxford: Cleveland Press, 1986

Kenney, P. *Rebuilding Poland: workers and communists 1945–1950*, Ithaca and London: Cornell University Press, 1997

Kersten, K. *The establishment of communist rule in Poland 1943–1948*, Berkeley: University of California Press, 1991

Kieniewicz, S. *The emancipation of the Polish peasantry*, Chicago and London: University of Chicago Press, 1969

Kirby, D. *The Baltic world 1772–1993. Europe's northern periphery in an age of change*, London: Longman, 1995

Komarnicki, T. *The rebirth of the Polish republic: a study in the diplomatic history of Europe 1914–1920*, London: Heinemann, 1957

Korbel, J. *Poland between East and West*, Princeton, N.J.: University Press, 1963

Korboński, A. *The politics of socialist agriculture in Poland 1945–1960*, New York: Columbia University Press, 1965

Korboński, S. *The Polish Underground State 1939–1945*, Boulder, Colo.: East European Monographs, 1978

Kurczewski, J. *The resurrection of rights in Poland*, Oxford: Clarendon Press, 1993

Labedz, L. (ed.) *Poland under Jaruzelski*, New York: Scribner, 1984

Latawski, P. (ed.) *The reconstruction of Poland 1914–23*, London: Macmillan, 1992

Lepak, K. J. *Prelude to Solidarity: Poland and the politics of the Gierek regime*, New York: Columbia University Press, 1988

Leslie, R. F. *Polish politics and the revolution of November 1830*, London: Athlone Press, 1956

Leslie, R. F. *Reform and insurrection in Russian Poland 1856–1863*, London: Athlone Press, 1963

Leslie, R. F. (ed.) *The history of Poland since 1863*, Cambridge: University Press, 1980

Lipski, J. J. *A history of KOR: the Committee for Workers' Self-Defence*, Berkeley: University of California Press, 1985

Lucas, R. C. *Forgotten holocaust: the Poles under German occupation 1939–1944*, New York: Hippocrene, 1990

Markovits, A. S. and Sysyn, F. E. (eds.) *Nation building and the politics of nationalism: essays on Austrian Galicia*, Cambridge, Mass.: Harvard University Press, 1982

Micewski, A. *Cardinal Wyszyński: a biography*, San Diego, Calif.: Harcourt, Brace, Jovanovich, 1984

Olszewski, A. K. *An outline of Polish art and architecture 1890–1980*, Warsaw: Interpress, 1989

Polonsky, A. (ed.) *The Great Powers and the Polish Question 1941–1945. A documentary study in Cold War origins*, London: London School of Economics and Political Science, 1976

Polonsky, A. *Politics in independent Poland 1921–1939. The crisis of constitutional government*, Oxford: Clarendon Press, 1972

Porter, B. *When nationalism began to hate: imagining modern politics in nineteenth-century Poland*, New York: Oxford University Press, 2000

Raina, P. *Poland 1981: towards social renewal*, London: George Allen and Unwin, 1985

Rothschild, J. *East central Europe between the two world wars*, Washington, D.C.: University Press, 1974

Rothschild, J. *Return to diversity: a political history of east central Europe since World War II* (2nd edn), New York and Oxford: Oxford University Press, 1993

Senn, A. E. *Lithuania awakening*, Berkeley: University of California Press, 1990

Stachura, P. D. *Poland in the twentieth century*, London: Macmillan, 1998

Stachura, P. D. (ed.) *Poland between the wars*, London: Macmillan, 1999

Stehle, H. *The independent satellite: society and politics in Poland since 1945*, New York: Praeger, 1965

Stokes, G. (ed.) *From Stalinism to pluralism: a documentary history of eastern Europe since 1945*, New York: Oxford University Press, 1991

Sugar, P. F. and Lederer, I. J. (eds.) *Nationalism in eastern Europe*, Seattle and London: University of Washington Press, 1971

Syrop, K. *Spring in October: the story of the Polish revolution 1956*, New York: Praeger, 1957

Thaden, E. C. *Russia's western borderlands 1710–1870*, Princeton, N.J.: University Press, 1984

Thomas, W. and Znaniecki, F. *The Polish peasant in Europe and America*, 2 vols., New York: Dover, 1958

Torańska, T. *Oni* ['Them']: *Stalin's Polish puppets*, London: Collins Harvill, 1987

Trzeciakowski, L. *The Kulturkampf in Prussian Poland*, Boulder, Colo.: East European Monographs, 1990

Walicki, A. *Philosophy and Romantic nationalism. The case of Poland*, Oxford: Clarendon Press, 1982

Wandycz, P. S. *The lands of partitioned Poland 1795–1918*, Seattle: University of Washington Press, 1974

Wiskemann, E. *Germany's eastern neighbours: problems relating to the Oder–Neisse Line and the Czech frontier region*, London: Oxford University Press, 1956

Wynot, E. *Warsaw between the world wars: profile of the capital city in a developing land 1918–1939*, Boulder, Colo.: East European Monographs, 1983

Zamoyski, A. *Chopin: a biography*, London: Collins, 1979

Zamoyski, A. *Holy madness: Romantics, patriots and revolutionaries 1776–1871*, London: Weidenfeld and Nicolson, 1999

Zawadzki, W. H. *A man of honour: Adam Czartoryski as a statesman of Russia and Poland 1795–1831*, Oxford: Clarendon Press, 1993

Zawodny, J. K. *Death in the forest: the story of the Katyn Forest massacre*, Notre Dame, Indiana: University Press, 1962

INDEX

(regnal dates only of rulers are given)